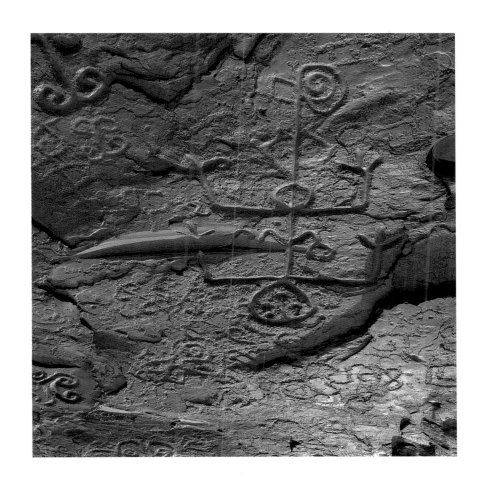

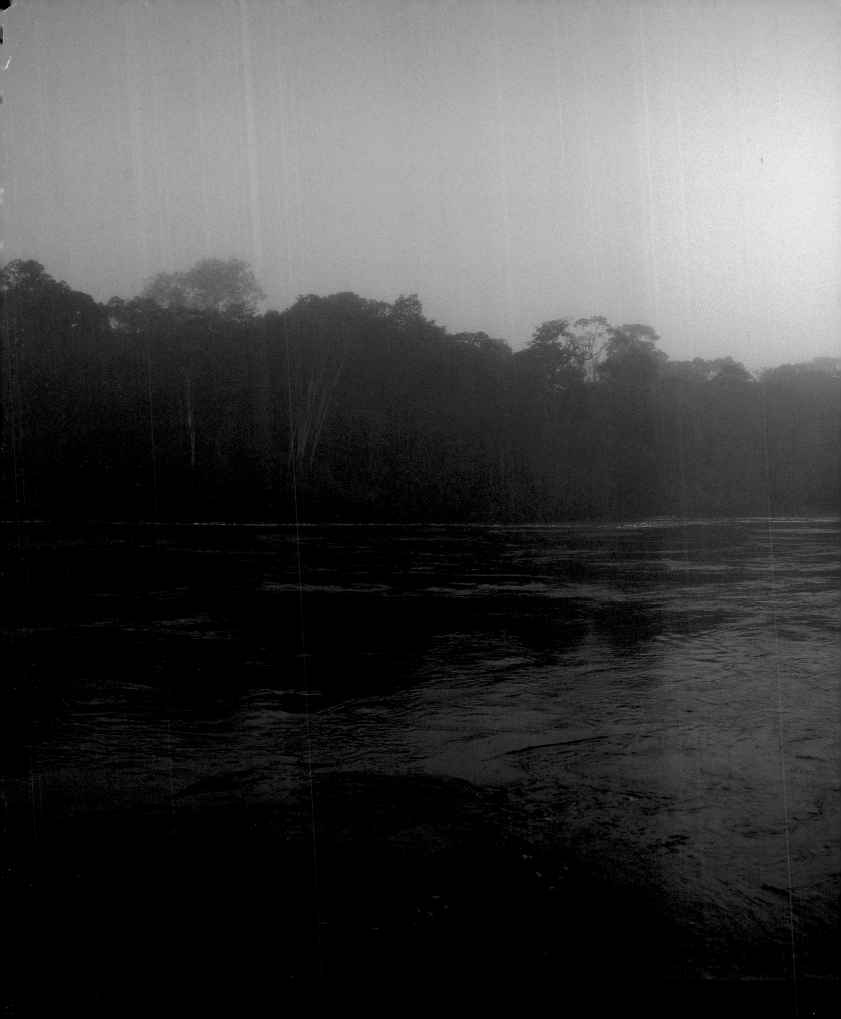

MAKUNA

PORTRAIT OF AN AMAZONIAN PEOPLE

KAJ ÅRHEM

PHOTOGRAPHS BY DIEGO SAMPER

SMITHSONIAN BOOKS
WASHINGTON AND LONDON

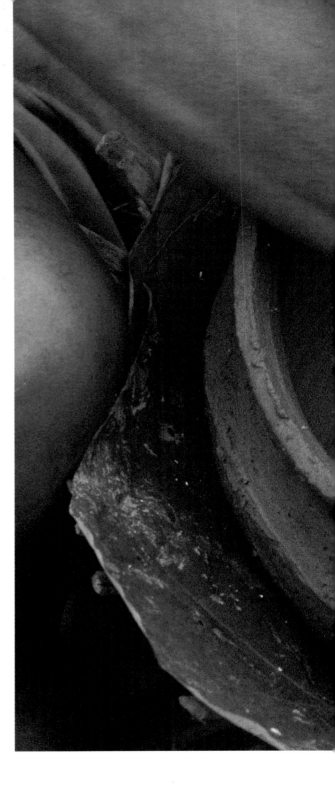

Editor: Robert A. Poarch
Designer: Janice Wheeler
Typesetter: Blue Heron Typesetters, Inc.
Printer: Tien Wah Press

Library of Congress Cataloging-in-Publication Data
Århem, Kaj.
   Makuna : portrait of an Amazonian people / Kaj Århem ; photographs by Diego Samper.
     p.   cm.
   Includes bibliographical references (p.   ) and index.
   ISBN 1-56098-874-6 (alk. Paper)
   1. Macuna Indians—Rites and ceremonies. 2. Macuna Indians—Religion. 3. Macuna
philosophy. 4. Shamanism—Uaupés River Valley (Colombia and Brazil). 5. Uaupés River Valley
(Colombia and Brazil)—Social life and customs. I. Title.
F2270.2.M33A68   1998
986.1'650049835—dc21   98-13898

British Library Cataloging-in-Publication Data avalable.

A paperback reissue (ISBN 1-58834-092-9) of the original cloth edition.

Manufactured in Singapore, not at government expense.
10 09 08 07 05 04 03   5 4 3 2 1

∞ The paper used in this publication meets the minimum requirements of the American
National Standard for Information Sciences—Permanence of Paper for Printed Library Materials
ANSI Z39.48-1984.

For permission to reproduce illustrations appearing in this book, please correspond directly with
the photographers. Unless otherwise noted, photographs are by Diego Samper. Smithsonian
Books does not retain reproduction rights for these illustrations individually, or maintain a file of
addresses for photo sources.

Financial support for this book was provided by the Swedish Council for Research in the
Humanities and Social Sciences, Längmanska Kulturfonden, Magn Bergvalls Stiftelse, and Kanung
Gustaf VI Adolfs Fond för Svensk Kultur.

Cover: **Woman with ritual black face paint. The thick angular pattern on the lower cheeks is characteristic of women's ritual paint.**

Page i: **Ancient rock art near La Pedrera on the Caquetá River; these anthropomorphic engravings represent mythical beings associated with the creation of the world.**

Pages ii–iii: **Amazon Indians invest rivers with profound religious meaning; to the Makuna they are the paths of the ancestors connecting the living with their ancestral origin and the source of all life.**

Right: **Woman smoothing the clay surface before a pot is burned and dyed with the leaves of the *lulu* fruit, giving it a black, glossy surface.**

Overleaf: **A roundhouse seen from within. The majestic architecture represents the Makuna cosmos; the four central posts correspond to the world pillars supporting the sky. As sunlight enters and smoke from the domestic fires leaves the house through the roof's openings, sky, house, and cosmos merge.**

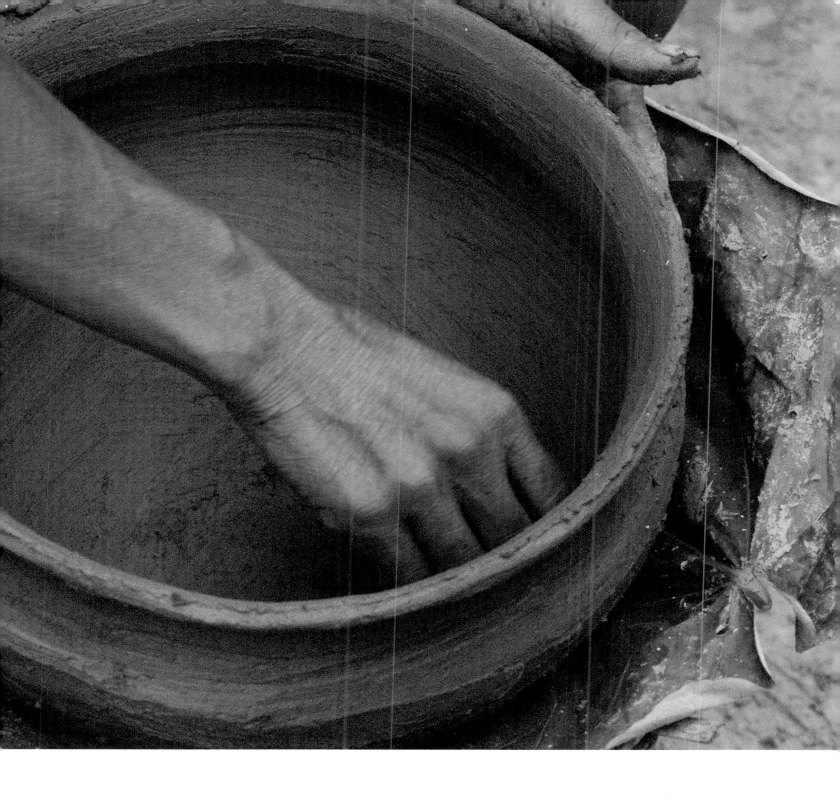

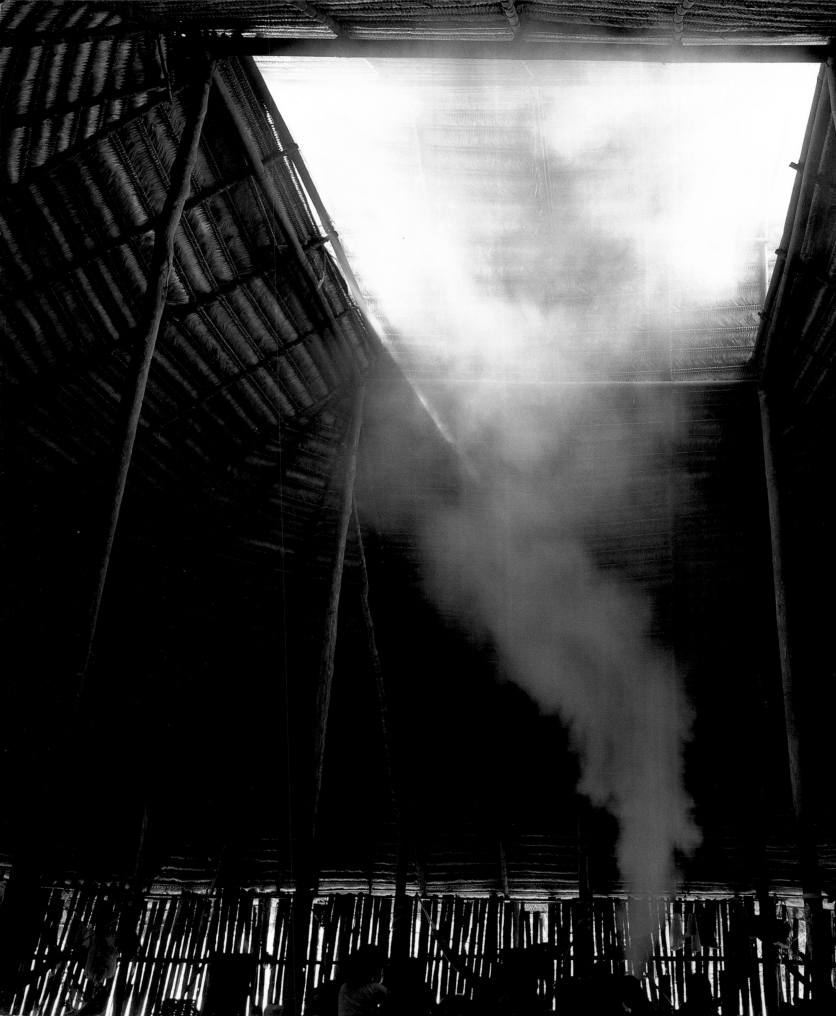

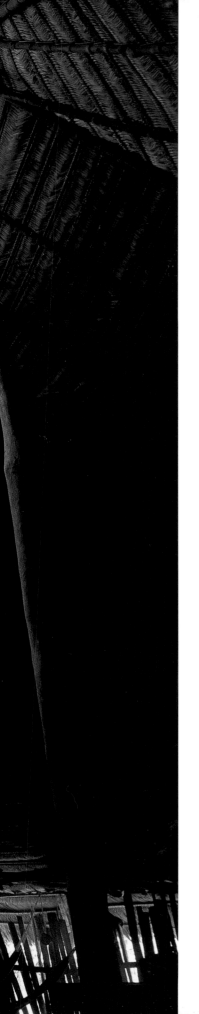

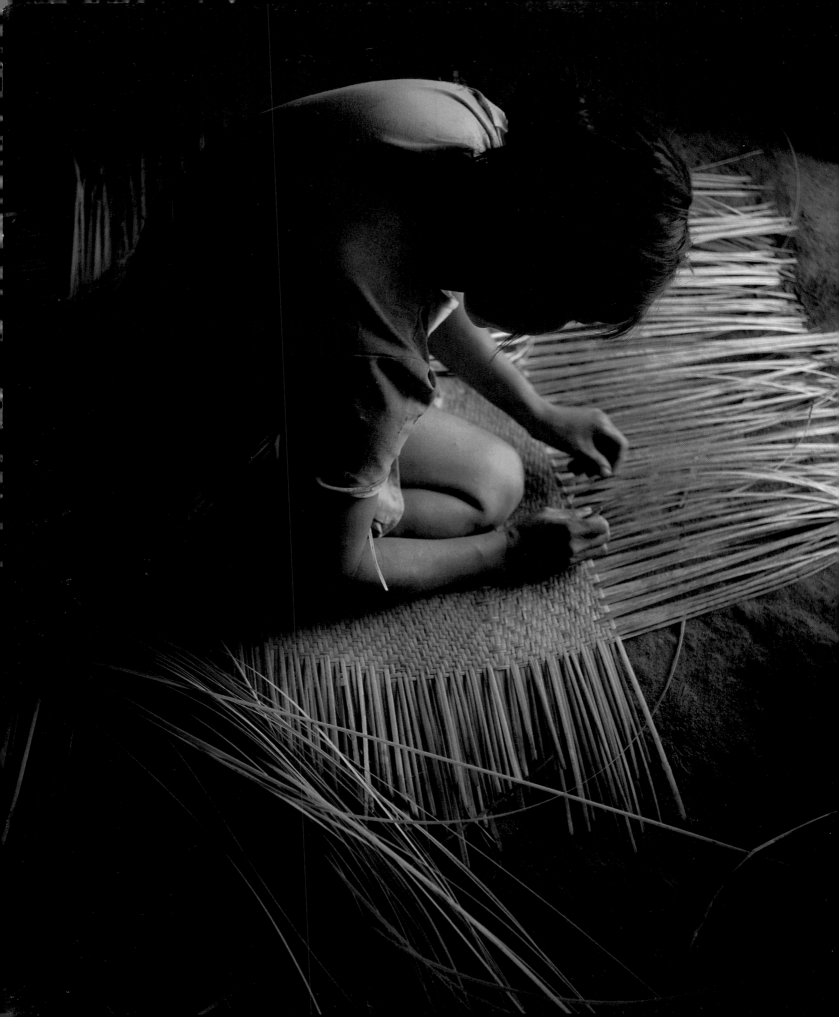

PREFACE

After centuries of reckless exploitation in the Amazonian rain forest and unprecedented persecution of its native inhabitants, only a handful of indigenous groups have managed to hold on to their ancestral land and traditional ways. The Makuna Indians, hidden in a remote part of the Colombian Amazon, are one such group. Though it describes a single people, this book has a more general relevance. The Makuna not only exemplify a type of society that, until recently, was widespread in the Amazon, they also illustrate the current plight of countless other Amerindian peoples struggling to maintain their lifeways and traditions in a world of turbulent change.

In text and images this book seeks to convey a sense of the richness of the Makuna culture. As an anthropologist, the author has spent extensive periods among the Makuna since 1972; the photographer has also visited and worked in Makuna communities on the Apaporis River since 1977. Drawn from over two decades of work the book provides a personal and factual account—a portrait—of the Makuna people. It focuses on Makuna cultural traditions, their notions about humanity and society, their perceptions of nature, and the way this vision guides their everyday life. The first part of the book offers a broad sketch of Makuna society placing it in a regional and historical context. Each of the subsequent parts deals with an important aspect of Makuna life in greater detail: their natural surroundings, domestic environment, mode of subsistence, and ritual life.

The apparent material poverty of the Makuna belies the spiritual richness of their culture. Their land is endowed with mythical significance and sacred value, which makes living intensely meaningful and gratifying. This enchantment of nature not only gives their life a poetic quality, but also turns their mode of living—the daily chores of hunting, fishing, and swidden cultivation—into a carefully integrated system of resource management worthy of our attention.

The last part of the text describes the gold rush presently sweeping through the Amazon and its particular effects on the Makuna. In the wake of the rubber hunters and coca barons, now gold miners encroaching on their ancestral lands cut down forest, pollute rivers, and defile their sacred places. The

A Makuna weaver.

Makuna fear that these menacing events forebode a catastrophic end of the world.

Tacitly implied in this apocalyptic vision is a powerful critique of Western industrial civilization. With their gentle wisdom the Makuna, along with other indigenous peoples, embody a radically different kind of humanity and an alternative vision of the world, suppressed but not yet eradicated by modernity. This book is offered as a testimony to one of these unobtrusive and resilient cultures in the hope that it may challenge some deep-rooted notions of reality and stimulate critical reflection on the current conditions of the world at large.

The text makes ample use of the published literature on the native peoples of northwest Amazonia. In particular it draws on the writings of Stephen and Christine Hugh-Jones—some of the finest extant works of Amazonian ethnography. It also owes a great deal to the scholarship and genius of the late Gerardo Reichel-Dolmatoff, patriarch of Colombian ethnography. By integrating the author's personal field experience with the published material of others, the book in a modest way summarizes existing knowledge of northwest Amazonia in general and provides new information on the Makuna in particular.

The author wants to express his gratitude to William Arens, Stephen Hugh-Jones, and Roy Willis for their helpful comments on earlier drafts of the text.

The greatest debt, however, is incurred to the Makuna themselves for their guidance, help, and generosity: Ignacio—shaman and teacher—and his family; Venancio, interpreter and companion; Pasico and Anisio and their families, generous hosts and friends; Domingo and his son Jaime; Waldemar, Emilio, Hernando, Amasio, Ricardo, and many, many others. Some of them will appear in the text under their proper names, others under fictitious ones. A special thanks goes to Carlos, son of Isaac, the great wizard, for his information on the Dance of the Spirits.

ORTHOGRAPHY

For the convenience of the reader, the orthography for Makuna words used in this book has been simplified.

Vowels	Consonants
a as in m<u>a</u>sk	b as in <u>b</u>ut
e as in <u>e</u>gg	k as in <u>k</u>ite
i as in <u>i</u>nk	d as in <u>d</u>ub
o as in <u>o</u>range	g as in <u>g</u>ot
u as in f<u>oo</u>d	h as in <u>h</u>ouse
ü similar to German gr<u>ü</u>n	m as in <u>m</u>an
	n as in <u>n</u>ose
	ng as in to<u>ng</u>ue
	ny as in Spanish ma<u>ñ</u>ana
	p as in <u>p</u>en
	r between English r and l
	s similar to English ts in boa<u>ts</u>
	t as in <u>t</u>ime
	w as in <u>w</u>ine
	y as in <u>y</u>am

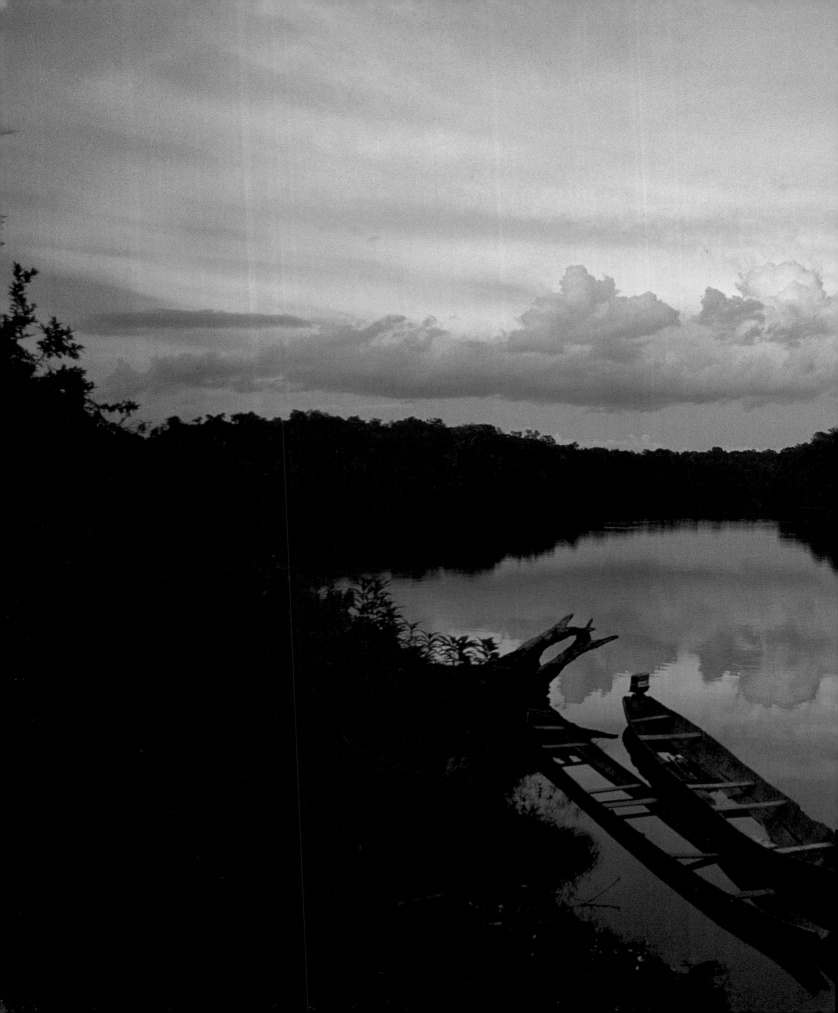

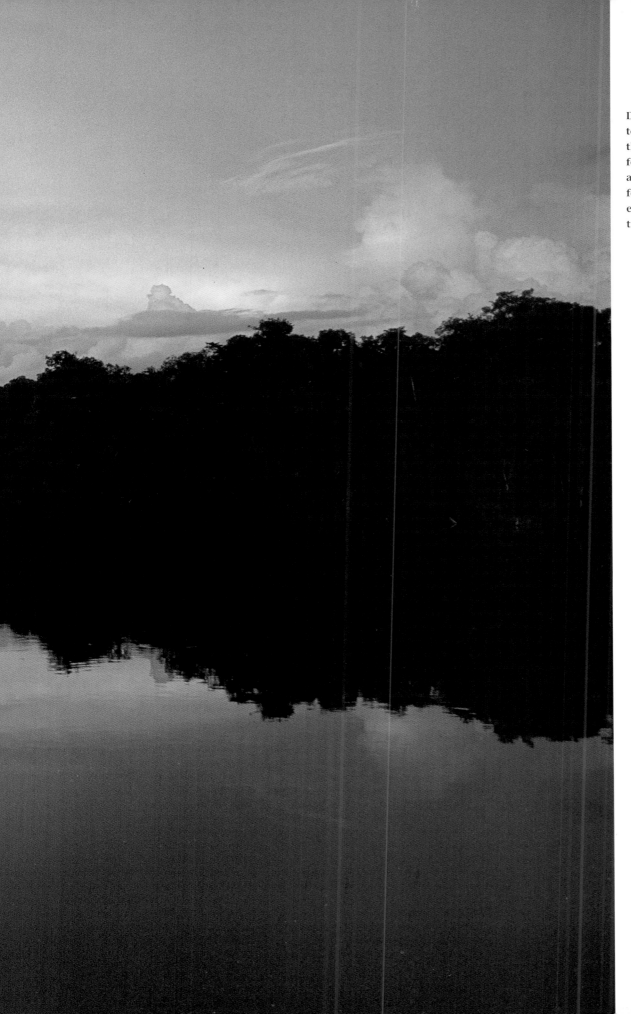

Dugout canoes moored to a landing. Rivers are the highways of the forest, and the canoe—a precious possession for the Indians—is the essential means of transport.

1
COMING HOME

In January 1972 I made my first journey to the Makuna. At the time little was known about them, and that primarily from visits by missionaries and traders. Reaching Makuna territory was difficult and not altogether safe. Starting out from Mitú, the capital of the Vaupés region in the Colombian Amazon, I recruited local Indians as guides along the way and paddled and trekked for about ten days. We ascended an upstream tributary of the Vaupés, then crossed the watershed between the Vaupés and Apaporis drainage systems, and entered the middle Pirá-Paraná River through one of its principal affluents, the rust-colored Colorado River. Below the confluence of the Colorado and Pirá-Paraná Rivers was San Miguel, a Catholic mission post, where I rested for a few days before continuing the journey.

The Pirá-Paraná, or *Waiya* (Fish River) in Makuna, is a blackwater river originating in the sandy upland soils of the watershed between the Vaupés and Apaporis Rivers. Its waters are dark, clean, and poor in nutrients. Yet its aquatic fauna and the forest it drains sustain a scattered population of some 1,000 Indians living along its shores and tributaries. Traveling down the Pirá-Paraná we passed only a handful of settlements. Then, as now, most Indians lived along the smaller tributaries.

The many waterfalls and rapids account for the inaccessibility of the Pirá-Paraná area and its relative isolation from the rest of the Vaupés region. Steering through one of these rapids I saw for the first time (on an erect rock in the middle of the river) the sacred petroglyphs at Nyi. Consisting of various engravings—stylized anthropomorphic and geometrical figures—they are said to depict the decorated body of the mythical being Nyi, the ancestral anaconda of the Taiwano people, who turned into stone as he danced in his underwater house.

Meandering rivers and lowland rain forest dominate the northwest Amazonian landscape. The Apaporis River is the axis of the Makuna world.

A few hours downstream from Nyi the yellowish water of the Komenya River flows into the dark current of the Pirá-Paraná. Just above the mouth of the Komenya is a magnificent waterfall, below which lies a pool of still waters covered with foam and floating debris. Hundreds of large, intensely azure morpho butterflies fluttered over the calm surface as we entered the Komenya River in bright sunlight. Paddling hard against the strong current, we then passed a series of difficult rapids, the last

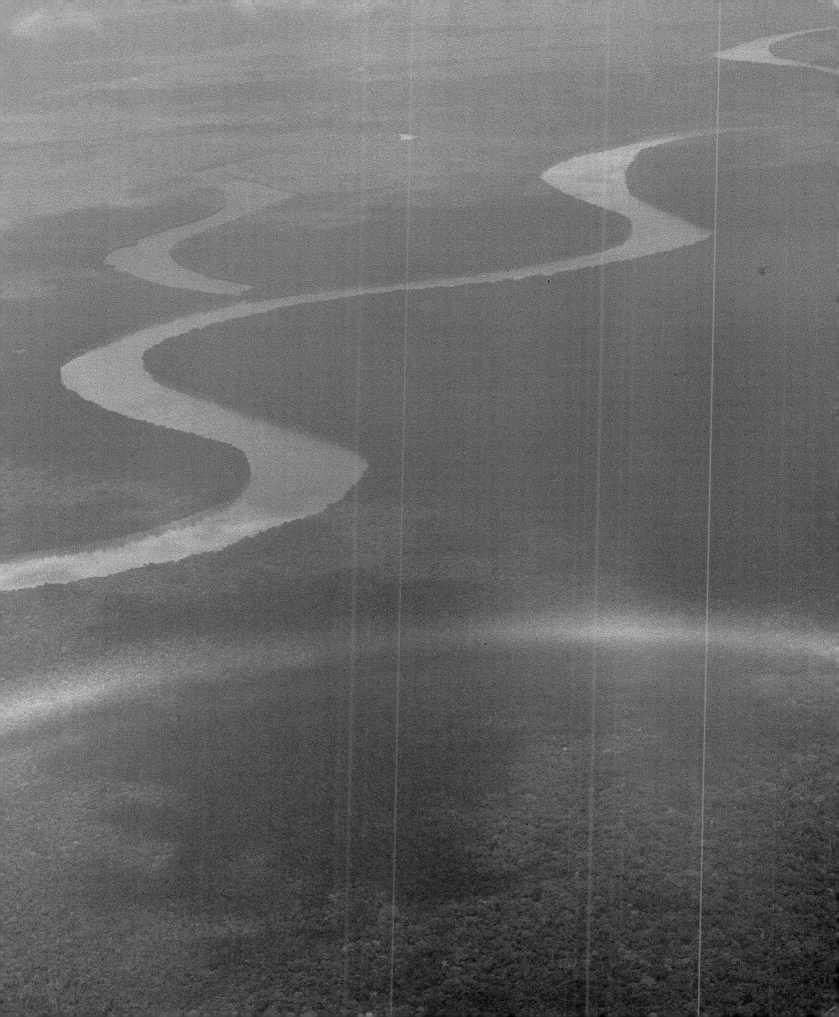

Below: A sacred place. Waterfalls are conceived of by the Makuna as houses of the ancestors and waking-up places of the dead.

Right: Rapids and water-falls make the rivers of northwest Amazonia difficult to navigate. In the past they protected Pirá-Paraná Indians from the destructive impact of slave raiders and rubber hunters.

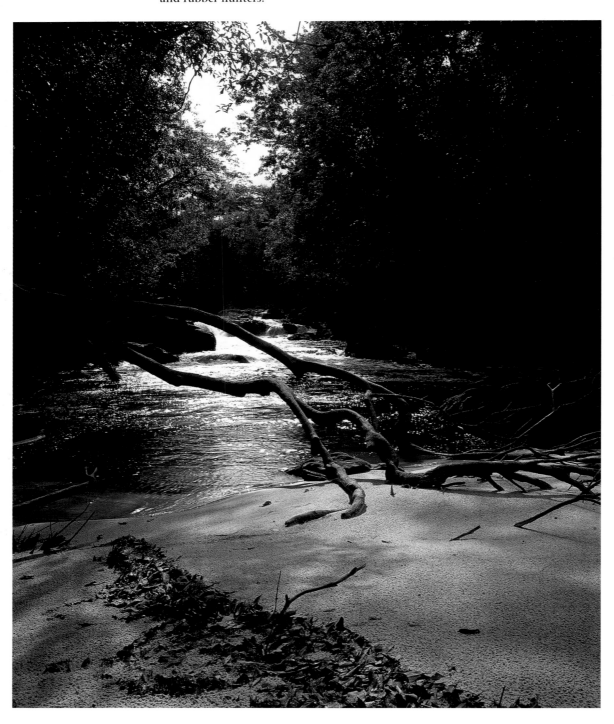

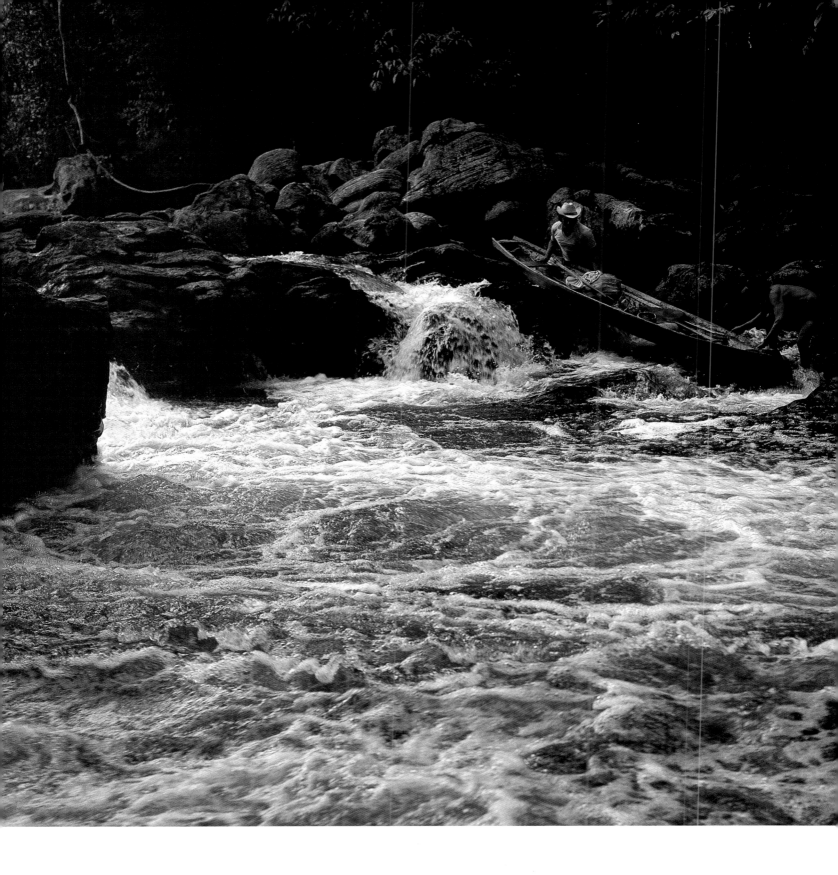

A longhouse settlement
at dawn, surrounded by
fruit trees and gardens.
The towering peach
palms reveal that the
site has been inhabited
for a considerable time.

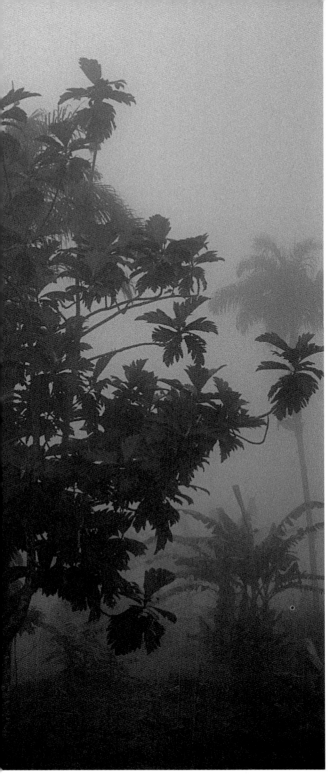

of which is called Thunder, named after another petrified ancestral being, rising above the surface of the river.

We encountered the first Makuna *maloca* (a traditional Indian multifamily longhouse) here just above the rapids. Its owner and headman, an old man called Luis, received us with customary hospitality and invited us into the cool, shady interior. We had a meal of dry manioc bread, hot pepper sauce, and manioc juice—the traveler's regular provisions among the Indians. Luis told us to continue upstream to the maloca of Ignacio, the headman and local leader of the Komenya Makuna, the appropriate person to receive a stranger such as me.

In the late afternoon, as the river took on the somber green color of the surrounding forest, we eventually reached Ignacio's settlement. At the canoe landing a swarm of yellow butterflies exploded into flight as we jumped ashore. From there I could see the silhouette of Ignacio's majestic maloca encircled by towering peach palms, groves of plantains, and other fruit trees. A soft, rhythmic sound of women grating manioc and men pounding coca leaves emanated from within the maloca. A group of children came running down the path to meet us. The entire scene radiated of familiarity and warmth. As we walked toward the house, I had the strange but comforting feeling of coming home.

That first evening among the Makuna I tried to explain the reason for my presence. Ignacio, it turned out, was away on a long river journey. His teenage son, Venancio, who had spent several years in a missionary boarding school, received us and acted as translator as I told my story in Spanish to the assembled people. Drawing a comparison with Venancio's years in school where he and other Indian children learned Spanish among the whites, I said I wished to live among them and learn their language and way of life. "There is a lot you can teach me," I said. "Indians and whites ought to learn from one another. Only then can we begin to understand each other." My words may now sound idealistic and rhetorical, but I honestly meant them then and still do today.

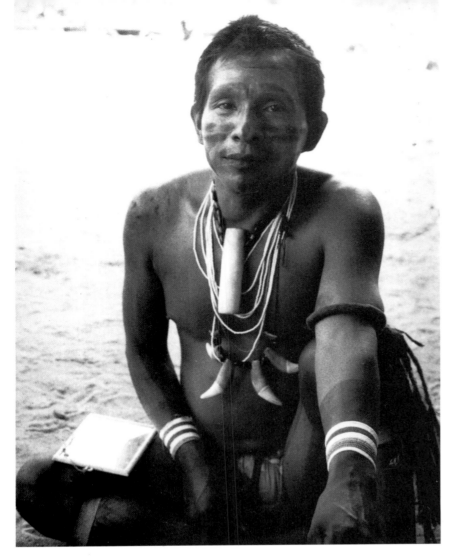

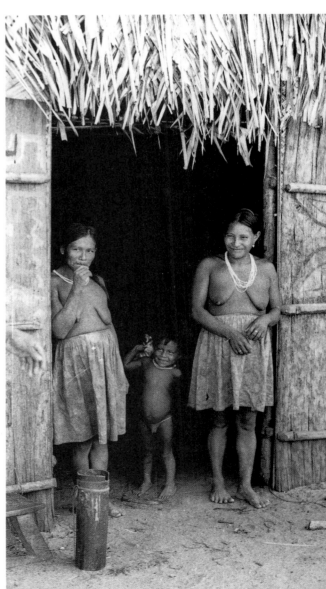

THE MIND'S EYE

For other, more mundane reasons than those I invoked, the people of Ignacio's maloca allowed me to stay among them. To many of them I represented a potential source of trade goods and a link to the world of the whites. Gradually, however, I began to see that to the Makuna elders my presence meant something quite different. After I had spent some months among the Makuna, an old man said to me in the typical frank manner of the elders, "It is good that you have come, we had been expecting you." This utterance was evidently a response to my words on the eve of my arrival. My arrival confirmed, as it were, their conviction that they had something to teach me. In my initial discourse I had also unwittingly invoked the principle of reciprocity so central to Makuna life. According to their way of thinking, the fact that some Makuna, like Venancio, had been to school with, and worked among, the whites implied that whites would come to stay among them. In this sense I *was* expected.

Looking back, it now seems to me that the old man's comment also revealed an awareness of the value of their own culture, which another Makuna would later formulate differently: "The whites only see with their eyes, but we can see with our mind." Through shamanic thinking, chanting, and participation in rituals the Makuna can enter a world—an invisible world of spirits—that is closed to whites. To obtain this "mind's eye" became the ultimate objective of my stay among them, and they generously accepted to teach me. More than twenty years later, I now realize I will never attain this objective, but I believe I have caught a glimpse of that other, distinctly Makuna reality.

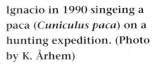

Ignacio in 1990 singeing a paca (*Cuniculus paca*) on a hunting expedition. (Photo by K. Århem)

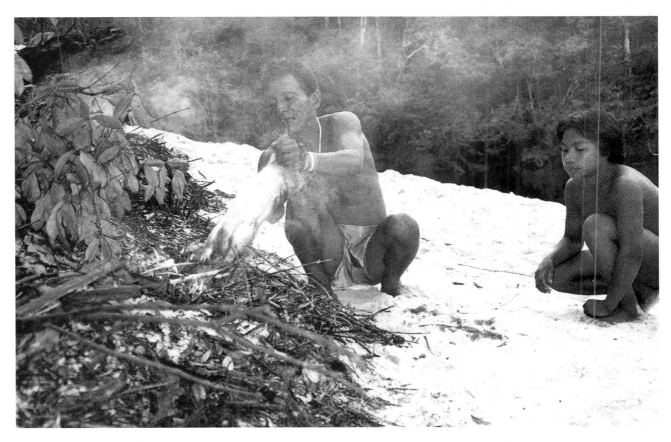

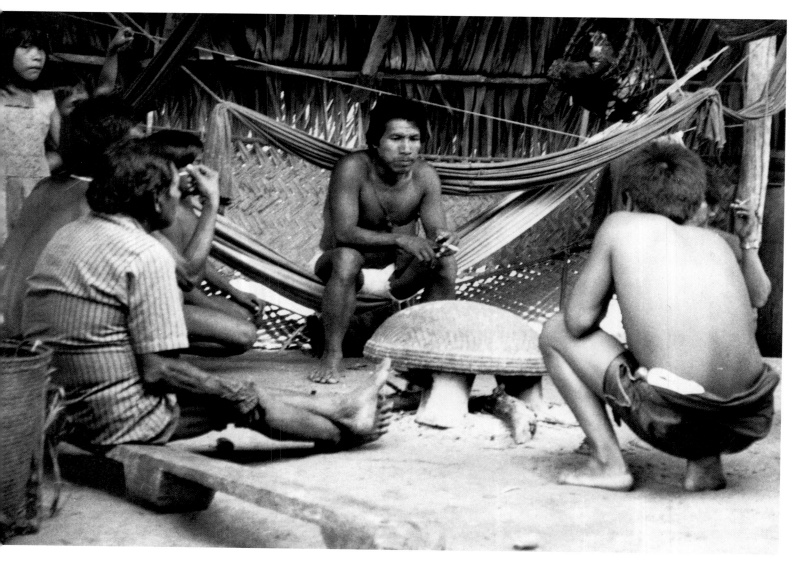

Ignacio's son, Venancio
(center), deliberating
with elders while young-
sters listen. As usual in
such situations, the men
are chewing coca and
smoking. (Photo by K.
Århem)

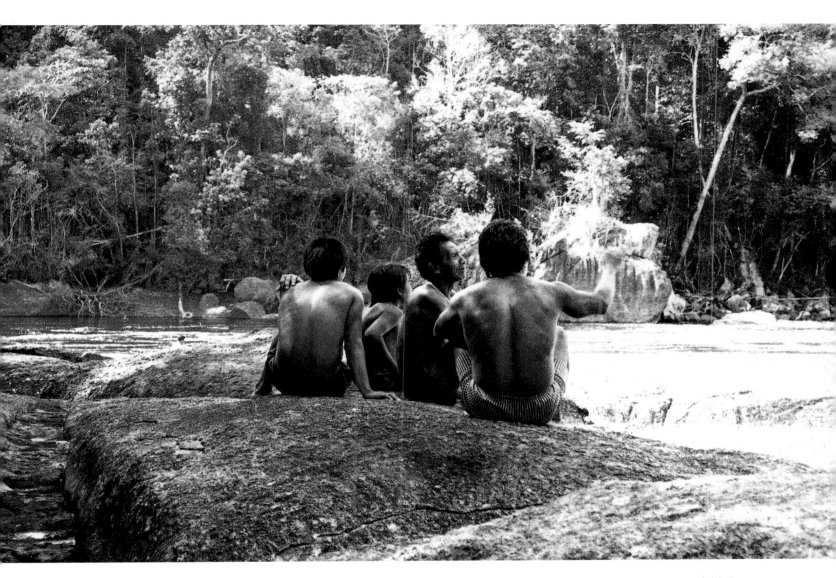

Ignacio instructing his children and grandchildren about the lore of the land. (Photo by K. Århem)

2
THE
MAKUNA
WORLD

To the casual visitor the immense forest of northwest Amazonia may seem a wild and perilous country. Yet for the Makuna Indians, the forest is their principal source of livelihood and a never-ceasing fount of creative imagery and cultural inspiration. The rain-forest environment has nurtured their particular philosophy of life and vision of the world, which is as different from ours in spirit as the forest is from the city. Only by suspending the ingrained beliefs of our civilization can we perceive reality the Makuna way.

In the Makuna world every tangible form is more than it appears. The visible world of ordinary experience also has an invisible and intangible dimension that the Makuna refer to as *he*—the world of powerful spirits and deified ancestors. In this other dimension, rocks and rivers are alive, and animals and plants are people. Known through myth and controlled through ritual, the *he* world contains the primordial powers of creation that ultimately govern the present. The Makuna shaman, both human and superhuman, has the capacity to see into this timeless and changeless spirit world. Through their rituals and shamanic acts the Makuna continually enlist these powers to maintain life and renew cosmic order.

Theirs is a boundless universe of continuities and relatedness, in which rivers and forests, humans and animals, living and dead, all form part of an integrated whole, an encompassing community of beings and things. The Western distinction between nature and culture dissolves and looses its meaning. It is a world of strange beauty and unsettling wisdom, utterly alien and peculiarly familiar.

PEOPLES OF THE VAUPÉS

A roundhouse in a clearing in the forest. To the Makuna, the immense forest of northwest Amazonia is their whole world.

The Makuna are one of some fifteen indigenous groups in the Vaupés region of the Colombian Amazon speaking a language of the Eastern Tukano language family.[1] The Colombian Vaupés, delimited by the Vaupés River and its tributaries in the north and the Apaporis River in the south, encompasses an indigenous population of between 15,000 and 20,000 people, mainly Eastern Tukano speakers, but

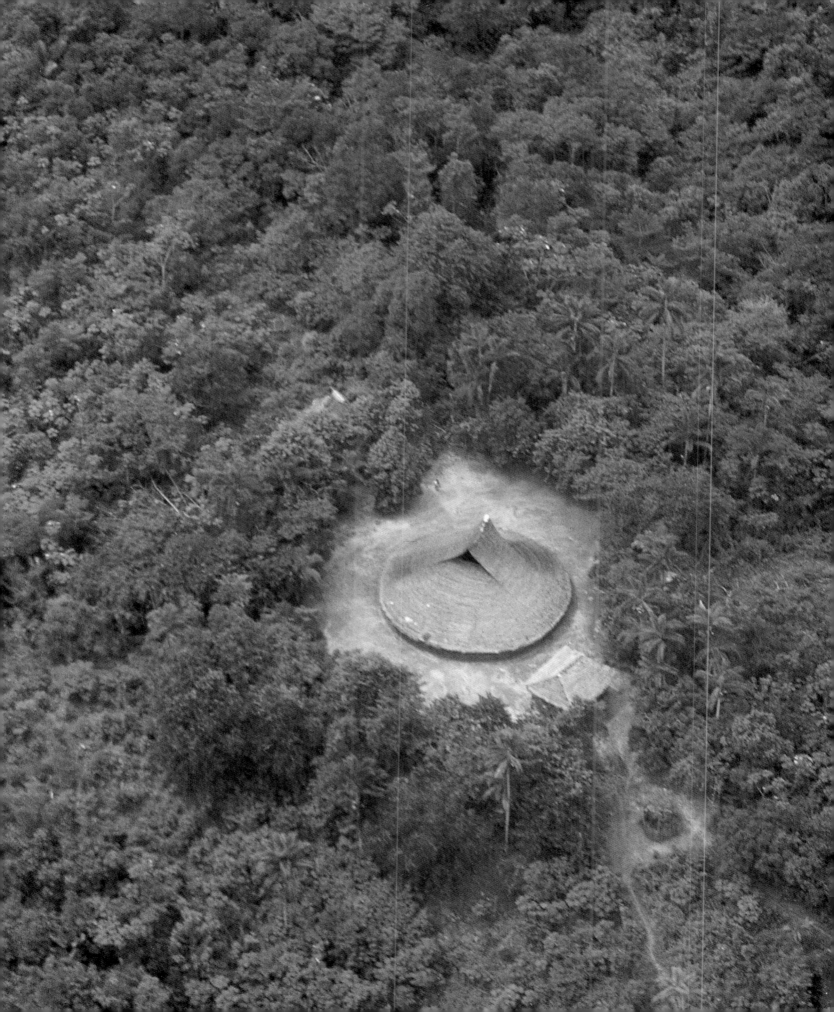

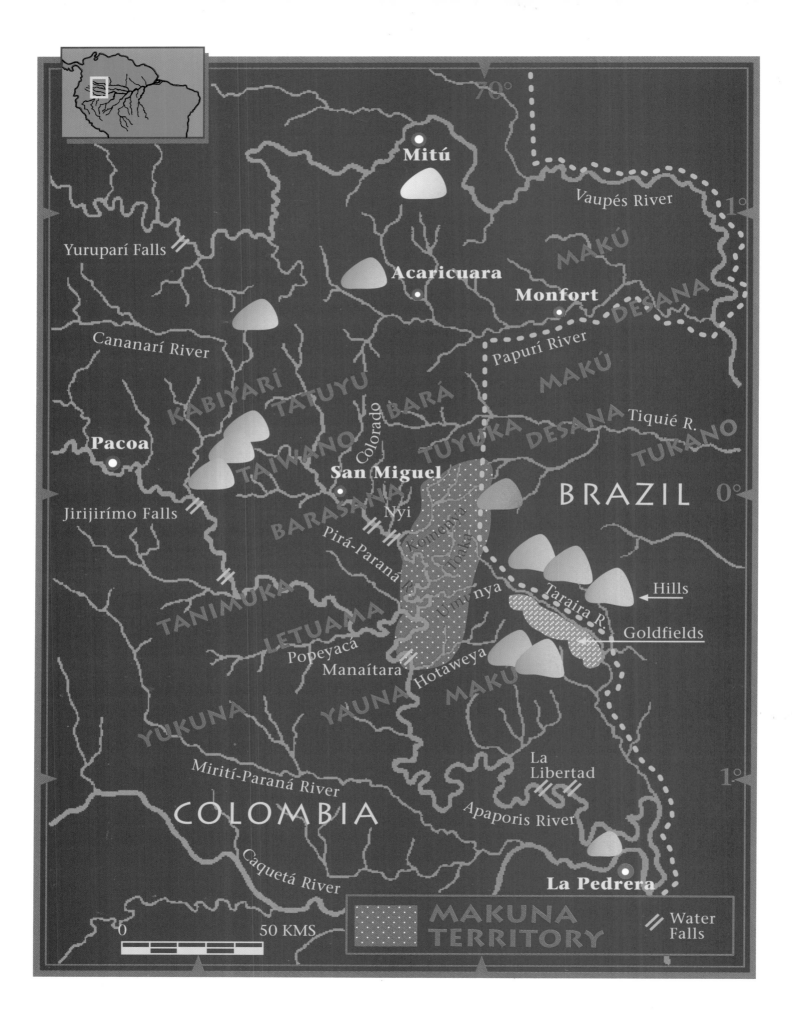

Mitú

Acaricuara

Monfort

Vaupés River

Yuruparí Falls

MAKÚ

DESANA

Cananarí River

Papurí River

MAKÚ

KABIYARÍ

TATUYU

BARÁ

Colorado

TAIWANO

Tiquié R.

Pacoa

TUYUKA

DESANA

TUKANO

BARASANA

San Miguel

BRAZIL

0°

Ñyi

Komeña

Jirijirímo Falls

Pirá-Paraná R.

Toaka

Hills

Umuña

Taraira R.

TANIMUKA

Goldfields

LETUAMA

Popeyacá

Manaítara

Hotaweya

MAKÚ

YUKUNA

YAUNA

Hotaweya

La
Libertad

Mirití-Paraná River

Apaporis River

1°

COLOMBIA

Caquetá River

La Pedrera

50 KMS

0

MAKUNA
TERRITORY

Water
Falls

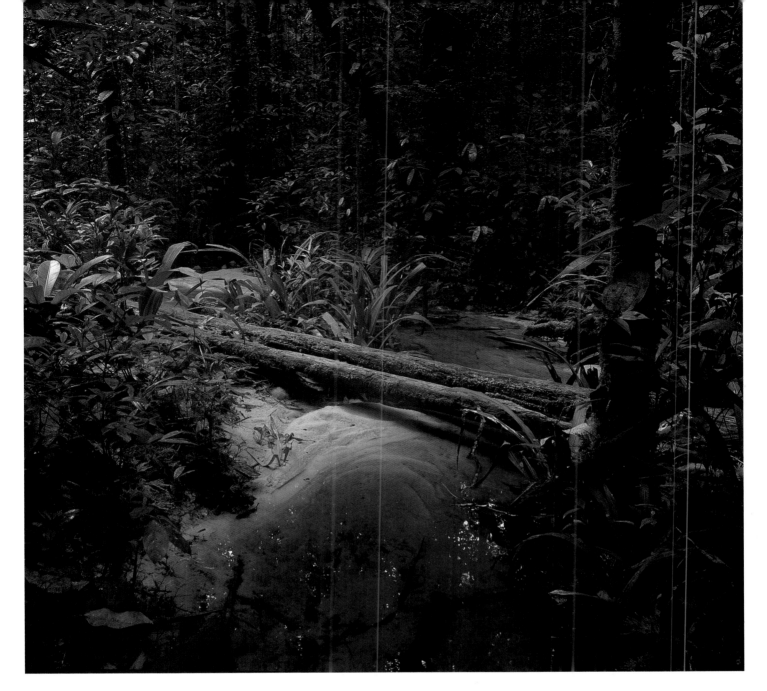

Fed by the tropical rains
and colored by the red,
sandy soil, countless
streams and rivulets
flow through the forest.

also some Arawak speakers and scattered Makú communities. The Tukanoan
and Arawakan groups are all riverine and sedentary, subsisting on shifting
cultivation, fishing, hunting, and gathering. Manioc, a cultivated root
plant, is the staple, and fish provide the bulk of the protein in the diet.
In contrast, the seminomadic Makú, living in small, mobile camps in the
interfluvial forest, depend more heavily on hunting and gathering. They
occasionally hunt for the riverine Tukanoans in return for cultivated plant
food. Despite the fact that most Makú groups today cultivate their own
swiddens, they are still considered an inferior people. The Makuna call
them *hosa masa* (servants).

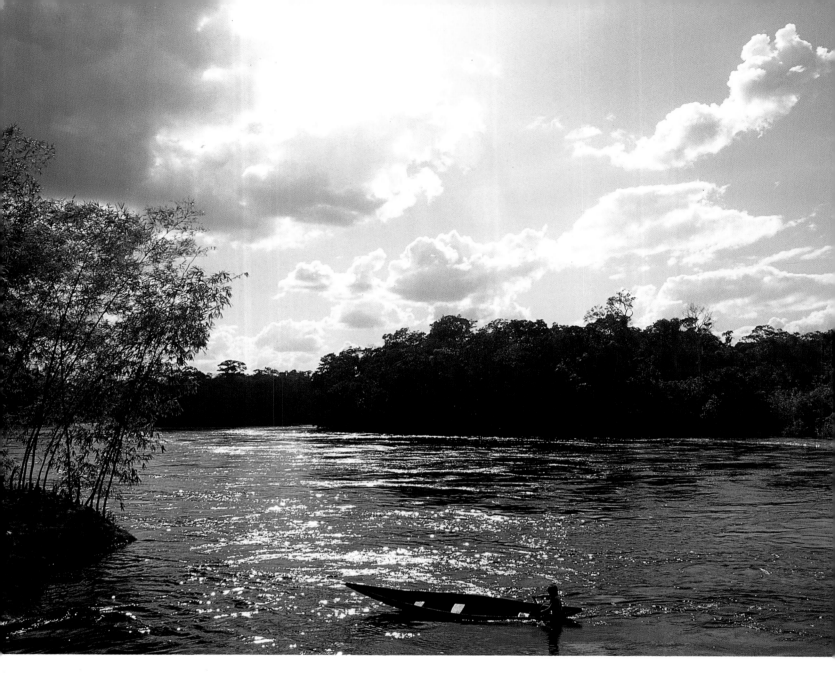

View of the Pirá-Paraná River, a tributary of the Apaporis River. Meaning "Fish River" in Makuna language, the Pirá-Paraná sustains an indigenous population of more than one thousand individuals, mainly living along tributaries and small feeder streams.

The forests between the Vaupés and Apaporis Rivers are Indian country. Native settlements and villages are widely dispersed and, in the interior, especially, contact with whites is limited and sporadic, although traders and missionaries have traversed this area since the seventeenth century. Trade and commerce center around a handful of mission posts and the two principal towns in the region: Mitú, the administrative center of Vaupés, and La Pedrera, a bustling frontier town on the lower Caquetá River below the confluence with the Apaporis River.

The Makuna inhabit a stretch of densely forested land along the lower Apaporis and the left-hand tributaries of the lower Pirá-Paraná River, which flows into the Apaporis. The largest concentration of Makuna live along the

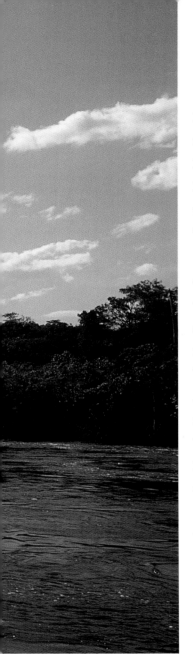

Komenya River. This area in the heartland of the Vaupés region harbors many small Indian groups speaking different Tukano languages. The Komenya Makuna's closest neighbors are the Barasana, Taiwano, Tatuyo, Bará, and Tuyuka, all closely interrelated and part of the same social and cultural universe. On the Apaporis River the Makuna live adjacent to the Tukano-speaking Letuama and Tanimuka and the Arawak-speaking Kabiyarí.

Each of these Indian groups is subdivided into a ranked set of patrilineal clans reckoning descent on the father's side from a named, mythical ancestor conceived of as a *hino* (anaconda). Such a group of clans, modeled on a set of brothers and ranked in order of seniority from elder to youngest, forms an exogamous unit with a distinct language. According to the general Tukanoan custom, a man should marry a woman speaking a different language—a practice known as linguistic exogamy. In actuality, however, there is no absolute fit between the language group and the exogamous group. The Makuna, along with the Cubeo on the northern banks of the Vaupés River, for example, intermarry among different exogamous groups speaking the same language.

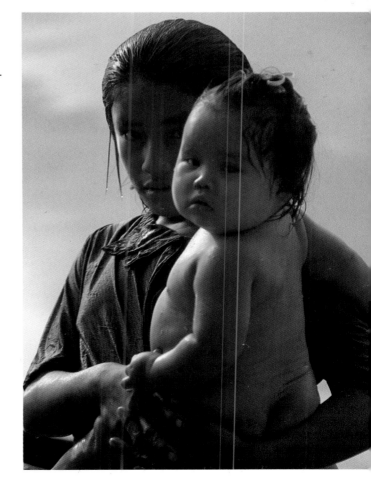

Mother and child.

All of the peoples of the Tukanoan social universe are in a sense relatives. The different exogamous groups are classified as *bai/kien masa* (elder or younger brothers), among whom intermarriage is prohibited, or as *tenyi masa* (affines), among whom marriage is prescribed. There is also the third category, *hakoria* (mother's children), which occupies an intermediate and ambiguous position in the system; it consists of groups and individuals that, from the point of view of any ego, are neither brothers nor appropriate affines (i.e. potential partners in marriage exchange). The relationship system prescribes marriage between cross cousins, which in the Tukanoan kinship terminology roughly means marriageables. The rule states that a man should marry a father's sister's daughter or mother's brother's daughter.

This rule goes with a normative ideal of sister

exchange, which implies that men classified as affines are expected to exchange real or classificatory sisters—kinswomen classified as sisters—in marriage. Families that have intermarried over generations have close, relaxed relations, and the exchange aspect of a marriage may be downplayed or temporarily suspended. In other words, a kinswoman may be given away in marriage to a close affine on the understanding that she will be reciprocated at a later date, either in this generation or the next. In contrast marriages between distant affines or families living in different territories may not be as congenially accomplished. If a man has no exchangeable kinswoman, nor a marriageable cousin in the locality, he may be forced to capture a wife from a group of unrelated and potentially hostile affines. Raids for women among neighboring and distant groups were probably common in the past, and may still occur today. But this is a risky and often dramatic venture likely to trigger retaliation and counter raids.

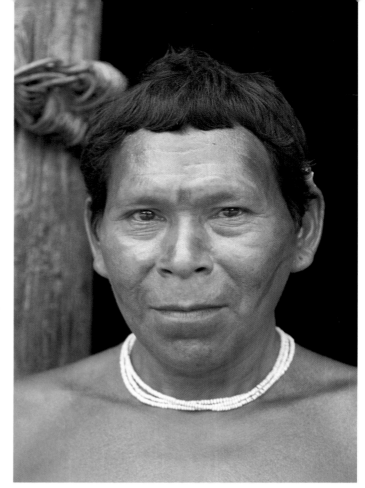

Middle-aged man.

Traditionally, and still to a significant extent, life in the Pirá-Paraná area revolves around the maloca—the multifamily longhouse.[2] The maloca tends to be composed of a core of close male kin, their wives, who move in upon marriage, and their children—in effect, an extended family centered on a patrilineage. The *ühü* (headman) and owner of the maloca is always a senior member of the clan group inhabiting it. Since no hereditary offices exist among the Tukanoans, the headman position is open to any resourceful and ambitious man. The exemplary headman is industrious, wise, well versed in traditions, and known for his ritual expertise. His authority rests on his success in guiding and protecting his following; if he fails to live up to expectations his following simply disperse. Particularly influential headmen occasionally succeed in gaining authority over a larger group of people, sometimes an entire river territory.

Tukanoan society is strikingly egalitarian and undifferentiated. Its elaborate complexity most clearly shows in its ritual organization and spiritual life. In Pirá-Paraná each locality has its officiating shamans, ritual chanters, and dancers. There are two kinds of shamans: *kumua* (protective) and *yaia* (curing)—the latter literally meaning "jaguars." Both claim direct access to

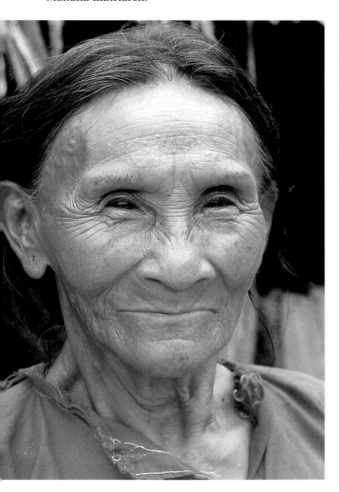

Makuna matriarch.

the invisible *he* world. Shamans communicate with the spirits, supervise rituals, and use their mental powers to prevent and cure illness. They never use medical plants or other material medicines. The curing shaman instead blows spells and sucks out pathogenic substances from the patient's body. The *yuamü* (chanter)—literally the "voice of the shaman"—and *baya* (master dancer) perform only during the many communal rituals, ensuring cosmic order and protection from evil and misfortune.

Since every adult man—including headmen, shamans, and other ritual experts—is a hunter and fisherman, and every woman is a cultivator and mother, each maloca is largely a self-sustained economic unit. The various households in the multifamily maloca engage in their own daily chores. Unity among all the members of the maloca only occurs during the communal meals at dawn and dusk, and during periodic, collective labors, such as clearing the swidden land and constructing and repairing the house itself.

The integration of these semiautonomous settlements into the wider Tukanoan society is accomplished and reinforced primarily by the many conspicuous communal rituals involving several different settlements and clan groups. During the pan-Tukanoan *dabucurí* (food giving) rituals and the Makuna masked dances, great quantities of food are exchanged and redistributed among intermarrying clans, thus symbolically underpinning their interdependence and the necessity of peaceful alliances. In all rituals copious amounts of coca, powdered snuff, and *chicha*, a beer made from manioc or other root crops, are consumed. These are the men's ritual foods replacing ordinary food during ritual events.[3] Particular potions of *keti bare* (spirit food)—shamanized coca and snuff—are also allocated by the officiating shaman to reinvigorate and infuse spiritual powers to the participants. At particularly important events, *yagé*, a hallucinogenic drink, is served to initiated men.[4] This drink is said to bring the men into contact with the *he* world and enable them to communicate with its powerful spirits.

At the heart of traditional Tukanoan culture is what is generally known in Vaupés as the Yuruparí cult. During the large-scale Yuruparí rituals, men play large palm flutes and trumpets representing deified ancestors.[5] The instruments are literally spirits of the *he* world. There are two kinds of Yuruparí instruments: *he büküra*, the ancient and most sacred ones played at the

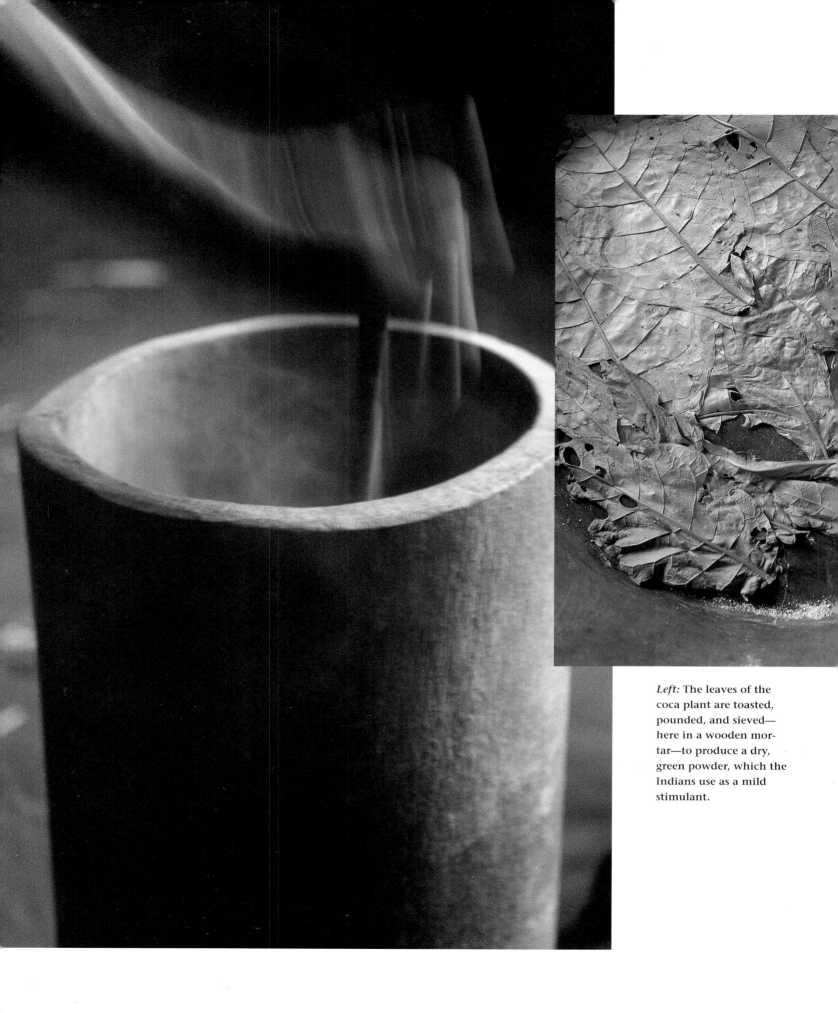

Left: The leaves of the coca plant are toasted, pounded, and sieved—here in a wooden mortar—to produce a dry, green powder, which the Indians use as a mild stimulant.

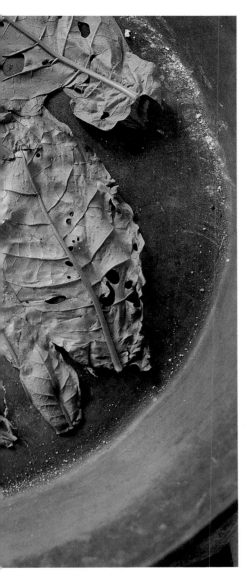

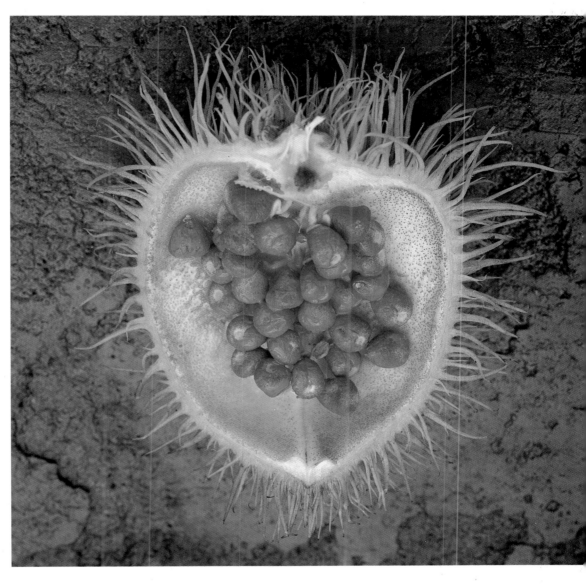

Above, left: Tobacco leaves being toasted on the clay griddle for snuff. Snuff and coca powder are referred to as spirit food, intimately tied to male identity and the spiritual power of men.

Above, right: Opened fruit of the *achiote* tree (*Bixa orellana*). The seeds contain red pigment used principally for decorating baskets and basketry trays.

elaborate initiation ceremony where boys become men, and *he rika samara*, the less sacred instruments played to celebrate the seasonal harvest of particular fruit. The fact that women and children are prohibited from seeing the instruments has contributed to the mystical and secret aura that surrounds Yuruparí rituals. The early missionaries misunderstood the Yuruparí cult and regarded it as a form of devil worship. According to the Indians, the instruments represent the sacred body of the clan ancestors, and as such are supreme, tangible symbols of the unity of the clan and the whole exogamous group. The Makuna say that the ancient Yuruparí instruments are the heart and soul of the clan. The annual Yuruparí ritual where the sacred instruments from various clans and local communities are brought

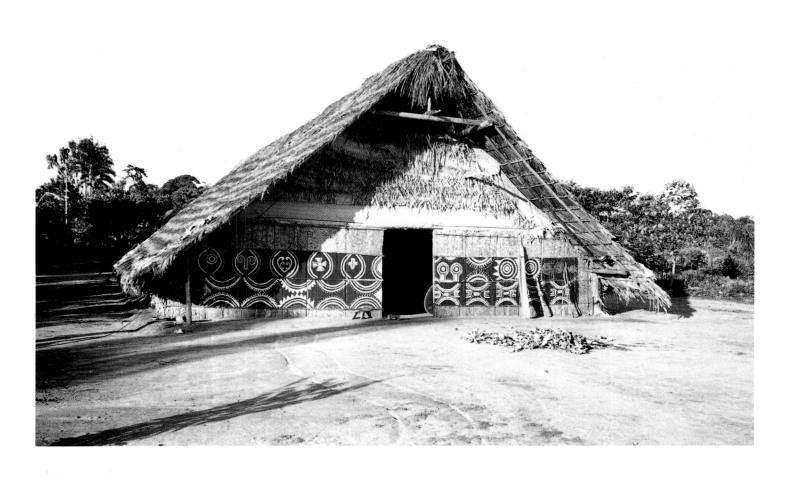

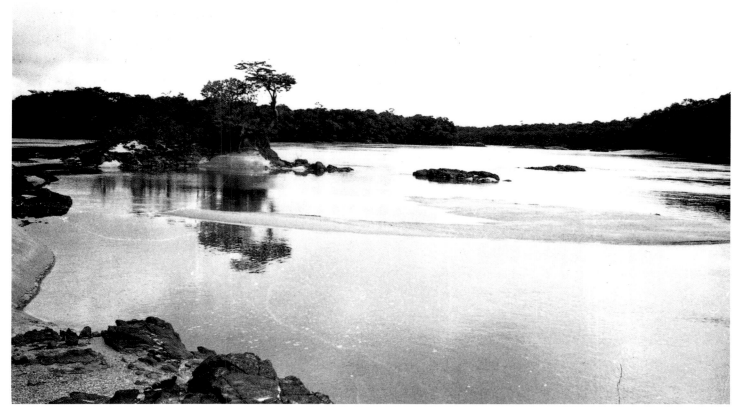

Above, left: Maloca with
a decorated front wall.
(Photo by K. Århem)

Below, left: Manaítara:
the sacred birthplace
and waking-up house of
the Water People on the
Apaporis River. (Photo
by K. Århem)

together in a single, joint ritual performance provides the fullest expression
of the identity of the Makuna as a people.

THE MAKUNA

Makuna individuals identify themselves by the name of the clan or wider
exogamous group to which they belong. The name *Makuna* is of Geral origin—the generalized Tupi trade language of the Amazon—and used only
by outsiders. Like the vernacular names of other tribal groups in the Vaupés
region Makuna refers primarily to the language group, or the set of clans
sharing a common language. According to the general Tukanoan model,
the language group corresponds to the exogamous unit of clans related as
brothers. This, however, is not the case with the Makuna. Currently, the
500 or so Makuna speakers in the Pirá-Paraná and Apaporis River basin are
grouped into two exogamous and intermarrying units named after the two
principal clans in each group, the *Ide Masa* (Water People) and the *Yiba
Masa* (Land People).[6] Together, the two exogamous units comprise some
twelve to fifteen extant clans.[7] It is said that the language spoken today by
the two groups was originally proper to the Water People. The term *Makuna*
can thus have two senses. In a strict sense it refers to the Water People as an
exogamous and originally language-bearing unit and, in a wider sense, it
refers to all the Makuna-speaking clans. The relatively well defined territory
and a long history of close intermarriage among the Makuna speakers have
given them a sense of collective identity. I generally use the term *Makuna* in
the wider sense to refer to the whole language community.

According to Makuna origin myths, the earliest ancestors of the various
clans were born as anacondas at a point in the east that they refer to as *Ide
sohe* (Water Door), where the rivers flow out of this world. The ancestral
anacondas swam upriver from there following the large river that the
Makuna call *Ohengü riaka* (Milk River), and then they entered the Apaporis
and later the Pirá-Paraná, which to the Makuna represent the axis of their
territory. At various points along the Apaporis and the lower Pirá-Paraná,
and the principal tributaries of the latter—the Umunya, Toaka, and
Komenya Rivers—the ancestral anacondas came up on land and turned into
people. These sites, called *masa yuhiri wiri* (waking-up houses) are the birthplaces of the different clans. To ordinary people these mythical places manifest themselves as rocks and rapids in the rivers, or as tapirs' salt licks in

the forest, but to shamans they are huge malocas, beautifully decorated and full of men wearing the complete ritual regalia, including shining macaw feather headdresses.

Makuna say that at death the soul of the deceased travels to the waking-up house and comes alive as a spirit person. At the birth of a boy child the spirit of a deceased grandfather, or in the case of a girl child that of a grandmother spirit, travels from the house of the dead to the house of the living and enters the body of the newborn child, who thus becomes identified with the dead ancestor whose name it receives. This notion of the soul's cyclical journey between the houses of the living and the dead is expressed in the practice of naming children after deceased relatives two generations removed. Thus, the birth names of its members form part of the clan's spiritual wealth.

The waking-up house of the first ancestor of all Water People clans, known as *Ide Hino* (Water Anaconda), is a huge underwater maloca at Man-aítara, an island set in the midst of a series of rocks and rapids in the Apaporis River below the mouth of the Pirá-Paraná. The individual ancestors of the various Water People clans traveled upstream from this point, founding other malocas. At the mouth of the Toaka River on the lower Pirá-Paraná, the Ide Masa clan proper received from their ancestors the clan goods—Yuruparí flutes, gourds of beeswax, coca, tobacco, yagé pots, and ritual dance regalia—that allow the present-day clan members to live and protect themselves from spiritual dangers. This sacred wealth kept in an invisible maloca at the mouth of the Toaka comprises the spiritual weapons, or *küni oka* (defenses), of the clan. Therefore the Toaka River is referred to as the *ide ma* (water path) or "lifeline" of the Ide Masa clan.

The Yiba Masa are the proper owners of the Komenya River. A salt lick at the mouth of the Komenya called *Itara* is their waking-up house, where their clan ancestor emerged into this world and where the souls of their dead return. Here their ancestral spirits bestowed spiritual wealth, sacred goods, and Yuruparí instruments upon the first Yiba Masa people. Like the Toaka River for the Water People, the Komenya is the ancestral territory of the Land People, their life-giving water path that connects the living with the dead and the present with the mythical past.

Today both Land and Water People live on the Komenya River. Less than a handful of malocas remain on the Toaka River, because several genera-

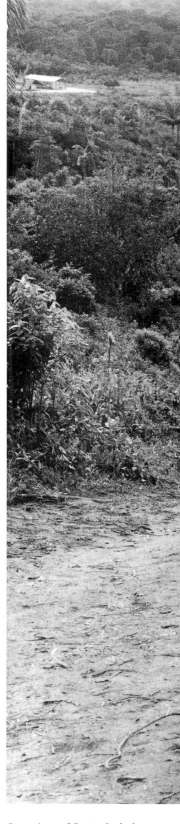

Overview of Santa Isabel village. This picture was taken at the inception of a Dance of the Spirits as the masked dancers approach the dance house. (Photo by K. Århem)

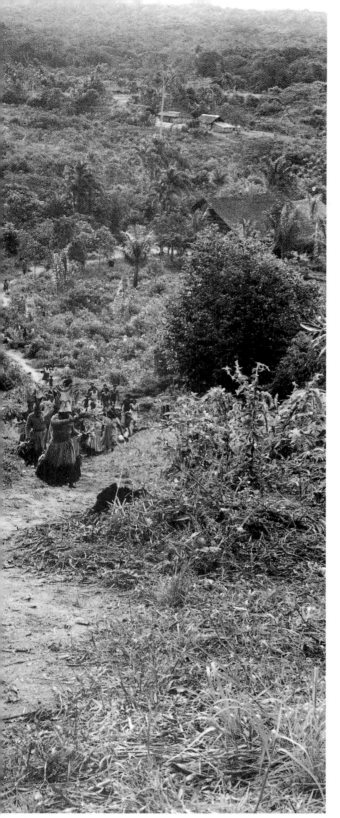

tions ago the Water People were forced to move to the Komenya, fleeing the persecution of rubber hunters. In the early part of the twentieth century they sought refuge among their Yiba Masa allies, with whom they had intermarried for generations, forming a numerically and politically stronger community. Bringing their Yuruparí instruments and other ritual goods from the Toaka, the Ide Masa clan settled on the Komenya, where they are found today.

The Water and Land People are, according to Makuna tradition, proper marriage partners. A well-known Makuna myth tells how Yiba, the ancestor of the Land People and son of a dog mother—appearing alternately as a jaguar, an anaconda, and a human being—married Yawira, Water Anaconda's daughter. Water Anaconda is the owner and guardian of all water animals. Yiba lives in the forest and is the owner and guardian of the land animals. While hunting in the forest, so the story goes, Yiba encountered Yawira collecting fruit and instantly fell in love with her. He captured her and brought her to his house.

Since Yawira was a water being, belonging to the river world, she found it difficult living with Yiba at first. His raw, wild forest food made her thin and ill. "Your food is no good," she said to Yiba. "It is not real food. I am going to my father's house to bring you some real food." She left and then returned with manioc and other cultivated plants that are still grown in the gardens today. Because Yiba did not know tobacco or coca, he smoked and chewed the leaves of wild trees. Therefore Yawira returned to her father's underwater maloca and brought tobacco leaves and coca plants for Yiba to cultivate. But Yiba thought that the tobacco leaves were fish and ate them. He became ill, vomited, and defecated outside his house. A tobacco plant grew from the spot where he had defecated. Yiba also received yagé and ceremonial feather headdresses from his father-in-law. In return he offered Water Anaconda smoked meat. Later Water Anaconda invited Yiba to a ritual dance in his underwater house. Yawira gave Yiba a magical substance that turned him into an anaconda and allowed him to swim in the river. Yiba brought *wasoa* (hevea fruit) to his father-in-law to be distributed during *wasoa basa* (the dance of the hevea fruit). To reciprocate Yiba then invited Water Anaconda and his people to *wamii basa* (the dance of the umarí fruit) in his own house. This time Water Anaconda brought fruit from his

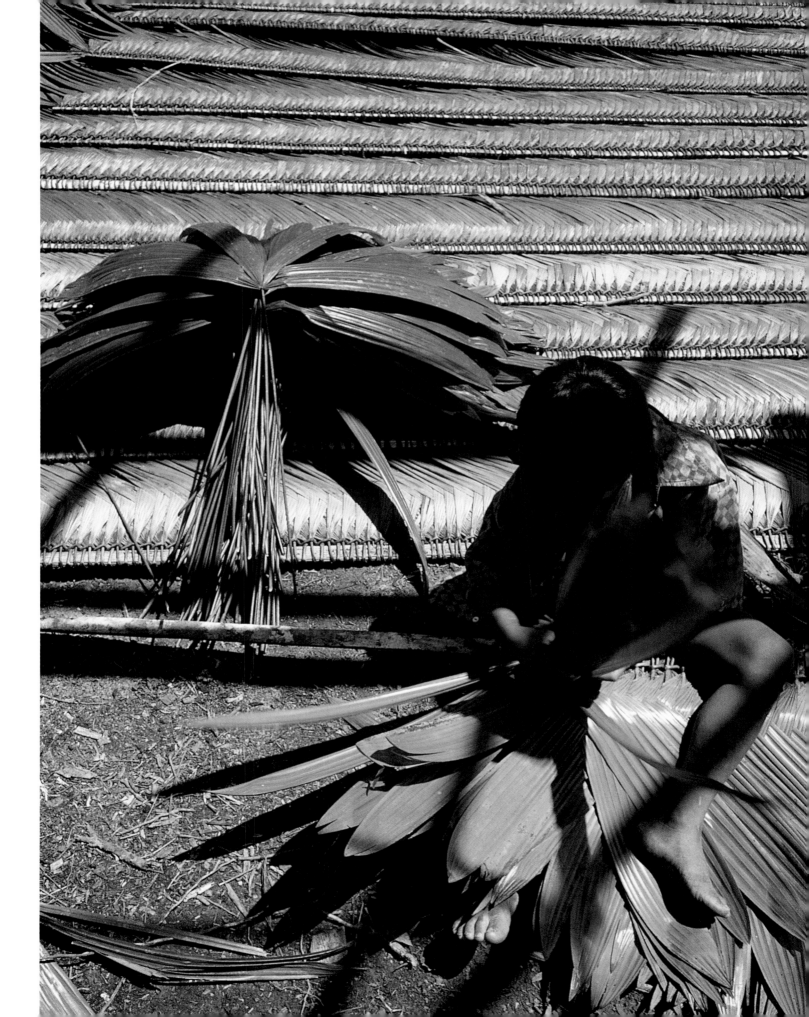

Man weaving palm fronds for the roof of the maloca. Various species and techniques are used according to the availability of palms and the personal preference of the house owner.

underwater gardens. Thus the Makuna received their ritual dances, yagé, and the sacred dance regalia.

This much abbreviated fragment of the epic myth about Yiba and Yawira, recounted in a multitude of different versions, conveys a significant message about Makuna identity. The marriage between Yiba and Yawira established the primordial alliance between the Land and Water People and brought about a creative conjunction between different cosmic domains— land and water, forest and river. Through this union society was born, and the alliance between the beings of the forest and the river was consolidated by the exchange of foods, ritual goods, and dances. When Yawira brought cultivated plants, spirit food, and ceremonial paraphernalia from the river world up onto land and into this world the Makuna culture as we know it today emerged. The manioc and other cultivated food plants, coca, tobacco, and yagé, along with the sacred goods and the ritual dances, the myths and the shamanic knowledge, are the cultural riches of the Pirá-Paraná peoples, which still sustain and give meaning to their lives.

THE RESILIENCE OF TRADITION

Between January 1972 and December 1973 I lived with the Makuna of the Komenya River (literally Axe River). I stayed mostly in the magnificent maloca of Ignacio of the Ide Masa clan. In his mid-forties he was an influential shaman and the principal headman of the Komenya Makuna. In his house I was offered a place to sling my hammock and store my goods. Throughout my stay Ignacio and his two wives generously shared their food with me and patiently explained the mysteries of Makuna culture. In return I brought them desired goods and needed medicines. I think it is no exaggeration to say that over the years we forged a friendship, which has allowed me to return to Komenya several times.

Subsisting by shifting cultivation, fishing, hunting, and gathering of wild forest food—including frogs and insects—the Makuna then led an austere but gratifying life. Some 250 people, equally distributed between Land and Water People clans as well as a few Tuyuka families, lived in twenty settlements along the banks and tributaries of the Komenya River. The daily chores were largely tuned to the rhythms of nature, the alternating pulse of floods and dry spells, and the breeding and fruiting seasons of animals and plants. Men hunted, fished, and crafted weapons, tools, and baskets;

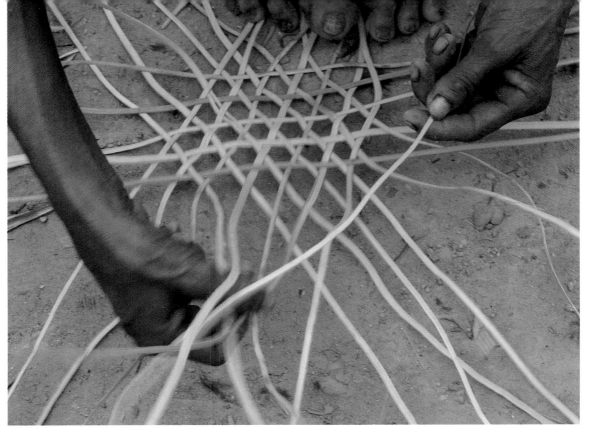

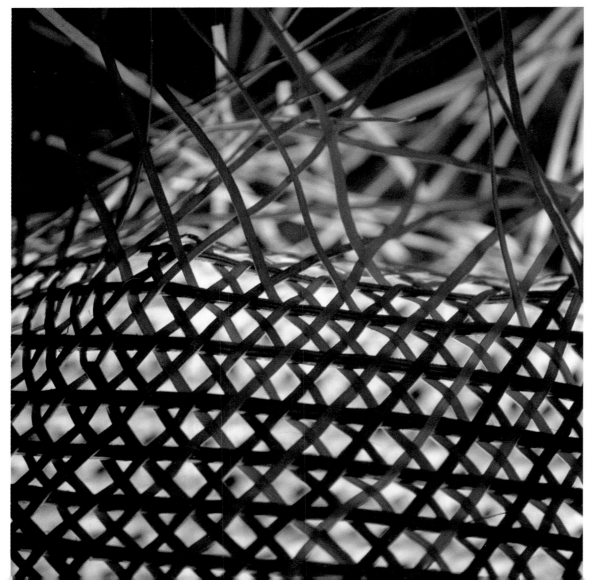

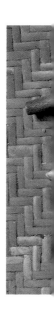

Above, left: Beginning of a basket.

Below, left: Nearly completed basket.

Right: Polished and decorated nut (from the *Astrocarym* palm) used as container for blessed red body paint.

Below: Snail-shell container and bird-bone tubes for tobacco snuff; the snuff is blown through the tube by one man into each of the nostrils of another.

Below, right: Blowpipe, darts, and wooden quiver. Along with the shotgun, the blowpipe is still an important hunting weapon among the Makuna. Birds and monkeys are killed with the darts, smeared with deadly *curare* poison.

women tended children and the cultivated gardens, cooked, and made all of their pottery. Frequent rituals, small and large, punctuated daily life and invested practical activities with deep religious meaning; the cosmic blended with the social and the sacred was always a part of the mundane.

Makuna men and women manufactured and used most of the traditional Indian tools and artifacts, including baskets, pottery, blowguns, bows and arrows, and fish spears. The goods that they could not produce themselves, such as fish hooks, nylon lines, knives, axes, metal pots, and clothes, were obtained from traders who occasionally traveled up the Pirá-Paraná and Apaporis Rivers. The Makuna sold or bartered hides, manioc flour (farinha), or worked periodically for white rubber merchants on the Mirití and upper Apaporis Rivers. Several Makuna men had spent many years—some ten or fifteen—working for white patrons, whom the Makuna saw more as a source of desired trade goods than as a threat. Encounters with traders and missionaries were sporadic and transient; there was no school, no shop, and no chapel in their territory. The nearest white settlements were La Pedrera on the Caquetá River and Mitú on the Vaupés River, both several weeks' distance away.

The Makuna depended on relatively simple tools, handled with competence, and an impressive knowledge of the local environment for survival. Their food consisted mainly of manioc bread, fish, and meat, supplemented by vegetables, fruit, nuts, and insects. During my prolonged initial stay among them, I never went hungry for long, nor suffered any serious deficiency or illness.

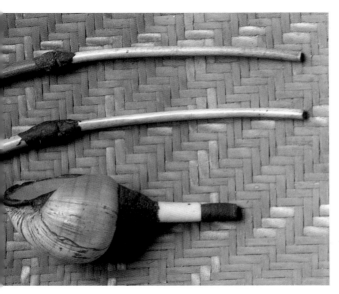

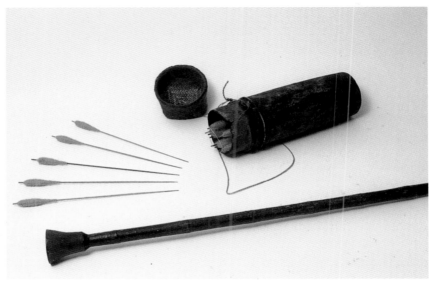

By 1988, more than fifteen years after my first visit, the population was now regrouped into three nucleated villages and only a few large, traditional malocas remained. In each village there was a small school house and a chapel built by the inhabitants themselves, and in the largest village, Santa Isabel, were now also a shop and a rudimentary but functioning airstrip. Local teachers, paid by the Catholic mission, today provide elementary instruction in Spanish. The Makuna children learn to read, write, and count, and mission-trained catechists give a simple religious service every Sunday in the chapel.

The villages have brought a new authority structure to the local community. The headmen of the remaining malocas are still influential in local politics, but each village now also has a *capitan* who is appointed by community members and recognized by the regional authorities as the official village spokesperson. Though this position is new, those who occupy it are senior men of traditional standing—prestigious headman and shamans. Thus the old and the new blend in with the emergent power structure of the village communities.

The presence of the state and the church in the communities is manifest in the proliferation of new civic and religious functionaries—including village headmen, schoolteachers, catechists, village secretaries, health promoters, and representatives of local development committees and youth clubs. Paradoxically, it may seem, the increased integration of the native communities into the regional administrative framework has also entailed a greater measure of Indian self-determination. In the late 1970s a considerable part of the Vaupés region (3,354,097 hectares, including the whole Pirá-Paraná area) was declared a *resguardo* (protected area) guaranteeing the Indians legal rights to their traditional lands. Though this change represents a momentous improvement of their juridical status in the national context, most Makuna remain unaware of the new legislation's full significance.

On the surface daily life appears much the same today as in the early 1970s. The men still fish and hunt while the women still work in the manioc gardens. The rhythm, pattern, and techniques of subsistence are unaltered. Yet the local economy has undergone great changes. Government restrictions on fur trading and a short-lived revival of the rubber economy in the mid-1970s induced many young men to seek temporary employment with white rubber patrons and traders.

One young man, Bere, who lives in a small community in the headwaters of Komenya, told me on my return in 1988 that he and his family had suffered many hardships after I left the area in the mid-1970s. "From where could we get our trade goods when you had gone?" he exclaimed. "We were poor, very poor." Together with his younger brother he went to work on the upper Apaporis for a white rubber patron known as Monolopez. They worked for two years before running away. "We could not stand it anymore," he said, showing me a long scar on his left arm. "My boss struck me here with a machete, almost cutting my arm off. He beat and mistreated us all the time. We worked hard, from dawn to long after dark. Sometimes we returned to camp after midnight, and still he hit us." Bere was full of resentment when he told his story but also proud of the trade goods he had acquired from the rubber camp. "Look here," he said, pointing at his worn-out shirt and tattered pair of trousers, "I brought this from the camp." He also showed me hammocks, a machete and axe, and a set of cooking pots. Apart from a small house and two canoes, these are the greater part of Bere's material possessions.

Several other Makuna men had experiences like Bere's. To defend themselves against the rubber patrons and avoid being forced into debt bondage the people along the Komenya in the late 1970s decided to form village communities. Encouraged by the Catholic mission, they founded the village of Santa Isabel on the lower Komenya and, upstream, two other communities, Santa Rosa and Puerto Amazonas.[8] The formation of these administrative villages, endorsed by the regional authorities in Mitú, enabled the Indians to defend their interests against unjust exploitation by the rubber patrons.

The need for a constant supply of trade goods remained, however. In the early 1980s when the coca trade reached the Pirá-Paraná region, the Indians turned to it as a new means of obtaining coveted trade goods. The Makuna and their neighbors traditionally cultivated and used the leaves of the coca plant as a mild stimulant and as an important ritual substance.[9] Raw material for chemically refined cocaine, coca now also became a lucrative crop for the drug trade. The coca boom engaged several young Indian men in the Komenya area, and much of the traditional garden land was turned into coca plantations. The young men cultivated the plants and transported the harvested leaves to the white *coqueros* who had established themselves on the upper Pirá-Paraná. Successful Indians obtained great quantities of trade goods. A few even employed fellow Indians on their plantations or sold trade goods for profit in the community. Shotguns, transistor radios, watches, and outboard motors trickled into the Makuna community, each item drawing the external world nearer.

The coca trade created tensions and cleavages as well as economic opportunities in the community. Like most forces of change it was both a blessing and a burden. For example, some men spent most of their time cultivating coca for the coqueros, neglecting food production for their families. Drugs like liquor and *basuco* found their way into the villages, adding to the stresses on community life.[10] There was also an exodus of young men going to work for coqueros in various parts of Colombia. When they returned, many now speaking a rudimentary Spanish, they brought new concerns and demands to their home villages.

The coca boom declined as suddenly as it rose. In the mid-1980s the coqueros abruptly left the area, apparently because of the combined fall in the black-market price, pressure from the Catholic mission, and prosecution by civil authorities. Soon life in Komenya reverted to the rhythm and pattern of the preboom days. Young men returned from their working sojourns in different parts of the country to marry local girls and settle down in their natal communities. Upon returning to Komenya in 1988 I was impressed that practically all recent marriages conformed to the traditional pattern of exchange among close relatives (cross cousins).

The changes in Makuna society that I have witnessed over the past twenty years are only the latest in a much longer and turbulent history of contact with outsiders. By the mid-eighteenth century, Spanish and Portuguese explorers had already traversed the interfluvial forests between the Vaupés and Apaporis Rivers, probably following the course of the Pirá-Paraná River. Soldiers, slave raiders, and *bandeirantes* from Brazil had by then harried the native groups in the region for at least a century. Indians were captured and forced to work on colonial plantations along the Brazilian coast and in settlements along the Amazon River and its major tributaries. Traders and backwoodsmen crossed the forest in search of quinine bark, sarsaparilla, vanilla, chocolate, indigo, and rubber. New diseases against which Indians had little resistance followed in the wake of the colonization process. As a result the native population of the Vaupés and upper Río Negro was severely depleted by the end of the nineteenth century.

Little is known about the first encounters between Indians and whites in the Pirá-Paraná area. The Makuna are first mentioned in the chronicles of the Portuguese explorer Tomas Antônio Ribeiro-Ferreira, who in 1776 reported of "Mucuna" settlements along the Apaporis River.[11] But it was not until the turn of the twentieth century that the German ethnographer Theodor Koch-Grünberg, who traveled the Pirá-Paraná and Apaporis Rivers, provided the first detailed and reliable account of the Indian groups in the region. He not only mentions various Makuna-speaking groups but also visited and described the location of several Makuna malocas that can still be found today.

The great rubber boom had reached the northwest Amazon during Koch-Grünberg's travels. The terror and turmoil it caused continued well into the 1920s. Mostly affecting the Caquetá and Putumayo River basins south of the Vaupés River, the destruction was also felt among the Makuna and their neighbors. Thousands of Indians were forced to work for white rubber barons, and those who fled from the rubber camps were usually captured and brutally executed. Groups that resisted the initial raids were massacred. From 1900 to 1910 some 40,000 Indians—probably more than half of the Indian population in the entire northwest Amazonia—died as a consequence of the activities of rubber companies such as the infamous Casa Arana, later renamed the Peruvian Amazon Company.[12] Competition from rubber plantations in Southeast Asia in the 1920s caused a dramatic decline in rubber exploitation in Amazonia. Petty rubber patrons, however, continued to exploit Indians in the northwest Amazon to the mid-1970s.

Makuna historical traditions tell of a time before the arrival of the whites when raiding and warfare were common among the native groups in the region.[13] Stories and legends recall countless battles with their traditional enemies, the Tanimuka and Yauna. These violent conflicts seem to have been motivated by cosmological and shamanic notions rather than by any competition for scarce resources or politics. To the Makuna the Tanimuka and Yauna were "jaguar people," sorcerers and evil spirit beings who posed a threat to social and cosmic order. Their shamans were said to

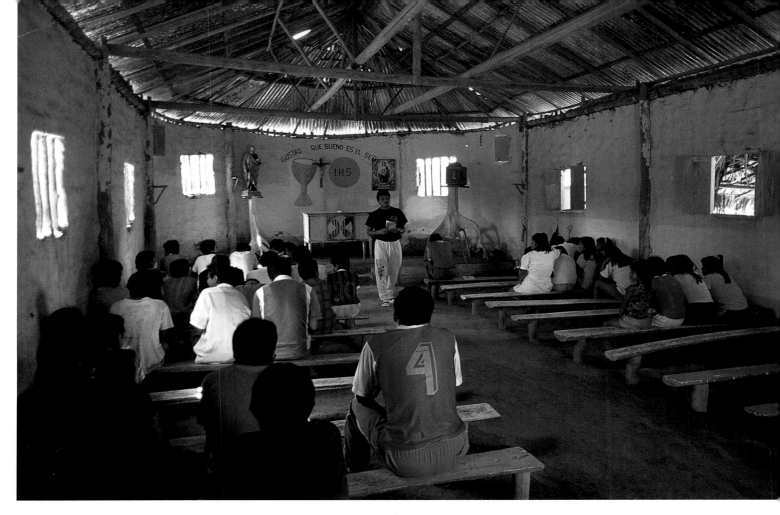

Sunday mass at Piedra Nyi, Pirá-Paraná. Profound changes have occurred among the Makuna over the past twenty years; many traditional longhouse communities have been replaced by villages, each with a school, a cooperative shop, and a chapel.

send disease, misfortune, and death to their enemies. The Makuna of today can point to sites where battles were fought and enemy groups defeated. They say that at one point the Yauna were almost completely exterminated but a powerful Makuna shaman who pitied them decided to cease the hostilities. As a result the Makuna and the remaining Yauna intermarry peacefully today.

These tribal wars were a prominent part of indigenous life in the region. For defense purposes settlements were much larger in the past—a single maloca could hold one hundred or more people—and war leaders occasionally exercised considerable authority over entire territories. The Makuna, just as the other Tukanoan groups in the Pirá-Paraná area, show traces of a hierarchical ideology of chiefs, chanters, warriors, shamans, and servants, which contrasts with their current egalitarian political practice.[14] It is possible that this political ideology was once put into practice by powerful chiefs subjugating war captives as servants or slaves, which is not altogether improbable in light of our present historical knowledge about the Amazon valley. Warlike chiefdoms, ruled by great chiefs and organized into ranked strata of aristocrats, priests, warriors, and slaves (mostly war captives), did exist in the upper and central Amazon valley at the time of the Spanish and Portuguese conquests. Perhaps the imaginary chiefdom implied by Makuna political ideology mirrors these sixteenth-century Amazonian chiefdoms.[15]

The personal memories of elder Makuna individuals stretch back to the turn of the twentieth century when the appearance of white rubber hunters and traders from Brazil and Peru caused unrest among the Indians and resulted in a series of moves from the Apaporis and lower Pirá-Paraná Rivers to more inaccessible tributaries and headwaters. In the early decades of this century a group of Water People—including Ignacio's grandfather and his family—moved from their homeland on the Toaka River to the upper reaches of Komenya to escape the incursions of the rubber hunters. But the whites continued to penetrate the Pirá-Paraná area, pursuing the free Indians to the most remote parts. Below the present village of Santa Isabel there is a hill known as the Port of the Whites where rubber hunters once kept imprisoned Indians in a fortified camp.

By the 1940s, when Ignacio was a child, times had changed. The rubber economy was on the decline after a short resurge during World War II. The brute violence of earlier decades had also been replaced by a system of debt bondage, which lasted until the 1970s. Small-scale rubber patrons and merchants tempted the Indians with trade goods that were paid by working in the rubber camps. For a pair of trousers, a shirt, and a handkerchief, Ignacio's father had to work for two years in a camp on the Apaporis. Ignacio told me his father had profoundly resented the whites ever since. When the regional authorities urged the Pirá-Paraná Indians to move farther down on the Apaporis in order to become a more manageable labor force in the post-war rubber industry, a group of Makuna headed by Ignacio's father refused.

Instead Ignacio's father withdrew deeper into the headwaters of the Komenya. Since he did not want his children to learn Spanish, he also refused to send his children to any of the mission schools that had begun to appear in various parts of the Vaupés region. "That is why we lived hidden in the forest and why I never learned to speak any Spanish," Ignacio explained.

Ignacio decided to move from the headwaters of Komenya to its lower reaches and renew contact with white traders and missionaries in the 1950s. He also sent one of his sons, Venancio, to the mission school in La

Pedrera on the Caquetá River. Venancio was the first Makuna from Komenya to attend school and learn Spanish. Now several of Ignacio's sons speak, read, and write Spanish. Yet he has kept some of his children from school in an effort to reduce influences from the outside world and to strengthen old Makuna traditions. One of his young sons is currently training to become a shaman and a chanter like Ignacio himself.

Similar stories are told about early contact with the whites by other Makuna, like Joaquín, now a middle-aged headman living in a traditional-style maloca on the Apaporis. When Joaquín was a young boy, a white rubber hunter took his father to a work camp on the upper Apaporis. After several years of hard labor Joaquín's father deserted the camp and returned home. Sometime later, when the white patron came to round up defectors and recruit more men, he was ambushed and killed. Fearing retaliation, many Indians hid in the forest and headwaters of the Pirá-Paraná. Others, like Joaquín's father and his family, moved down the Apaporis to seek protection under other, less brutal patrons. The lower Apaporis, which had been virtually depopulated since the rubber boom at the turn of the twentieth century, began to be repopulated in the 1940s and 1950s. Makuna families, such as Joaquín's, reclaimed the ancestral land since the Apaporis is the mythical birthplace of the ancestral founder of the Water People clans.

There have been sporadic missionary activities along the Vaupés and Apaporis Rivers since the mid-eighteenth century.[16] Ribeiro-Ferreira reported seeing various mission villages along the Apaporis in 1776. Starting in the 1850s, Carmelite and Franciscan missionaries made repeated attempts to civilize and nucleate the Indians on the Vaupés and its principal tributaries. They founded mission villages that were soon abandoned after strong resistance from the Indians and white traders who felt threatened. The Salesians and Montfortians gained a permanent foothold in the Vaupés region in the early part of the twentieth century. They regrouped the Indians into mission villages, burned malocas, and suppressed ancient rituals. The Javerianos replaced the Montfortians in 1949 and have controlled, for the most part, both the missionary activities and the secular education in the region ever since. Today the attitude of the Catholic church toward the Indians has changed and become more sensitive to their needs and cultural values.

In the late 1960s Bible translators of the Summer Institute of Linguistics—a branch of the Wycliffe Bible Society—first entered the region, establishing themselves among most of the Indians groups. They made contact with the Makuna and opened an airstrip on the Komenya River in the early 1970s. Since then translators have worked and intermittently lived among the Makuna. The activities of the Summer Institute of Linguistics, consisting mainly of Bible translation and linguistic work (the creation of simplified indigenous orthographies), have been rather inconspicuous compared to the Catholic missionizing. Yet the sheer presence of outsiders, regardless of their degree of interaction, has had a profound impact on indigenous life in the region.

Although the Catholic mission has a long history in the Colombian Vaupés, its presence was only intermittent in the Pirá-Paraná area until the

Young girl in a cotton dress. Cloth and cotton dresses are in great demand among the Makuna, traded for manioc flour and—increasingly—gold.

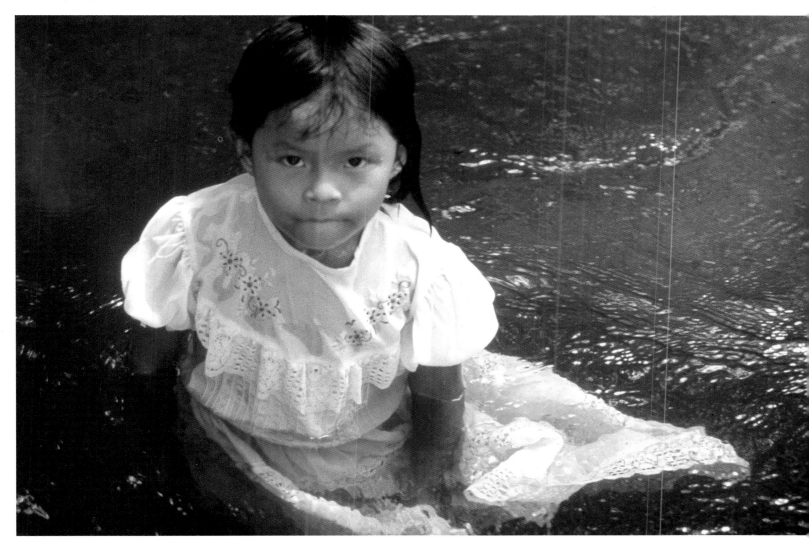

1970s. Over the past twenty years the influence of the Catholic church on the native communities in the Pirá-Paraná area has been pervasive. The missionaries have been instrumental in encouraging the Indians to regroup into nucleated villages, build schools and chapels, construct airstrips, and cut trails through the forest, thus connecting the different villages with one another and with the outside world. The success of their labors, however, has depended less on the promise of spiritual returns than on the material rewards they have brought in the form of remunerated work and improved access to trade goods.

Despite the dramatic changes over the past few decades and the progressive opening up of their society to outside influences, Makuna traditions remain vital and compelling. Ritual life is not only intact but seems to have intensified as a reaction against the mounting pressures from the outside. Many of the rituals performed during my earlier stay are now conducted with renewed fervor. Makuna culture seems to provide a remarkably stable conceptual framework for interpreting and validating current events. Conversely, traditional notions are reshaped and given altered meanings by new experiences. In this way the Makuna try to make sense out of a changing reality and, at the same time, to control and direct it. Nurtured by the past, Makuna cultural traditions are vigorously alive in the present.

On the Apaporis, local Indians have established a cooperative brown sugar processing plant. The Makuna are increasingly looking for sources of cash to obtain coveted trade goods.

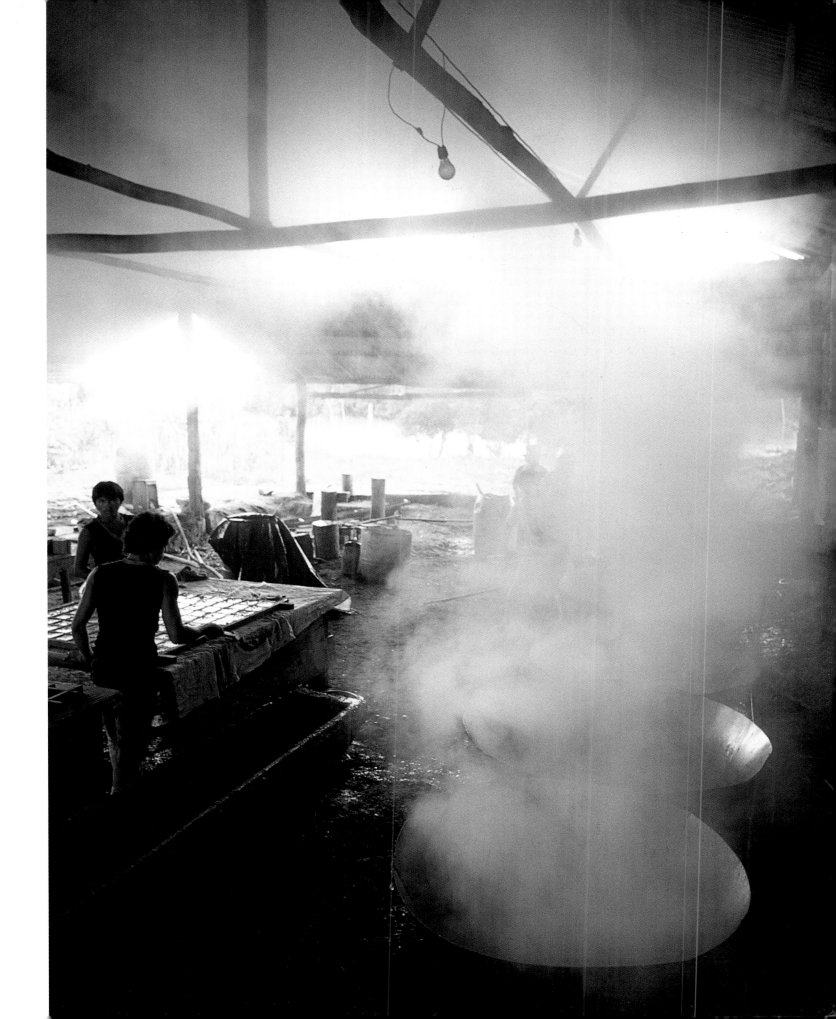

3
THE
LAND

The Makuna sometimes describe their cosmos as an immense wasp nest divided into layers, each forming a world unto itself. The middle level is the earth inhabited by human beings, plants, and animals. The upper layers form the sky world. The sun, moon, stars, thunder, and lightning, which to the Makuna are powerful spirit beings, inhabit the uppermost levels of the sky. The level immediately above the earth, called the path of the wind, is the abode of vultures and swift-flying raptors. The layers beneath the earth constitute the underworld, which is peopled by ants, worms, frogs, and the soulless corpses of the dead. A celestial river runs across the sky and a chthonic river traverses the underworld. Each day the sun travels the celestial river from east to west, and each night it follows the underworld river from west to east, completing a cosmic circuit.

The Makuna earth is flat and circular like the clay griddle on which women bake bread in the maloca. Along the edge of their world is an imagined circle of hills supporting the sky and protecting its inhabitants. There are four gateways at each of the cardinal directions and one in the center that allows access into and out of the world. *Ide sohe* (Water Door) is the gateway in the east where the sun rises every morning and where earth fuses with the sky. It is the source of all life on earth and the mouth of the great *Ohengü riaka* (Milk River), which traverses the earth and collects all terrestrial waters. The gateway in the west, *Huna sohe* (Door of Suffering), is the end of the world. Associated with death and disease it is the entrance for the destructive forces of the underworld that periodically invade the earth. The gateways to the north and south are called *Warua soheri* (Rib Doors), symbolically relating the cosmos to the human body.

The lower part of the Apaporis River is perceived as the entry to the Makuna world, marking the beginning of their ancestral territory.

This mythical world is mapped onto major landmarks—hills, rivers, and rapids—of the Makuna territory. The mountains at Mitú and La Pedrera, the hills along the Taraira and upper Pirá-Paraná Rivers, the majestic falls at Yuruparí on the Vaupés and at Araracuara on the Caquetá Rivers define the extent of the known and named world and form the protective mountain wall encircling it. The Makuna say that the world begins at the falls of *Yuisi ngumu* (La Libertad) on the lower Apaporis and ends at

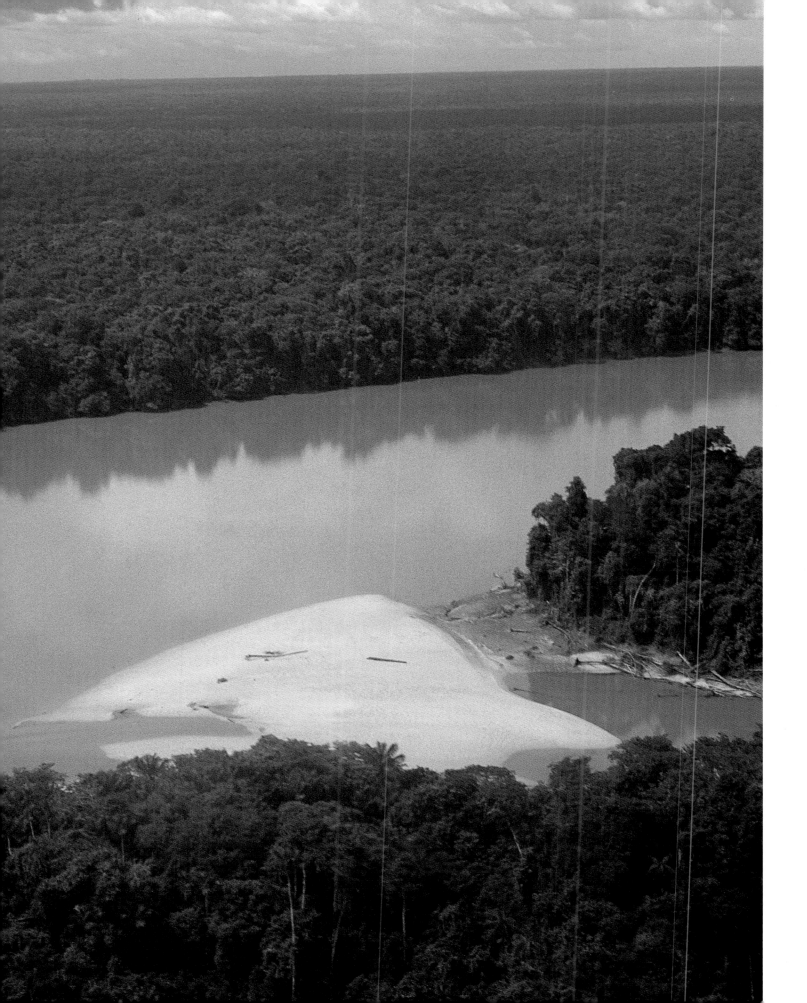

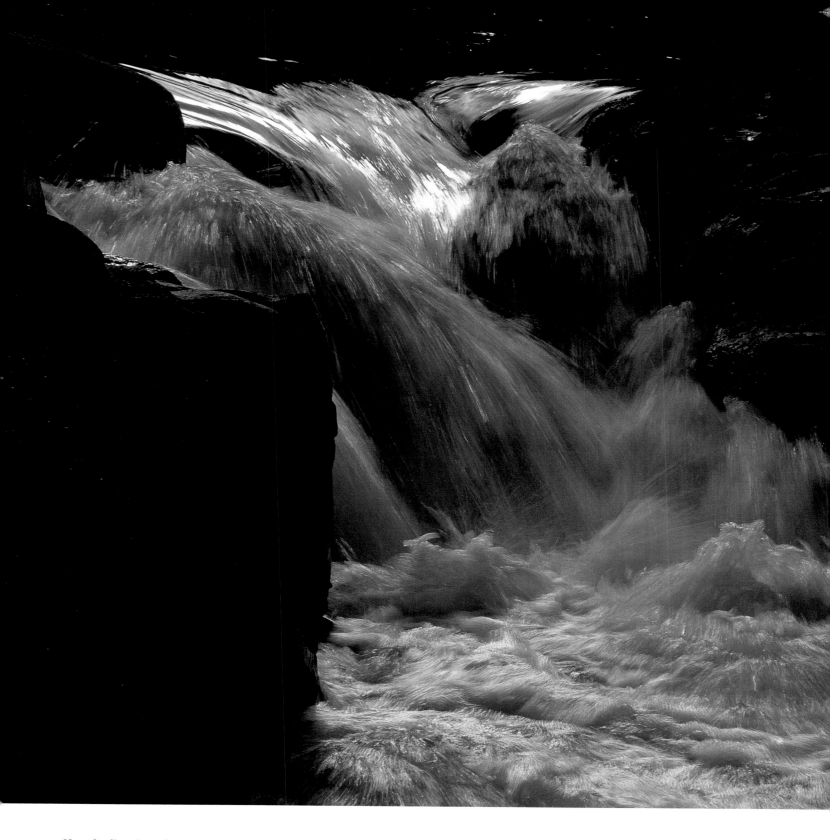

Hasa hudiro (Jirijirímo Falls) on its upper reaches. La Libertad is their Water
Door and Jirijirímo Falls their Door of Suffering. The end of the Makuna
world is the beginning of other worlds and other territories. The Jirijirímo
Falls is thus the Water Door of the Kabiyarí people on the upper Apaporis.

Jirijirímo Falls on the upper Apaporis. This majestic cascade— known as the Door of Suffering—is the place where Makuna territory ends and the souls of the dead leave this world.

In this way the adjacent but distinct territories of the various native groups of the Vaupés region are interlocked in a complex mosaic of imaginary worlds, each conceptualized as an immense maloca.

The Makuna live at the center of this universe and refer to themselves as *güdareko ngana* (people of the center). Their geographical and cosmological center is said to be close to the headwaters of the Komenya River, an uninhabited and rarely visited sacred site called *Tabotiro* (Place of White Grass). Those who have seen it say it is an open, treeless area in the midst of the forest, covered with shining white grass. In the beginning of time, here the ancestral beings measured the world and separated earth from sky. At Tabotiro, the Makuna believe, there is an invisible cosmic pillar reaching to the uppermost sky and extending deep into the underworld along which shamans may travel between the layers of the cosmos.

The ancestral territory of the Makuna-speaking clans stretches from the island of Manaítara on the Apaporis River to the great waterfall of *Nahu gohe* (Hole of the Manioc Bread) in the middle of the Pirá-Paraná, above the mouth of the Komenya River. Clan territories, defined by the water paths and birthplaces of the individual clan ancestors, further subdivide the area. The Indian groups living on the upper Pirá-Paraná, including the Barasana, Taiwano, and Tatuyo, are called *hode ngana* (headwaters people) while the more remote peoples living at the edge of the Makuna world, the Tukano, Cubeo, Yukuna, and Witoto, are called *tünima ngana* (people of the margin). Beyond their borders live only strangers and whites, demons and monsters.

The people of the center are like the inhabitants of a single maloca. The hills encircling them and the spiritual powers of their shamans protect the Makuna from the world beyond. When the shaman performs *wanore* (protective shamanism) his mind travels along this ring of hills, shielding the people of the center from outside dangers and evil forces. To the shaman, then, the world is a cosmic maloca, with hills for walls and the sky for a roof.

RIVERS OF HUNGER, RIVERS OF PLENTY

The flat, forested land of the Pirá-Paraná area in the heart of northwest Amazonia forms part of the ancient and weathered land formation called the Guiana shield. It is an area of meager soils and nutrient-poor rivers. Here and there dome-shaped mountains and steep rocks shoot up from the

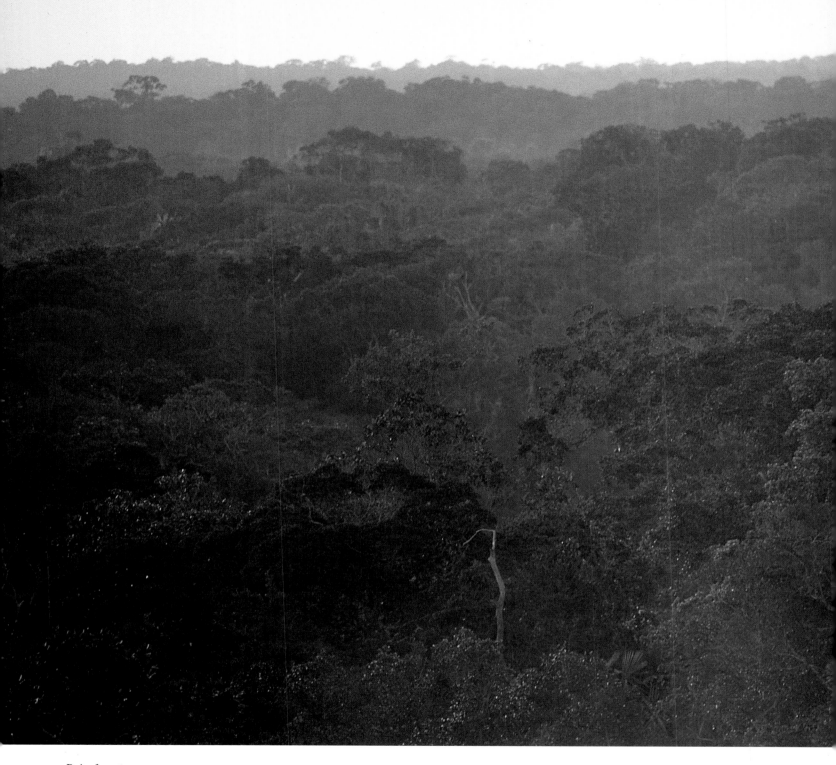

Rain-forest canopy.
Though growing on ex-
tremely poor soils, the
forests of northwest
Amazonia are perhaps
the most ecologically
diversified in the entire
Amazon basin.

otherwise undifferentiated forest cover. Yet nothing could be more mislead-
ing than this apparent uniformity of landscape: the Amazonian rain forest
is extremely differentiated, and its northwestern segment probably the
most varied and species-rich part of the entire basin.[1]

Biological diversity is the true wealth of the rain forest. Harboring more
than 80,000 plant species, of which more than 4,000 are trees, the Amazon
forest supports a formidable variety of microenvironments and a multitude

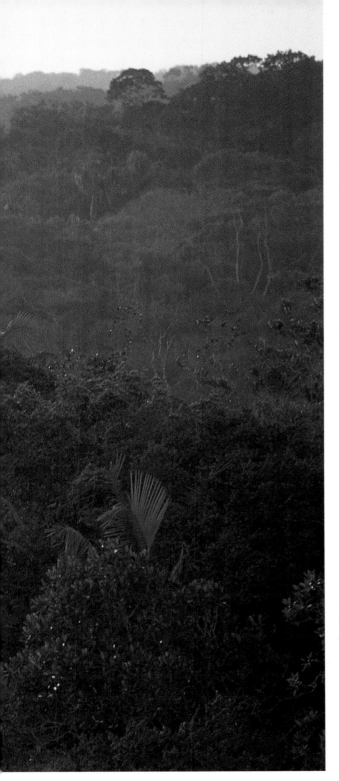

of life forms.[2] There are, however, relatively few representatives of each species. Populations are small and widely dispersed, often confined to a few localities. Compared with the plant and animal life in temperate climates, most tropical forest species are actually rare.

The lush vegetation of the Amazonian rain forest conceals the poor quality of its soils. The soil stores less than 10 percent of the nutrients in the rain forest. The rain-forest environment is a closed system that continuously and efficiently recycles the same nutrients. As soon as a leaf or branch withers and falls to the ground it begins to decay as microorganisms—fungi and bacteria—attack the debris and roots help the plants absorb the released nutrients. But precisely because the reabsorption process is so rapid, the soil is never effectively fertilized.

The hot and humid climate favors continuous growth and reproduction throughout the year. More than half of the rain that falls in the Amazon is recycled directly from the forest's immense quantity of green foliage. In the Vaupés region temperatures range between 20°C and 35°C, and the average annual rainfall exceeds 2,500 mm (100 inches). Though the Makuna distinguish a whole series of wet and dry seasons, identified by seasonal fruit and

Right: The hot and humid climate favors continual growth throughout the year; the green foliage evaporates and transpires more than half of the rain.

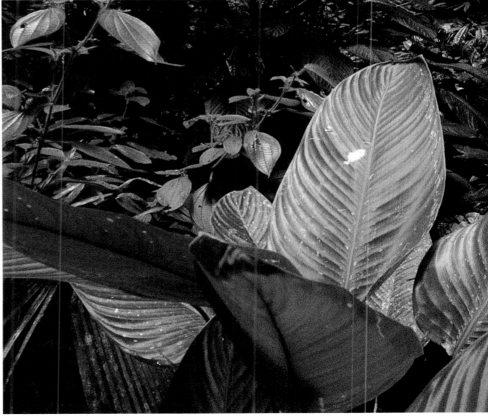

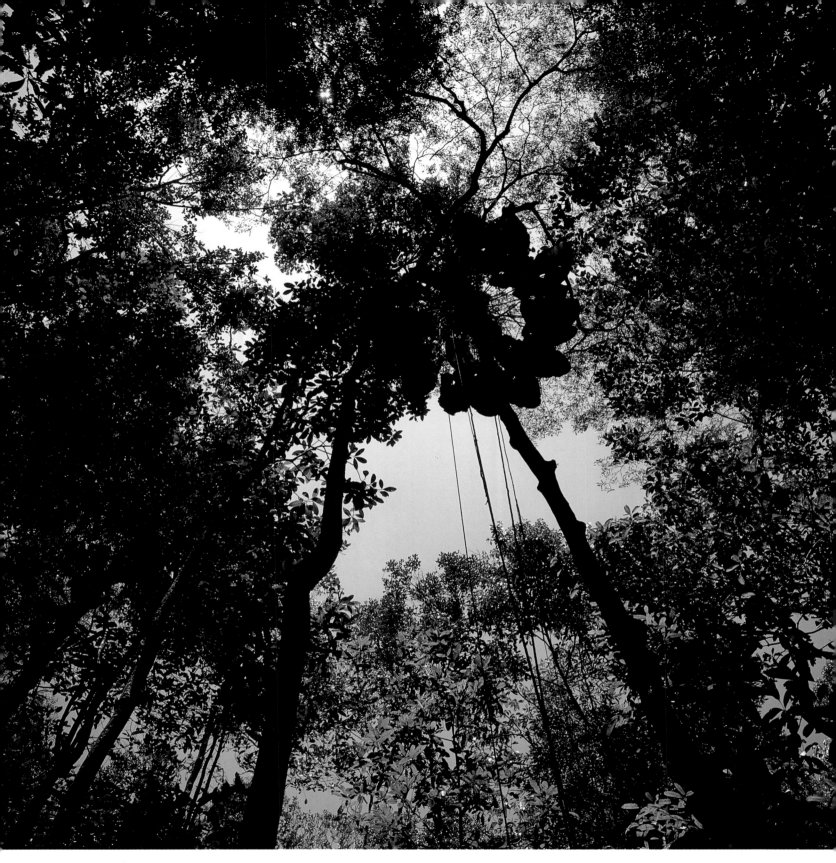

The roof of the forest is penetrated by a few, scattered giant trees reaching above the compact mass of foliage and revealing its vertical stratification.

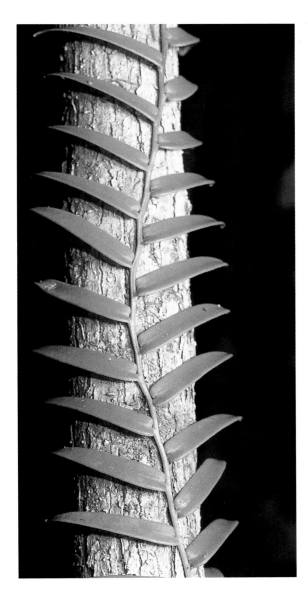

star constellations, the weather cycle in central northwest Amazonia is conventionally divided into two wet and two dry seasons. The long wet season lasts approximately from April to August, the short occupies a few weeks in October and November. The long dry season lasts from December to March, and the short for several weeks in September and October. Life in the forest is determined by this seasonal pulse, the periodicity of floods, fruiting seasons, and the reproductive cycles of migratory fish, frogs, ants, termites, and larvae, which all make up an important part of the Indian diet.

A characteristic feature of the tropical forest is its vertical differentiation and stratified structure. It forms a multilayered environment of trees, saplings, and other plants of different heights and sizes, each layer forming a distinct niche and biological community. A few scattered, giant trees reach above the dense canopy, making up the roof of the forest; below that are shorter trees and saplings; farther down there is a sparse understory of shrubs and seedlings; the forest floor is usually bare except for a thin litter of dead leaves, mosses, and fungi.

The canopy layer is so dense that the forest floor is in almost constant shade, protected from the scorching heat of the sun and the destructive tropical rain storms. The lush world of the canopy, which receives an abundance of light and rain, provides a favorable habitat for a variety of flying and climbing animals. Its wealth of leaves, fruit, seeds, and flowers sustains butterflies, bees, and wasps of all kinds; a spectacular variety of birds, including toucans, macaws, parrots, and hummingbirds; a whole range of

Faces of the forest: a climbing plant *(above)* **and a fallen seed** *(right)*.

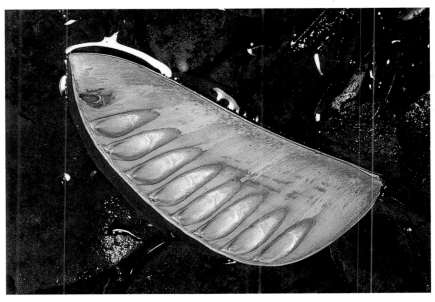

monkeys; and two genera of sloths, to mention only a few. In the deep shade of the forest floor, tapirs, peccaries, and agoutis rummage for fallen fruit, nuts, and seeds.

In the Amazon, forest and river are so closely linked, it is sometimes difficult to tell where one ends and the other begins. Animals have adapted well to the rain-forest environment with its myriad of waterways. Tree-dwelling species stay in the upper layers to escape flooding, while ground-living animals have developed an amphibianlike capacity for moving freely between land and water. The jaguar and its principal prey—tapirs, peccaries, and large rodents—are all excellent swimmers, while other predators such as anacondas, caymans, and otters live mostly in the rivers.

Even the fish depend on the forest for their food supply. At least fifty species in the Río Negro basin, and most large fish in the Vaupés River, feed almost exclusively on fruit that falls into the river.[3] Several of these species appear not to eat at all when their preferred fruit are out of season or the water has receded. Other fish feed on insects that fall into the river. According to one estimate, approximately one fourth of all the fish species of the Amazon, and possibly all young fish, feed on the thick layer of detritus and insects that periodically covers the surface of rivers and streams.[4]

No one knows how many species of fish exist in the Amazon basin, but 3,000 is an often quoted estimate, making it the world's most diverse collection of freshwater fish. In the Río Negro alone, into which the Vaupés River flows, there are more than 700 different species—mostly characins and catfish.[5] The river contains a variety of microenvironments and ecological niches that support localized populations of fish and aquatic mammals. Rapids and waterfalls form biological barriers between such animal communities; in northwest Amazonia the large characins, for example, seasonally migrate along specific routes bounded by the major cataracts of the main rivers. At the beginning of the wet season the fish descend the tributaries to spawn in the main river near the confluences. A second migration, known as *pirasemu,* takes place during the dry season when the fish ascend a main river, moving from one tributary to another in a long upriver journey that takes several years to complete.[6]

For the Indians the rivers are the highways and life-sustaining arteries of the forest. The seasonal floods determine fish migrations and spawning pat-

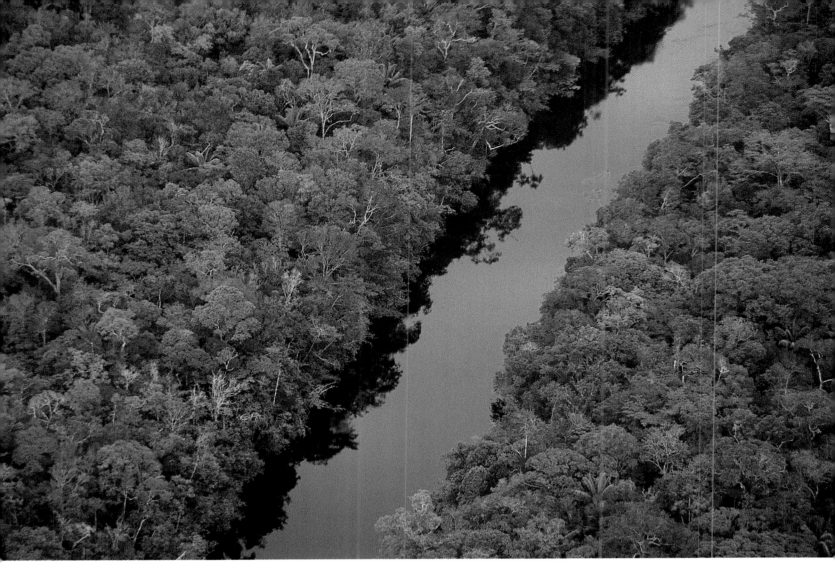

The Pirá-Paraná River is a nutrient-poor black-water river. Early explorers referred to the rivers of northwest Amazonia as rivers of hunger, yet to the Indians, the river is an abundant and unceasing source of food.

terns, which provide food for other animals living in or near rivers and streams, such as caymans, pacas, and peccaries, which all form an important part of the native diet. For groups like the Makuna the rivers are not only a source of food and the principal means of communication but also a link between the living present and the ancestral past. The mouth of the Milk River is the point of origin of humankind and the source of all life. Rivers are the "paths of the ancestors," formed as the primordial ancestors traveled from the Water Door in the east to the inhabited center of the earth, founding the waking-up houses of the various exogamous groups. In Makuna imagery the trunks and branches of the river system parallel their descent system; the string of mythical birthplaces along the river ideally forms a single line of descent with its apex at the mouth. The winding river and its moving current metaphorically embody the living body of the ancestral anaconda. The river that connects people living along the shores symbolizes their common origin and essential unity.

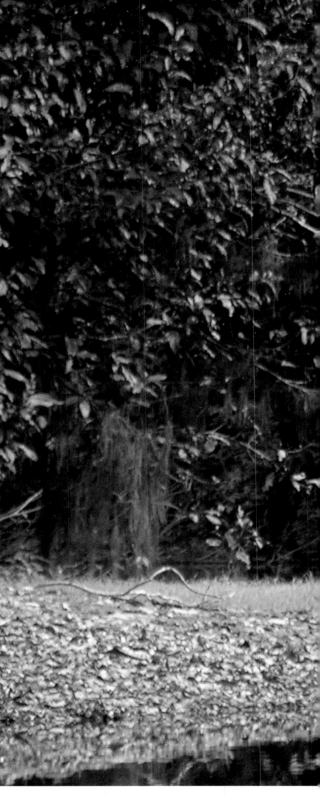

Ecologists for a long time have been making a distinction between two types of environments in the Amazon basin with different implications for human settlements: the floodplains, or *várzea,* and the interfluvial upland forests, or *terra firme.* The várzea, composing only approximately 2 percent of the total area, consists of the fertile valleys of the Amazon River and its major affluents. In contrast, the vastly larger terra firme consists of relatively poorer upland soils. Yet it is in these interfluvial forests that most of the Amazonian Indians are found today, adapting to the environment by living in small, mobile, and scattered settlements, and subsisting on shifting cultivation, fishing, hunting, and gathering. (The complex indigenous civilizations that once existed along the floodplains of the large rivers were destroyed by their Spanish and Portuguese conquerors.)

Three types of rivers—whitewater, clearwater, and blackwater—drain the Amazonian watershed and contribute to its environmental diversity. Whitewater rivers originate in the Andes and carry fertile sediments that are deposited downstream during the flood season. The whitewater rivers include the Amazon proper and its principal Andean source rivers and western tributaries. Clearwater rivers, such as the Tapajós, Xingú, and Tocantins, drain the Central Plateau of Brazil and parts of the Guiana highlands, carrying medium to low fertility sediments from ancient and leached land formations. Blackwater rivers drain the upland forests of northwest Amazonia where the soils are sandy and extremely acidic. The water of the Apaporis, Vaupés, Icana, and Río Negro is almost septically clean and devoid of nutrients; its black color comes from large amounts of undecomposed organic matter and dissolved chemicals from the vegetation.[7] Due to their poverty, early explorers referred to these rivers as "rivers of hunger."

Recent research on the Amazonian environment suggests that the dichotomy between várzea and terra firme is vastly oversimplified and fails to capture the complexity of environmental differentiations. Emilio Moran, an authority on Amazonian human ecology, argues that there are three types of várzea—estuary, lower floodplain, and upper floodplain—and several types of terra firme, including lowland savannas, blackwater ecosystems, upland forests, and montane forests, each with distinctive characteristics.[8]

The Río Negro basin (including the Vaupés and Pirá-Paraná drainage) is considered the poorest in the entire Amazon basin in terms of nutrient lev-

A dry-season beach. In the constantly hot and humid Amazonian climate the seasonal cycle reveals itself in dramatic variations between high and low river levels rather than in perceptible changes in precipitation.

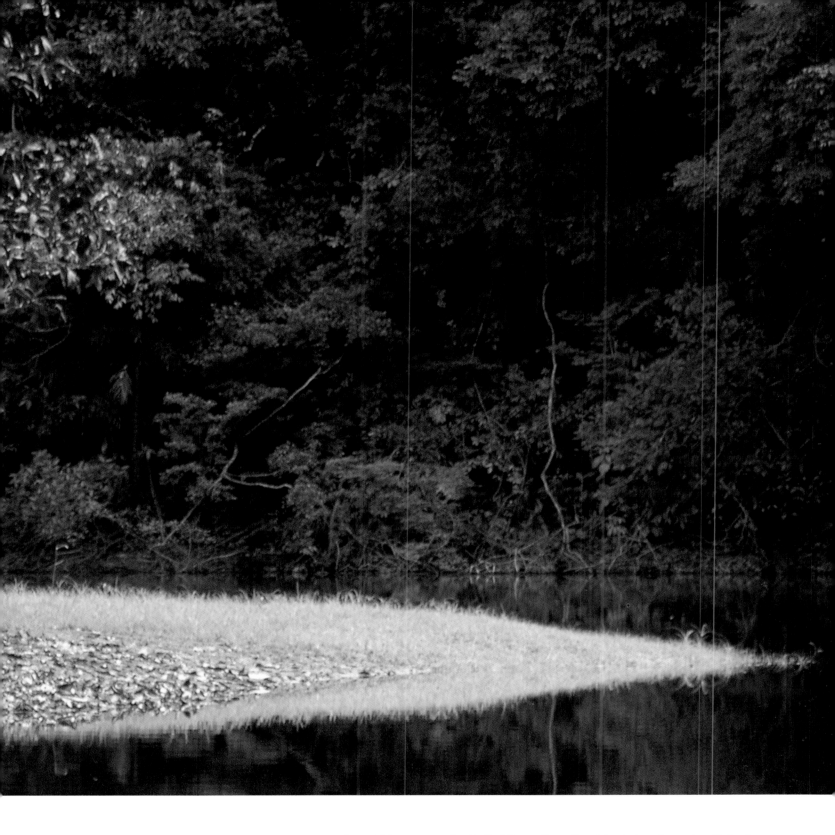

els and biomass productivity.[9] Recycling of nutrients is extremely efficient, but decomposition is slow because of the acidity of the soils and water. The vegetation contains high concentrations of toxic substances that protect the leaves, seeds, and fruit, thus reducing herbivore pressure and nutrient loss—conserving nutrients and making growth possible in the infertile soils. The result is widely dispersed and comparatively smaller populations of terrestrial and aquatic animals than in the richer upland forests and floodplains. In Amazonia as a whole the fauna of the northwest is spectacularly diverse. This is particularly notable with respect to the fish fauna: Río Negro is perhaps the most species-rich river in the Amazon basin (and in the world), yet, because most species are small in size, the total biomass is considerably lower than that of the silt-rich whitewater rivers flowing from the eastern slopes of the Andes.

Even within a small part of northwest Amazonia, such as the Pirá-Paraná drainage system, a gradient of local environmental variation can be discerned. Soils, flora, and fauna can vary substantially between the headwaters area and the lower reaches of a single river system. Certain fish do not extend beyond particular falls and rapids. Hunting and gathering become more important than fishing in the headwaters communities, while the opposite is true for the downstream and main-river communities.[10] Similarly, agricultural productivity generally declines from main-river to headwaters environments, and the varieties of crops as well as their size and quality change.

The blackwater environment of central northwest Amazonia clearly presents a formidable challenge to its native inhabitants. The fact that they have survived in the region testifies to their adaptive ingenuity and cultural creativity. By developing a rich variety of sophisticated social and cultural systems the Indians of northwest Amazonia have successfully responded to the challenge posed by the extreme conditions of their environment. To the Indians the "rivers of hunger" are the lifelines of their existence, a plentiful source of sustenance and mythical imagination.

ENCHANTED FOREST

For the Makuna nature is saturated with meaning and cosmological significance. Every place and landmark has a name, and each tells a story of its own. The world as the Makuna know it was created by *Romikumu* (Woman Shaman or Ancestral Mother) and by the *Ayawaroa* (primordial ancestors or Male Creators). In myth these powerful spirit beings appear in different guises, and their works and deeds are described in a bewildering number of ways from different perspectives and in changing contexts. One set of cosmogonic images depicts Romikumu as the world itself, and the Ayawaroa as the celestial bodies—sun, moon, stars, and thunder. Romikumu's ribs are the mountain ridges at the northern and southern gateways of the world, her breast milk and blood the rivers, and her vagina the Water Door in the east. The seasonal changes in the water level of the rivers correspond to her menstrual cycle, the opening and closing of her womb.

In other myths Romikumu and the Ayawaroa are beings living on the earth, humanlike but immortal and omnipotent. They are the *he* people, alternatively referred to as the Creators, Owners, or Children of the World; through their actions and deeds they created the world and all that is in it. The Ayawaroa traveled across the world from the Water Door in the east to the center creating rivers, rapids, hills, forests, and animals. Along the way they also made the first artifacts and ritual instruments. Thus the ancestors created the cosmos as a huge maloca and all the things and beings in it.

Creating the world, the ancestral beings established a cosmic division of labor between the sexes. Woman Shaman literally gave birth to the world, making the land and waters one with herself. The Ayawaroa, on the other hand, formed hills, rivers, and animals by means of their craft and the power of their ritual acts. Nature, in a very direct and concrete way, thus shares in the creative powers of the ancestors.

Before the mythical event known as *rodori menire* (the creation of the seasons) chaos reigned over the Makuna world. The *he* spirits alternately appeared as humans and animals; they were at the same time powerful shamans, jaguars, and anacondas. They preyed on their own kind, bred indiscriminately, committed incest, and ate their own children. The ancestors paid no respect to Woman Shaman, who responded by destroying the world with flood and fire. She then turned it upside down so that the sky became the earth; the old, drowned, and scorched earth became the underworld, now full of dried skulls and incinerated bones. From its ruins a new world and a new generation of living beings emerged. By flooding and burning the world Woman Shaman created the seasons that make life possible on earth. In this sense the myth marks the beginning of time and the creation of the present natural and social order.

As an opaque symbolic commentary on the biological process of death and regeneration and the seasonal rhythms of nature, the myth links the female menstrual cycle with the fertility of the land and the agricultural cycle of burning and planting the swiddens. On another level the myth can be seen as an accurate account of the evolution of the Amazonian rainforest environment. Scientists today believe that the Amazon forest evolved through a sequence of floods and dry spells during the Pleistocene glaciations and interglacial periods.[11] What is now tropical rain forest was once dry savanna and inundated floodplain. It is as if the Makuna creation myth, in its own veiled language, recalls this remote period of the prehistoric past.

The new world that emerged after the flooding and burning was flat, dry, and barren. First the ancestral beings recreated forests, rivers, and mountains, and then the living beings of the present. The rivers are described as the paths of the ancestors. As the Ayawaroa traveled from the margins toward the center of the earth, they pushed the primordial Yuruparí instruments before them into the still soft earth forming the river valleys. And as they played the sacred flutes, the saliva that dripped from their mouths became the rivers. At various places along the journey they stopped to rest, drink, dance, and to perform a variety of deeds. They brought night to the world, creating the diurnal rhythm. They built and thatched the first maloca, and fabricated the original artifacts and ritual regalia. Upon each of these sites they bestowed a name, thus giving the land a history and endowing it with meaning for its present inhabitants.

The mountains and conspicuous hilltops that rise above the surrounding forest are the posts and walls of the maloca cosmos that materialized from the sound of the Yuruparí flutes played by the Ayawaroa traversing the earth in search of its center. These hills and mountains are also the petrified bodies of the ancestral beings themselves, supporting the sky and protecting the people at the center. Makuna shamans continually offer blessed coca and snuff to the hills and blow fragrant smoke from cigars and burning beeswax in their direction to placate the ancestral beings who inhabit them.

The ancestors stopped as they reached the center, the home of Woman Shaman and from whence she ruled the world. She kept the creative fire in her vagina, and as long as she maintained it the Ayawaroa could not have intercourse with her. Through a series of cunning acts the Ayawaroa managed to steal her fire and impregnate her. Their work completed, the Ayawaroa rose to the sky and turned into thunder and lightning. Woman Shaman, realizing that she was pregnant, descended to the Water Door where she gave birth to the ancestral anacondas, the clan ancestors of the present generation of Makuna.

As the anaconda children grew up, they followed the rivers of the earth to their source at the center and then returned to the east. Repeating the creative journey of the first ancestors, they stopped at various sites along the way, danced, and gave birth to people at particular rocks and rapids in the rivers and salt licks in the forest. These became the birthplaces of the clan ancestors and the waking-up houses of deceased clan members. Waterfalls, hills, and rocky outcrops in the forest are also said to be the birth and dance houses of fish and game animals, where they seasonally gather to feast and reproduce.

The rivers and the forest of the Makuna territory teem with spiritual beings and mystical life. Nature is penetrated by ancestral powers and infused with the forces of creation. The water in the rivers and everything that grows in the forest contain the bodily fluids of the *he* people, partaking of the ultimate powers of life and death. Into the Komenya River, for example, flows a small stream of dark, reddish water, which according to the Makuna, contains the poisoned blood of a man-eating giant eagle once slain by the ancestral heroes. Higher up the Komenya, along another seemingly insignificant tributary, a great fire is said to have burned to death the first generation of initiates—the ritual protégés of the Ayawaroa. Its water is believed to contain the flames of this ancestral fire and the ashes of its victims. At Jirijirímo Falls the Ayawaroa felled the Water Tree that turned into the upper Apaporis River, its waters the trunk and branches. The headwater streams flowing from Tabotiro at the center of the Makuna world contain the menstrual blood of Woman Shaman. From the blood-stained soil at the Water Door, where she gave birth to the ancestral anacondas, grew the first palm tree, called the Palm of Life since it nourishes all fruit-eating animals of the forest and the rivers.

The numerous stories and named sites in the Makuna territory each provide a variation on the fundamental message that the land is potent because it is part of the ancestral body and the result of primordial creation. Everything that lives off the land partakes of its creative and destructive powers. It is essential for the Makuna to know these names and the messages they convey. Where waters are poisoned or contain the ancestral fire, the Indians may not fish. The fruit of the forest must be blessed—made safe by shamanic means—before they can be eaten, as must the edible animals that feed on forest fruit and fish that swim in harmful waters. In order to bless food, prevent and cure illness, and protect people from misfortune, shamans must know the mythical significance of their territory and its diverse life forms. Myth thus instructs on the blessings and dangers of the land.

LESSONS OF A SHAMAN

In Makuna natural history, all living beings are classified as either eaters or food, or predators or prey. The universe of living beings constitutes a trophic system, divided into *masa* (human beings), *masa bare* (human food), including all plants and animals, and *masa bari masa* (man-eaters), including those predators that, according to Makuna, feed on men. In shamanic language the *yai* (jaguar) epitomizes the category of supreme predators and *wai* (fish) the prototypical human food, thus forming a tri-partite system of cosmic classification based on the food chain:

eater	food/eater	food
yai	*masa*	*wai*
jaguar	people	fish

The limits of this system are defined at one extreme by the supreme predators, who prey on all living beings but are prey to none, and at the other extreme by the plants, which are only food. The intermediate trophic level encompasses most life forms, including human beings, who are at the same time both eaters and food. And since all animals to the Makuna are "people," the scheme also applies to any animal. From the point of view of game animals and fish, men are included among their "jaguars," while fruit, seeds, insects, and plant detritus are their "fish."

Not surprisingly, the supreme predator category, which includes jaguars, anacondas, and the major raptors, is considered extremely powerful and mythologically important. Curing shamans are identified with jaguars and are called *yaia*. In the Makuna shamanic universe these powerful predators are one and the same in different guises. Each are hunters of the different cosmic domains: jaguars in the forest, anacondas in the rivers, and raptors in the sky. As with their human counterparts—shamans—the cosmic

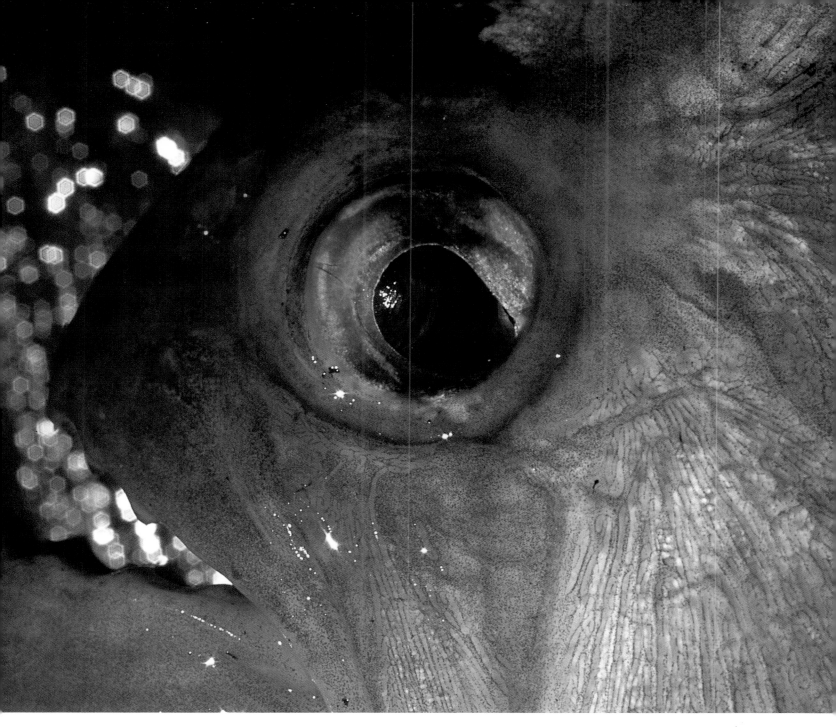

Close-up of a piranha. In Makuna cosmology, fish and men are closely related. Animals in general are conceived of as profoundly human; different species metaphorically represent different peoples.

hunters freely change shape as they move between the various layers and domains of the universe.

Here, then, is a fundamental ecological principle—the food chain—used as a cosmological template, a way of looking at the world. According to this conceptual scheme, fish are the preferred human food and all edible animals—the animals created to sustain human beings—are, in fact, related to fish. Accordingly, fish are subdivided into *wai ria* (small fish or fish children) and *wai* (big fish or adult fish), while game animals are known as *wai bükü* (old fish). The idea behind this peculiar classification seems to be that as the fish children are born in the birth houses of the rivers, they swim upriver and grow into mature fish, feeding on the ripe forest fruit that falls into the rivers. When the mature fish die they enter another existence, walk up onto land, and turn into forest animals. The life cycle of fish thus repeats the creative journey of the ancestral anacondas who traveled up the rivers of the earth, walked up onto land, and became people. In shamanic thought, fish, game, and humans are contextually and symbolically identified with one another.

As the *he* people made the original artifacts and ritual regalia at different places along their creative journey, all kinds of animals were created from the waste and leftovers of their work. Down from the ancestral feather crowns and chips and splinters from Yuruparí flutes turned into insects, fish, and game. Similarly, when the Ayawaroa cut down the Water Tree at Jirijirímo Falls that turned into the Apaporis River, the wooden splinters turned into fish and game. Different animals were created at different places by different creative processes. Local populations of the same species were created separately at various sites with specific implications for food blessing and shamanic curing. The fish in Komenya, for example, are different from the ones in the Apaporis, and each variety of game in the upper Pirá-Paraná area differ from those of the lower Pirá-Paraná. Each local variety of game and fish must be blessed in its own unique way before it can be safely consumed, which means that every shaman must know the local history of creation of every animal species in his dominion.

According to the Makuna, fish and game animals, like people, live in malocas in the rivers and forest—in rapids, salt licks, and hills. These invisible malocas are their waking-up houses where they gather to dance and drink chicha, and where they are born and breed. In these houses the animals keep their household goods and ritual regalia including baskets and pots, gourds of coca and snuff, sacred feather headdresses, and Yuruparí flutes. They appear as game and fish when roaming in the forest or swimming in the rivers, but in their houses they shed their animal guises and turn into people. Inside their houses they are spirit people, beautifully painted and dressed in full dance regalia. Makuna say that animals change appearance just as whites change shirts.

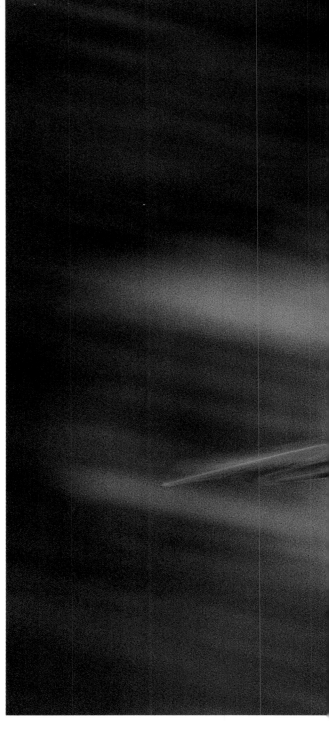

Blue-and-yellow macaw. Macaws are kept as pets in the settlements, fed, carefully groomed, and continually blessed by shamans to produce bright and gleaming feathers for the ritual feather crowns.

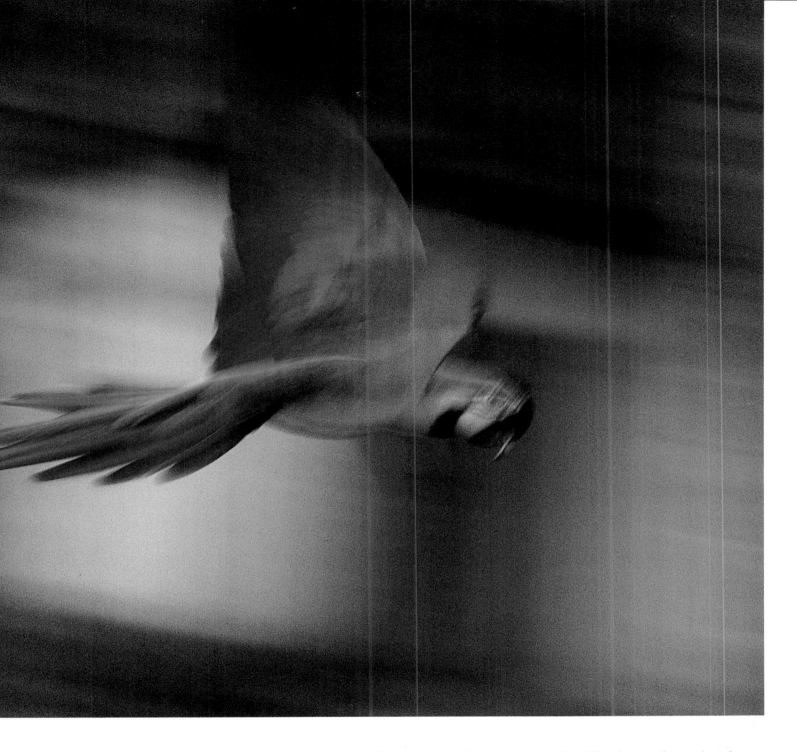

Like humans, animals form communities. They have cultivated gardens and use the river ports for collecting water and bathing. Each animal maloca also has its headman and owner who guards and protects its inhabitants. The *wai hakü masa* (guardians or fathers of the fish), for example, are the *hinoa* (anacondas) and *hawa* (stingrays) dwelling in the deep parts of rivers and lagoons. Animals seasonally gather in their dance houses to exchange food and play their Yuruparí flutes much like people do. Organized along the same lines as human societies, each species and community of animals has its own culture, knowledge, rituals, and goods that sustain life.

Animals are people in another dimension of reality.

In the words of Ignacio, himself a practicing *kumu* (protective shaman):

When the fish travel along the river they visit the fish of other houses, just like people visit one another in this world. The fish go to drink and dance in each others' houses. As they leave one house and enter another they take off the old dresses and put on new ones; each house is different, with its own name and history. The fish change accordingly. Even the river changes from one place to another; the water is here bitter and heavy, there light and sweet like the juice of sweet fruit. The fish also change with the season; in the appropriate season they perform forest fruit rituals, make *dabucurí* feasts, and play their Yuruparí instruments. Therefore the fish has to be blessed differently according to season and place, depending on when and where it was caught.

When a child falls sick, people say that an evil shaman sent illness upon the child. But no, it is the river itself and the fish in it that cause the sickness, because the child has eaten unblessed fish, or fish caught in prohibited places.

Though fish live in the river world they easily turn into birds, monkeys, rodents, peccaries, and other fruit-eating game animals. When food in the river is scarce, fish turn into birds and ground-living animals seeking food in the forest. With their baskets they collect food both in the river and the forest. That is why fish always have their stomachs full. In the river the fish dress like fish, on land they dress like game animals. Fish and game animals are *wai masa* (Fish People); they are the same, they just change dress.

Vultures feed on cadavers. To them a corpse is a river full of fish. The worms that live in the rotten corpse are the fish of vultures. In our vision the vulture eats worms and rotten meat; in the vision of the vultures they eat fish trapped in the river. Vultures are like white people: they have plates, cups, spoons, and frying pans in which they fry their fish. Certain parts of the rivers belong to the vulture where the fish are dangerous for human consumption because it is the food of the vultures. Thus what seems to be fish are actually worms.

The large game animals have their proper dance houses called *kawiri*—large, painted malocas in the salt licks where tapirs go to drink at night. Every year, at the time when summer ends and the winter rains begin, all the animals of the forest and the fish of the rivers come to these dance houses to drink and dance. Here animals of all kinds and shapes gather—forest animals, fish, jaguars, anacondas, and vultures. Even monsters, souls of dead people, and the spirits of living men—shamans, dancers, and chanters—participate in the dance. They come from all the directions and corners of the world, from the sky, and from the underworld. These houses are also called *basa büküa wiri* (birth houses of songs and dances) where all the ritual songs and dances that people posses today were born.

In the middle of the dance house stands the yagé pot. The animals drink the yagé and paint their faces and bodies, take coca and snuff, drink chicha, and dance in full ritual gear. Thus the animals receive their knowledge, and like human beings they have their own mind. When the animals dance they breed and multiply. When people dance in this world, our spirits also dance in the dance houses of the animals, and when the shaman blows over coca and snuff, he offers spirit food to the animals. If people do not dance and the shaman does not fill the gourds of coca and snuff in the dance houses of the animals, they will not reproduce and multiply.

Because the game animals dance and drink in their own houses, it is dangerous to kill them and eat their meat. Their bodies contain all the powerful substances they have consumed, the paint and the ritual ornaments they wear. All these substances and goods cause us to fall ill if we eat unblessed meat. Therefore the meat must be blessed before eaten; the powerful substances contained in the meat must be removed and restored to their proper places in the dance houses of the animals. The slain animal has to be converted into food by means of food shamanism. The person who knows how to bless food converts the tapir's meat into cassava bread or cultivated plants like plantain or pineapple. In former times only adults ate meat; it was considered too dangerous for children to eat.

At the mouth of the Komenya River there is a tapir's salt lick called *Itara*. Its owner and headman is *Yuta Wekü* (Cotton Tapir). What to us is a tapir's salt lick, a swampy, muddy place full of flies, is—in the eyes of the shaman—a big, beautifully painted maloca surrounded by a clean patio, groves of fruit trees and garden land where the tapirs grow their food. Inside the maloca is their big beer trough. When a particular fruit is in season the juice of this fruit turns into chicha and fills up the vessel. When the tapirs drink water in the salt lick, they really drink the chicha and juice of the fruit in season. When the trough is full of chicha, animals from all parts of the forest come to drink. Tapirs from different malocas visit each other; even anacondas and fish come from their underwater malocas in the rivers to drink and dance in the tapirs' dance houses. Dressed in full ritual regalia, playing the Yuruparí flutes, they enter with basket loads of forest fruit to drink and dance—just as people do in the harvest season of the wild forest fruit.

In our vision tapirs look like animals but in the vision of the shaman a tapir is a person dressed in animal skin. Thus, whatever people do in this world, tapirs do in theirs. Yet at the same time their world is the opposite of ours as if in a dream. When it is night in this world, it is daylight in theirs. What is dark and invisible to us is clear and bright to them.

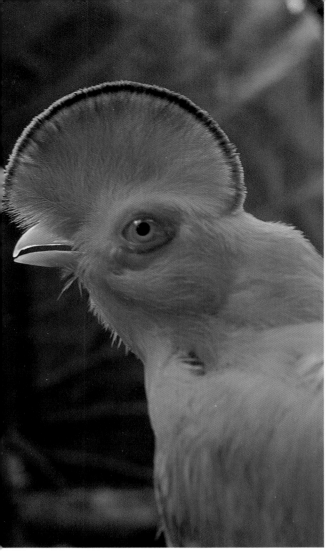

The elusive cock-of-the-rock inhabits the hills and rocky outcrops in the forest that the Makuna identify as houses of mythical heroes and ancestral beings.

In Makuna thought the world and all living beings in it have both a material, apparent form and an immaterial, spiritual essence, perceived by shamans but invisible to ordinary people. Rocks, rivers, and plants are living, embodiments of spirits and ancestral beings that continuously empower the whole of the cosmos. Human beings, game, and fish are different bodily manifestations of this spiritual essence, which flows between the various domains and life worlds of the cosmos. Changing from fish to game animal to human being and back again, all beings participate in an ever-changing circuit of life.

This reversible process of transformation between different life worlds, and between physical form and spiritual essence, lies at the heart of the Makuna concepts of birth and death. Each conversion is simultaneously a death and a rebirth, a passage from one life world into another. Birth is the embodiment of spirit, which the Makuna see as a creative movement from the undifferentiated spirit world into the life world of human beings. Death, in a sense, is just the opposite. It separates soul from body and involves a passage from the differentiated universe of corporeal forms to the undifferentiated world of spiritual essence. Birth and death are therefore movements between dimensions of reality.

The soul of a diseased person may easily turn into an animal. Much of the work of Makuna shamans aims at securing the cycling of souls within the human life world. Yet in life, as in death, human beings constantly run the risk of losing their souls—in dreams, during rituals, or when seriously ill—to the waking-up houses and life worlds of animals. If not properly protected the human soul may be stolen by the spirit-owners of the animals and turned into fish or game. A lost human soul becomes a gain to the animal world. Human deaths help replenish the game animals in the forest and the fish in the river.

The spiritual essence shared by humans and animals and, to a lesser extent, tree fruit, forms a sort of common pool of fertile powers upon which all life forms draw. The different classes of living beings have their own particular characteristics, shapes, and worlds, but the spiritual essence flows freely among them, animating their different forms of life. The Makuna cosmos forms an interrelated whole in which disparity in outer shape disguises an inner unity of spiritual essence. The Makuna call this fundamental oneness of reality the *he* world.

In this transformational universe there is no single, privileged perspective on the world, no single true representation of reality. All living beings are divided into eaters or food, and those who are predators from one point of view are themselves prey from another. The world looks radically different depending on one's point of view. What from one point of view looks like a river full of fish, from another is a rotten carcass full of worms; what for some appears to be a mudhole full of flies, for others is a beautifully painted maloca. In such a universe the human-centered conception of reality just becomes one of many, but all equally valid, important, and true. The world is multicentered, and a true understanding of reality requires the capacity to see it from different points of view, or rather from the points of view of different seers. Makuna shamans have this capacity to identify with different kinds of beings and see the world in a variety of perspectives.

Based on intimate knowledge and deep reflection, the Makuna concept of nature is very different from ours. Where we stress separateness and discontinuity between nature and culture, the Makuna emphasize relatedness and continuity. In their view humans, animals, and plants have the same origin, share in the same creative powers, and are—in a deep sense—essentially identical. All living beings are related and participate in a single cosmic society ordered by the same, pervasive principles and patterns. Nature and culture are fundamentally one. The norms governing the relationships among humans also apply to the relationships between humans and other living beings.

Myth invests the land with religious meaning and instructs the people how to use it. It teaches the women how to cultivate the swidden, gives the men the knowledge to hunt and fish without depleting the resources on which they depend, and shows them how to bless food and prevent illness. Makuna myths and subsistence practices encode their vision of the world, ensuring the well-being of the people. Knowledge of their mythical geography is essential for survival the Makuna way. The entire traditional medical system—their ideas about disease and therapeutic practices—rests on the specialized knowledge of the ancestral history of the land: the meanings, dangers, and blessings of each named site and every kind of edible or useful plant and animal.

Thus the enchanted world of the Makuna is local, confined to the known

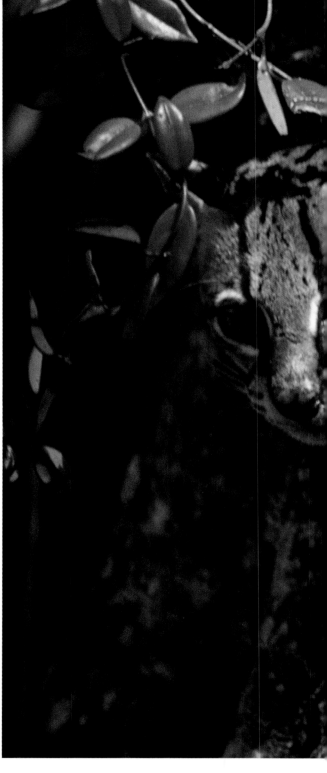

The ocelot, one of the large Amazonian predators—like the jaguar—that the Makuna associate with ancestral spirits and shamans; they are attributed with the power of creating life as well as causing death.

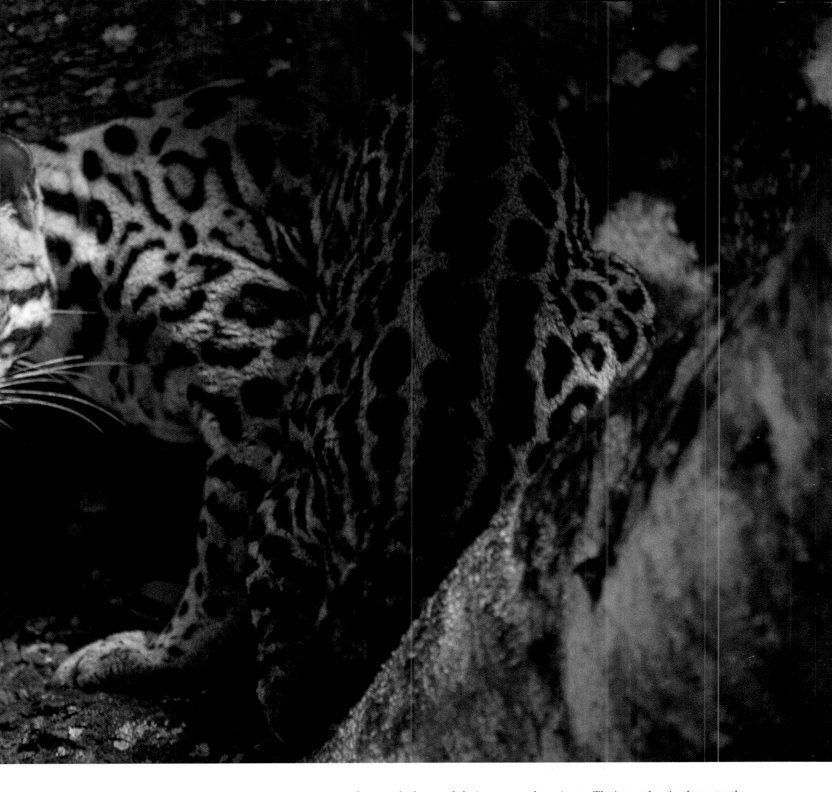

and named places of their ancestral territory. Their myths tie them to the land. Their world view, their shamanic knowledge, and their spiritual wealth are literally anchored in the soil. If torn from their land the Makuna would not only be deprived of their physical means of survival, but also the spiritual resources needed for coping with life in general. They would lose their culture and their soul as a people.

4
THE
LONGHOUSE

Located in a forest clearing, near a river or small stream, and often encircled by gardens and fruit-tree groves, the large traditional longhouse—maloca— is the center of the Makuna world, a whole village under one roof, communal dwelling, meeting place, and temple. The imposing beauty of its architecture makes the maloca a supreme manifestation of culture and human sociality in the endless expanse of forest. A network of well-trodden paths converges on the settlement. One leads from the river, where canoes are moored, to the front of the maloca; others emerge from the forest to the backyard of the settlement, where a variety of kitchen and medicine plants grow, including tobacco, gourds, peppers, yagé vines, and fish-poison plants.

The multifamily maloca was, until recently, the traditional settlement of all Tukanoan groups in the Pirá-Paraná area. Today malocas are sparsely distributed among the larger, nucleated village communities and the smaller, single-family settlements. However, two types of malocas, both of majestic proportions, are still found in the Makuna territory: the rectangular longhouse common in the Pirá-Paraná area, measuring up to 40 meters (130 feet) in length and 10 meters (33 feet) in height, and the roundhouse common along the Apaporis River, with a diameter of 20 meters (66 feet) or more.[1] A thatched roof of palm fronds covers the wooden structure and the eaves of the roof almost reach to the ground. The following description refers, unless otherwise specified, to the longhouse of the Komenya Makuna.

Constructed entirely from forest materials—tree trunks, palm leaves, vines, and bark—the maloca is well adapted to the tropical rain-forest environment. The roof, usually changed every six to eight years after rotting or becoming infested with bugs, is woven from the fronds of various palm species,

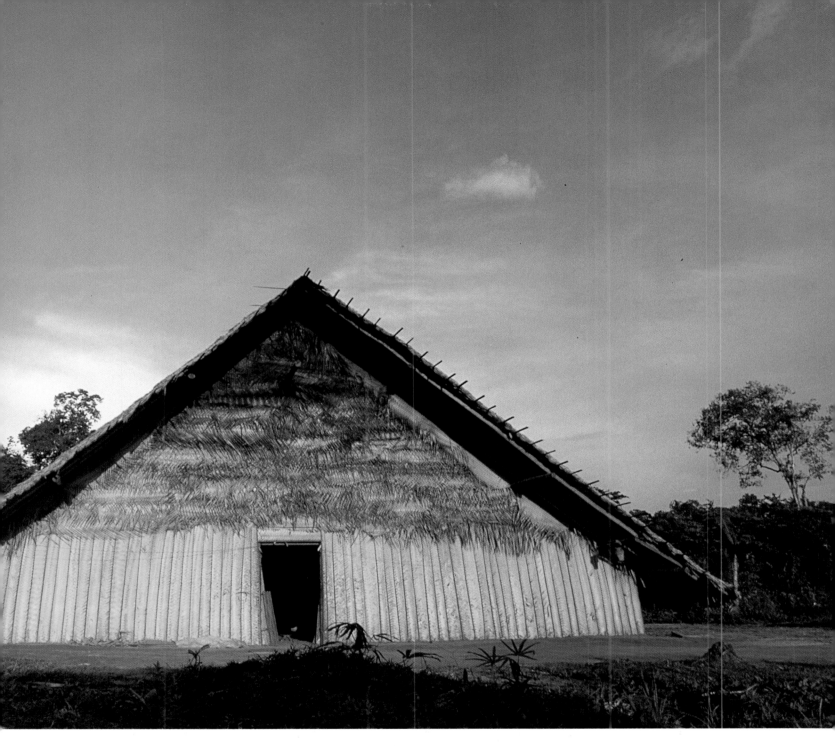

Front view of a typical
multifamily longhouse:
the center of the
Makuna world, a village
under one roof.

each emblematically associated with a particular clan. The supporting house posts, named after the clan ancestors, are made of a naturally termite-resistant wood. The low walls are made of woven palm leaves or bark. Sometimes the front is decorated with multicolored designs that depict sacred petroglyphs or the yagé-induced visions of its inhabitants. The maloca itself has only two entrances—one at the front called the "men's door" and one at the rear called the "women's door"—which ensure relatively dry conditions in the spacious interior. During the day, small fires smoulder in the two entrances producing a thick smoke screen that repels insects. At night, when a cool breeze from the forest sweeps through the maloca, the family hearths spread a cosy warmth throughout.

Each maloca has a headman, the leader and spokesperson of the group inhabiting it and usually the man who initiated its building. Together with an officiating shaman, he supervises its construction. As with so many other Makuna labors, the construction of a new maloca is a lengthy and collective process, punctuated by rituals and feasting. The house is usually built in the center of an abandoned garden after the crops have been harvested and the land successively cleared of logs and debris. Before trees and vines are cut, and before the leaves for the roof collected, the shaman asks permission from the spirit-owners of the forest. Many months later when the maloca is complete an inauguration ritual is performed during which the men of the maloca offer coca and snuff to the spirit-owners who provided the leaves, vines, and trunks. During this ritual, the soft, sandy ground of the new house is sprinkled with water and then hardened by the stamping feet of the dancers. The dance reenacts the origin myth of the ancestral *he* people walking across the earth, hardening its soil and creating mountains and rivers.

The dance of inauguration is also said to give life and soul to the new house.[2] As the shaman blows smoke from burning incense into the maloca, he literally breathes life into its body. He also blows spells to guarantee strength and durability, and to protect the house from wind, rain, and lightning, as well as attacks from evil spirits. In his chants the shaman invokes the ancestral underwater maloca of the Water People that, according to the Makuna, is eternal and alive—the living body of the Water Anaconda. After some ten to fifteen years and various replacements of the roof, the usually worn-out maloca is abandoned. If its headman dies or if an unusually high number of people of the house become sick or die, the maloca may be abandoned much earlier; the house is then said to be filled with sorrow and considered inauspicious. A new house site is chosen, usually not far from the old one.

The interior space of the maloca is divided by invisible walls and organized by tacit cultural rules. The front and central part of the house is used for public activities, ritual life, political affairs, and entertaining guests. The rear and sides are the domains of women and domestic life. These divisions are most marked during public rituals, when women are confined to the rear or the family compartments along the sides, while the men gather at the front and center to chew coca, smoke, and chant. At the most important rituals, such as the male initiation ceremony when the sacred Yuruparí flutes are played, women and children either leave or hide behind a screen at the back of the house.

In the domestic space and family area women process the manioc and prepare the meals. Along the side walls, extending from the back wall to the center of the house, are the various family compartments where people sleep and sometimes take private meals. On the back wall hang woven manioc presses used for squeezing manioc mash. Next to the women's door stands a large, communal clay griddle on which manioc bread is baked. Tripods for washing manioc pulp and big, blackened pots for boiling the manioc juice are also there. Outside each family compartment, usually separated from the central hall by a woven palm leaf wall, is a wicker stand for carrying the family's tray of manioc bread and pepper pot. Inside hammocks are slung round the hearth. From the roof above the fire hangs a rack for smoking meat and fish and baskets and bark-cloth bags for storing dried peppers. Leaning against the wall and stuck in the thatch are blowpipes, bows, arrows, shotguns, canoe paddles, fishing rods, traps, and other tools. Ripening plantains hang from the ceiling beams, clothes and blankets dangle from stretched vines, and other personal articles such as knives, beads, torches, batteries, mirrors, and combs are stored away in baskets or wooden chests.

The center of the maloca is sacred space. The area around the four central posts where rituals are performed is known as the *basa ma* (dance path). Clustered around one of the central house posts are wicker stands contain-

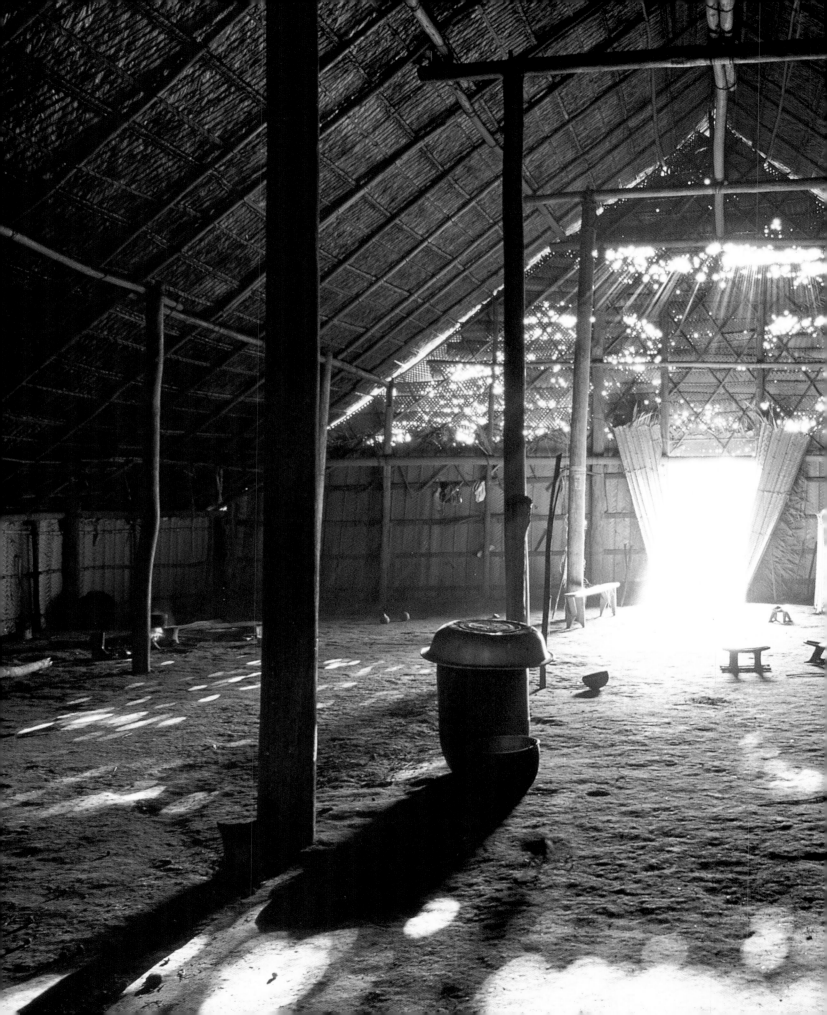

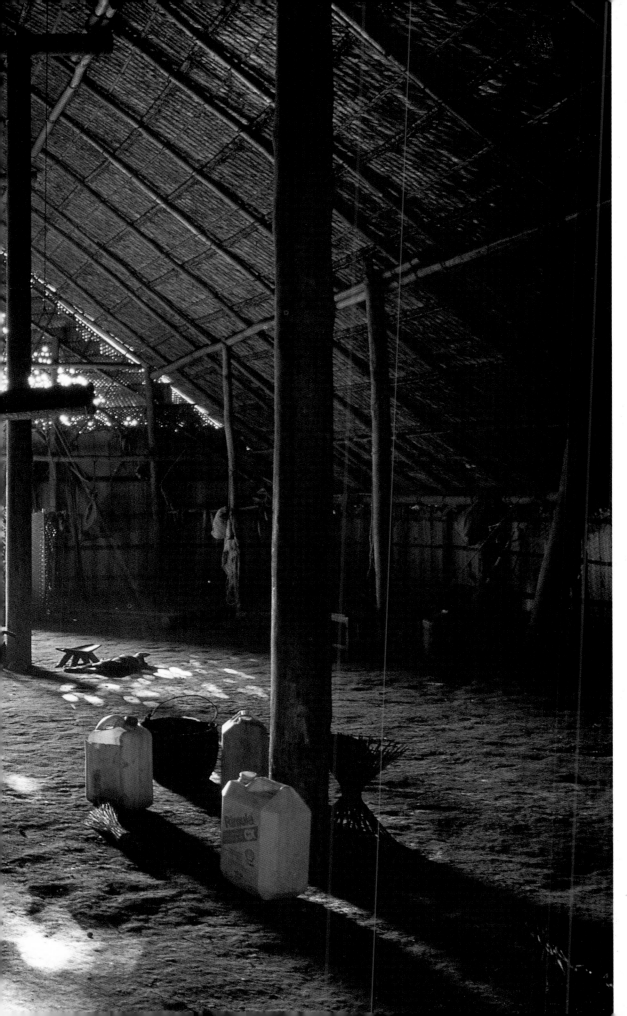

The seemingly spare but highly structured and symbolically charged interior of a longhouse, as seen from the women's door (rear). In the background, toward the men's door (front), is the public and ritual space. At the base of the house post at the right are the men's stools and the gourds of spirit food, and hanging from the ceiling is the box of ritual adornments.

ing gourds of shamanic substances—coca, snuff, beeswax, and red paint—
and the equipment for coca preparation. On the ground stands a canoelike
trough where chicha is fermented and stored during rituals. From a beam
hangs a finely woven palm leaf chest containing the ceremonial headdresses, eagle feathers, ancient cigars, snuff, and other sacred goods associated with ritual and shamanism. More rattles, feathers, and musical instruments—panpipes, reed flutes, and deer-bone flutes—hang from branched
sticks lashed to the front house posts. Nowadays colorful calendars are
often nailed to one of the posts.

The sacred center is also the burial place of important men—headmen
and shamans. Other men, women, and children are buried close to the
compartments they occupied. The maloca, therefore, is a dwelling for the
living and dead, humans and spirits.

The size of the longhouse reflects the prestige of its headman and the
strength of his following. There are accounts of immense longhouses
in the past holding up to 150 individuals representing an entire lineage or
local clan group. Today the number inhabiting a longhouse is relatively
small: fifteen to twenty closely related people, including a father and his
married sons, or a set of married brothers, their wives and children.
Ignacio's longhouse was rather typical in terms of size and composition.
Ignacio had two wives occupying distinct compartments in the rear of his
house. He stayed with one, but provided impartially for both and his eight
surviving children. The young widow of Ignacio's father lived with her
small children in the house of one of his brothers; she often came to visit,
staying for long periods in his maloca. Two of Ignacio's half brothers, born
of different mothers, also lived in his maloca. One was married with a small
child and the other was a bachelor. Three households, a total of fifteen
persons, lived in Ignacio's maloca on a permanent basis. Often, though, the
house contained many more people since close and distant relatives—kin
and affines—periodically came to stay with him.

While the architectural form of the maloca has remained relatively un-
changed for generations, the dress and adornments of its inhabitants have
changed considerably over the last century. In the past adult men wore
long hair in a bound braid down their backs. They had small ear plugs—
some still do today—and possibly a lip plug. A quotation from Alfred Wallace, the British naturalist and early explorer of the Amazon, describing his

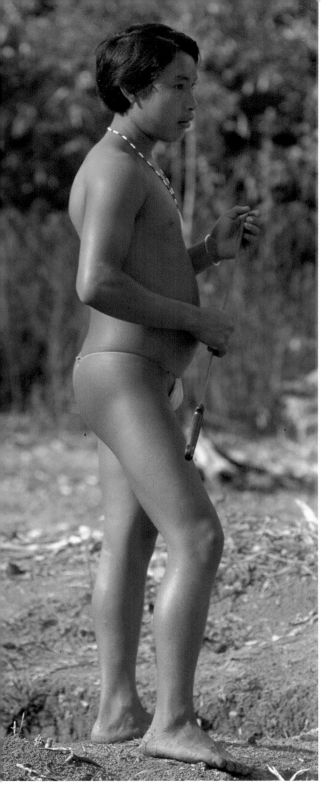

Young man with machete. Until recently the loincloth was the characteristic clothing for men, and is still worn by boys and old men.

arrival at a longhouse on the Vaupés River in the mid-nineteenth century, provides an idea of how the Makuna could have looked before the arrival of the whites:

On entering this house, I was delighted to find myself at length in the presence of the true denizens of the forest. . . . The women were absolutely naked; but on the entrance of the "brancos" they slipped on a petticoat, with which in these lower parts of the river they are generally provided but never use except on such occasions. Their hair was but moderately long, and they were without any ornament but strongly knitted garters, tightly laced immediately below the knee. It was the men, however, who presented the most novel appearance. . . . Their hair was carefully parted in the middle, combed behind the ears, and tied behind in a long tail reaching a yard down the back. The hair of this tail was firmly bound with a long cord formed of monkeys' hair, very soft and pliable. On the top of the head was stuck a comb, ingeniously constructed of palm-wood and grass, and ornamented with little tufts of toucans' rump feathers at each end; and the ears were pierced, and a small piece of straw stuck in the hole; altogether giving a most feminine appearance to the face, increased by the total absence of beard or whiskers, and by the hair of the eyebrows being almost entirely plucked out. A small strip of "tururi" (the inner bark of a tree) passed between the legs, and secured to a string round the waist, with a pair of knitted garters, constituted their simple dress.[3]

In the early 1970s Makuna men were still dressing much as in Wallace's account except a piece of cotton cloth had replaced the bark-cloth *tururi*. Women were wearing richly colored skirts, leaving the upper part of the body bare. The men wore their hair short, while the women had it long and loose, occasionally held with a bright-colored plastic comb. Today, however, only very old men and young boys are occasionally seen in loin cloth. Shorts and shirts among men and cotton dresses among women have become more fashionable.

Both men and women still take pleasure in adorning themselves with brightly colored bead collars and painting their faces with *ngünanyi* (red vegetable dye). Face painting is to the Makuna a creative artistic activity. Patterns and designs seem to be freely invented, and individuals change their designs daily. The red face paint is also considered magically protective. Sometimes women accentuate their hair and jaw lines with *we* (black dye). When men go to hunt in the forest and women to work in the gardens, they carefully paint themselves in protective red designs. At particularly critical occasions—during sacred rituals, setting off on long journeys, or carrying out difficult and dangerous work—a special blessed red paint, often kept in the house for generations, is applied. During dances, hands, feet, and knees are also stained with the black dye, and basket weave patterns are traced on the legs and arms to symbolically identify the ritual

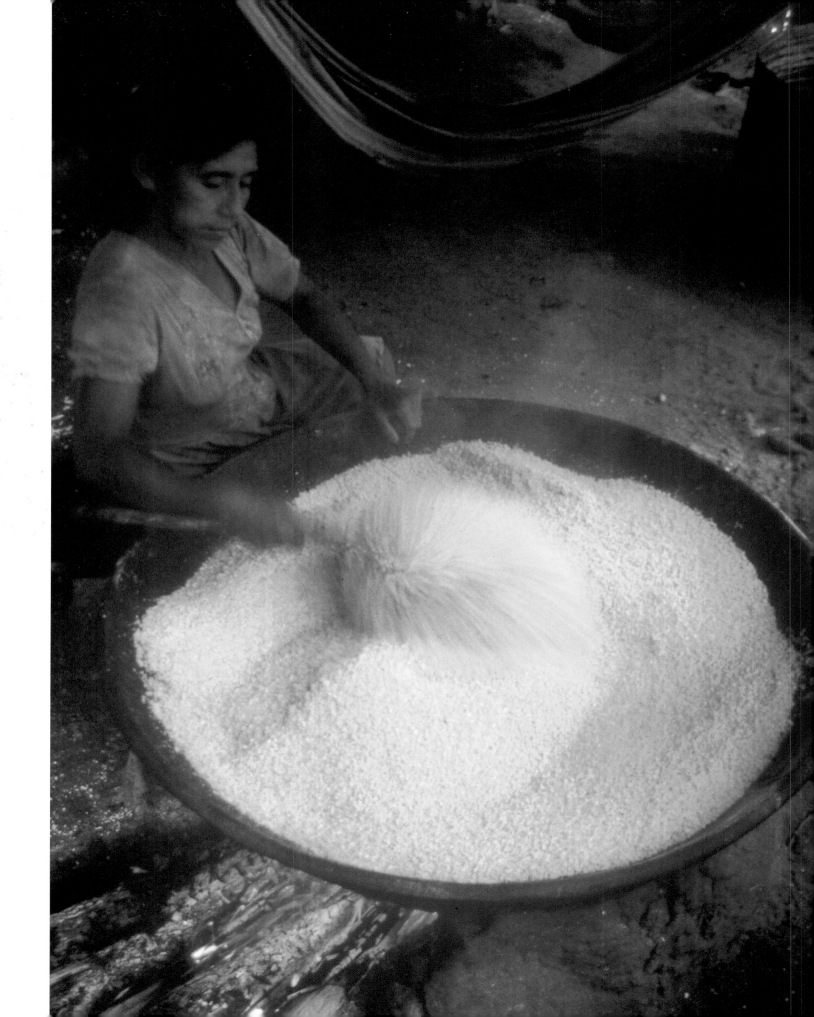

Left: Woman toasting manioc flour (farinha) on the clay griddle. In the morning the women of the longhouse alternate to bake cassava bread on the single, communal stove.

Right: Man painted for ritual dance with red dye extracted from the leaves of a cultivated vine (*Bignonia chica*). Designs are individual elaborations on common patterns. The paint itself is considered to have protective qualities.

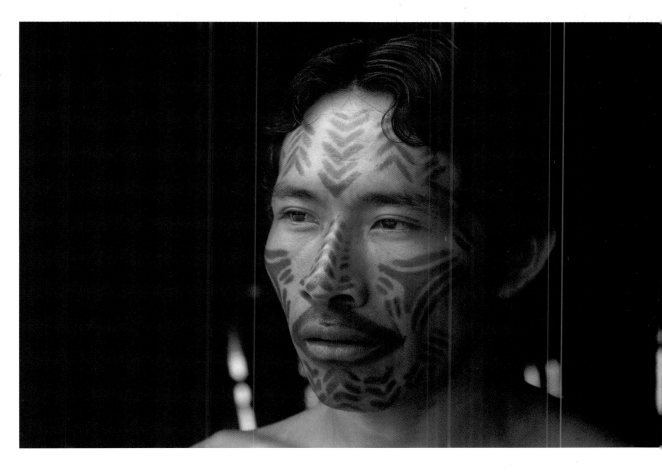

participants with the *he* spirits. The dye remains on the skin for weeks, leaving a visible trace and bodily imprint of the ritual experience, which gradually wears off as the individuals resume ordinary human status.

THE DAILY ROUND

The inhabitants of the maloca stir before sunrise, when the air is still chilly and dusky. Women rise first, kindle the fires, and then go to the stream to bathe and fetch water. The headman signals the beginning of the new day by opening the front door. As the bleak light of dawn penetrates the house, one after another of the men and young boys get up to take their morning bath in the cold river, believed to make their bodies hard and strong. Screams and laughter are soon heard from the canoe landing, and a drum-like beat resounds through the forest as the boys playfully strike the surface of the water with their hands—a habit (common to all Indians in the area) that recalls the sound of the swimming anaconda.

When the fire in the big oven blazes and the griddle is heated, men and

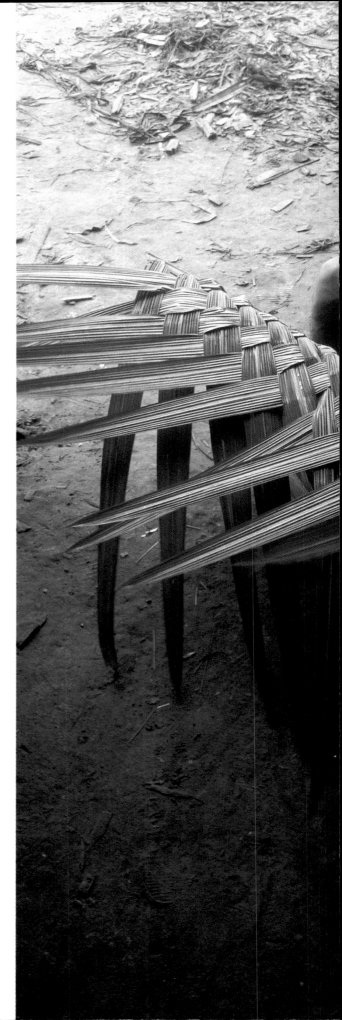

children gather around it to warm and dry themselves. The smell of newly baked bread soon fills the house, and pots of fish, meat, and vegetables boil over the family hearths. The women bring basket trays of manioc bread and pots of food and pepper sauce to the center of the house. The headman calls everyone to the communal breakfast. Men eat first, then the women and children. Squatting in a close circle around the food laid out on fresh banana leaves on the ground, they dip the bread in the pepper pots and grab pieces of meat and fish with their hands, smacking with gusto and peacefully chatting as they eat. When the meal is finished the women collect the trays and pots and put them away in their different compartments. The men wash their hands, rinse their mouths in water, and take the obligatory pinch of coca, without which no meal is complete.

As the morning wears on, men and women go off on their different pursuits. While most men go hunting and fishing, or scouting for wild fruit or other forest produce, a few usually stay in the house to rest, weave a basket, or repair some tool or weapon. Women and children leave for the gardens, and as the sun begins to burn the sandy plaza the whole settlement is for a few hours strangely silent and deserted.

At noon the women begin to return, soaked in sweat and loaded with manioc tubers and garden fruit. They bathe, and while still half immersed in the cool water, wash and peel the manioc tubers. In the house they prepare a small meal for themselves and the children, and then they usually take a short rest before they begin to process the manioc—a long and arduous task, which takes the rest of the day. The tubers are grated, sieved, and squeezed into a dry mash that is separated from the juice and baked into bread. The juice is boiled into a tasty drink that is cooled and served at dusk.

In the afternoon when the men arrive, the house revives and fills with excited chatter. The successful hunters hand over the game and fish to their women, who clean, slice, and cook it for the afternoon meal. While the pots of meat and fish boil over the fires, the men laugh and joke as they report on the day's events to each other and the attentive women and children. Senior men bless the food before it is served. The residents then gather for a late afternoon or early evening meal that marks the end of the day; the rest of the evening is reserved for the spirit food of men—coca, snuff, and puffs on sweet-smelling cigars. The two main meals of the day—in the morning and afternoon—thus structure time by separating day from

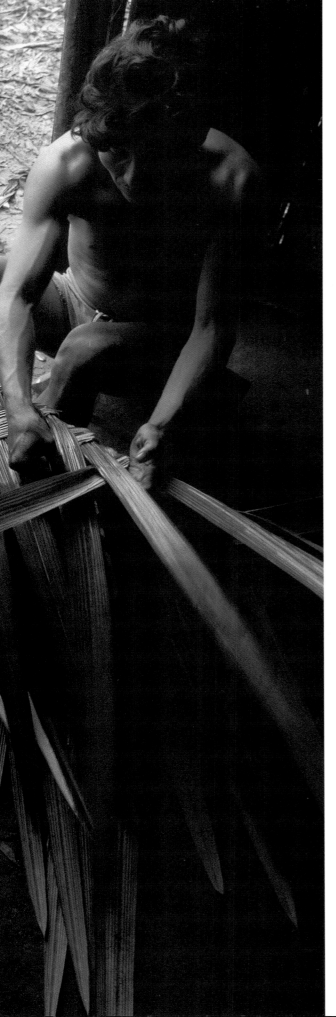

night. Each in itself carries a message about the structure of society and the complementary roles of men and women; to be complete the meal must contain the manioc bread provided by women and the fish and meat procured by the men.

As the light fades, the men leave to pick coca leaves in the nearby gardens. Their work in preparing the coca in many respects corresponds to the women's processing of manioc during the day; again the gender tasks are complementary and symbolically significant. The fresh coca leaves are toasted until dry and brittle, then pulverized in a mortar and mixed with the ash from tree grape leaves. The powdered mixture is then pounded in a long, hollow balsa cylinder. When ready, the green, dustlike powder is tipped out in a gourd and shared among the men. For the men this moment marks the culmination of the day.

Seated on stools in the dark maloca barely lit by the burning torch in the center, the men then pass the coca around, occasionally puffing on freshly rolled cigars and inhaling powdered snuff. The headman sits facing the other men with the bowl of coca at his feet. The men's ceaseless sharing of coca, cigars, and snuff, their low-key talk, and the long moments of silence give their gathering a solemn character. Evening is a time for reflection, for blessing, curing, and exchanging knowledge among men. After a long day's physical work, when the men have been separated in various individual pursuits, the evening gathering unites them and enhances their sense of community.

In the sacred center of the maloca the spiritual traditions of the community are forged, shared, and passed on to the younger generations. A day without the men gathering around the spirit food is an incomplete one, like a meal without coca or a body without a soul. The deep calm, the reflexive contemplation, the mythical discourse, and the shamanic activities performed for the good of the community radiate a profound spirituality, which contrasts with the hectic work and merry atmosphere in the maloca

Man weaving a few palm fronds together to serve as a simple but useful backpack. During the day, some men usu- ally stay at home resting, weaving, or repairing some tool or weapon.

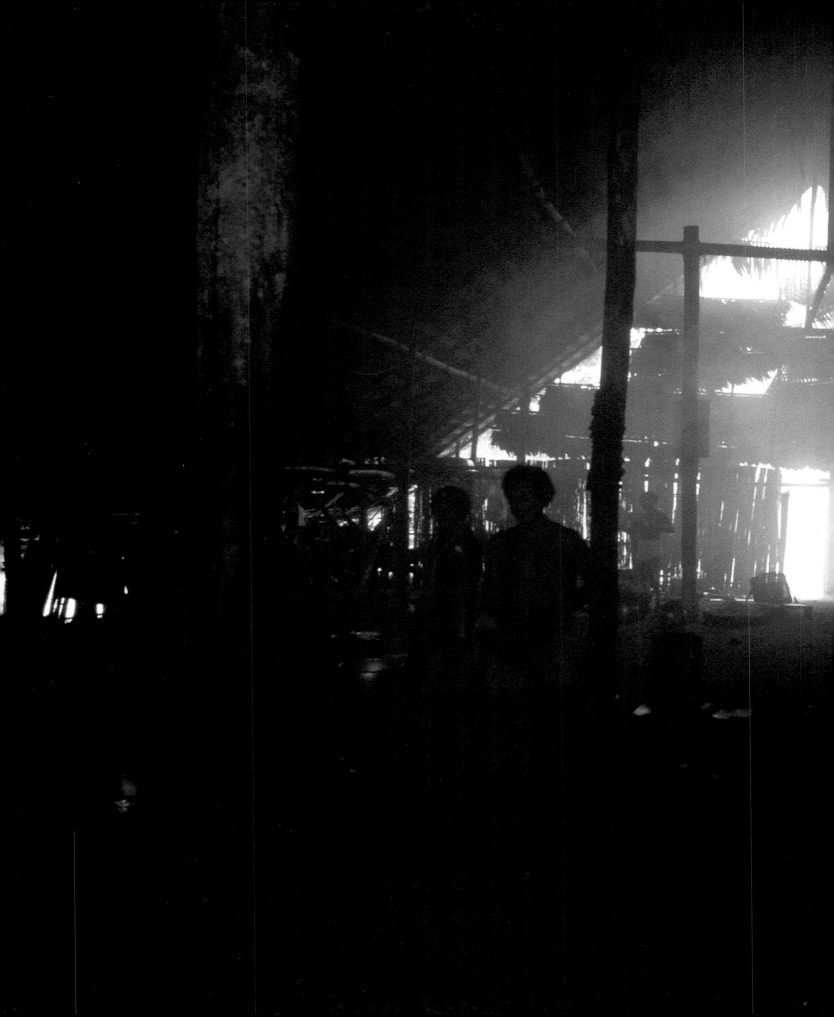

during the morning and afternoon. After a few hours, when women and children have long since fallen asleep, the headman dissolves the gathering. "The night has come," he says. "We have eaten and smoked together, it is time to rest." The headman extinguishes the torch, closes the doors of the longhouse, and the men retire to their hammocks.

RICHES OF THE HOUSE

Makuna artifacts, orderly spaced throughout the interior of the maloca, communicate significant messages about the society and culture of which they form a part. Every piece of pottery and basketwork, each tool, weapon, and ritual ornament, condenses in its form utility, aesthetics, and meaning. Usually simple in design and serving the most practical of purposes the *gaheoni* (goods of the house) express and reinforce Makuna identity.

The basketry of men and the pottery of women are the two fundamental indigenous crafts. Like hunting and gardening they epitomize the symbolic division of labor between the sexes. Woven baskets, trays, sieves, and manioc presses are all manufactured by men and then used by women in gardening and household work. Manioc tubers are carried in baskets from the garden to the house, the grated mash is pressed through the sieve, squeezed through the manioc press, baked on a large clay griddle, and then served on a tray. All pottery—including the clay griddle used to bake bread—is made by women. Pots are used for cooking fish and meat, manioc juice, and pepper sauce. Other clay vessels are used by men for storing arrow poison, toasting coca leaves, and serving yagé during rituals. Except for the big and carefully molded yagé pot, which is decorated with geometrical designs in a pale yellow mud color, the vessels are all simple and functional in form and covered with a black glaze.

The sexual division of crafts is grounded in Makuna cosmology. Earth and soil are associated with female fertility and women's work. Women are cultivators, potters, and cooks—mothers of the garden crops, creators in clay, and masters of domestic fire. Pottery, baking, and cooking are all female tasks involving the creative use and transformative power of fire. Through fire, moist clay is transformed into pots, manioc flour is baked into bread, and raw fish and meat become food. According to Makuna metaphysics, pottery, baking, and cooking are all distinct expressions of the

Right: Woman making a cooking pot. Pottery is an exclusively female craft; along with cultivation, manioc processing, baking, and cooking, it is intimately associated with female identity and symbolically related to women's procreative capacities.

Overleaf: In the afternoon the men gather in the darkening longhouse to prepare coca. A heap of dry tree grape leaves is set aflame to produce ashes for mixing with pulverized coca leaves.

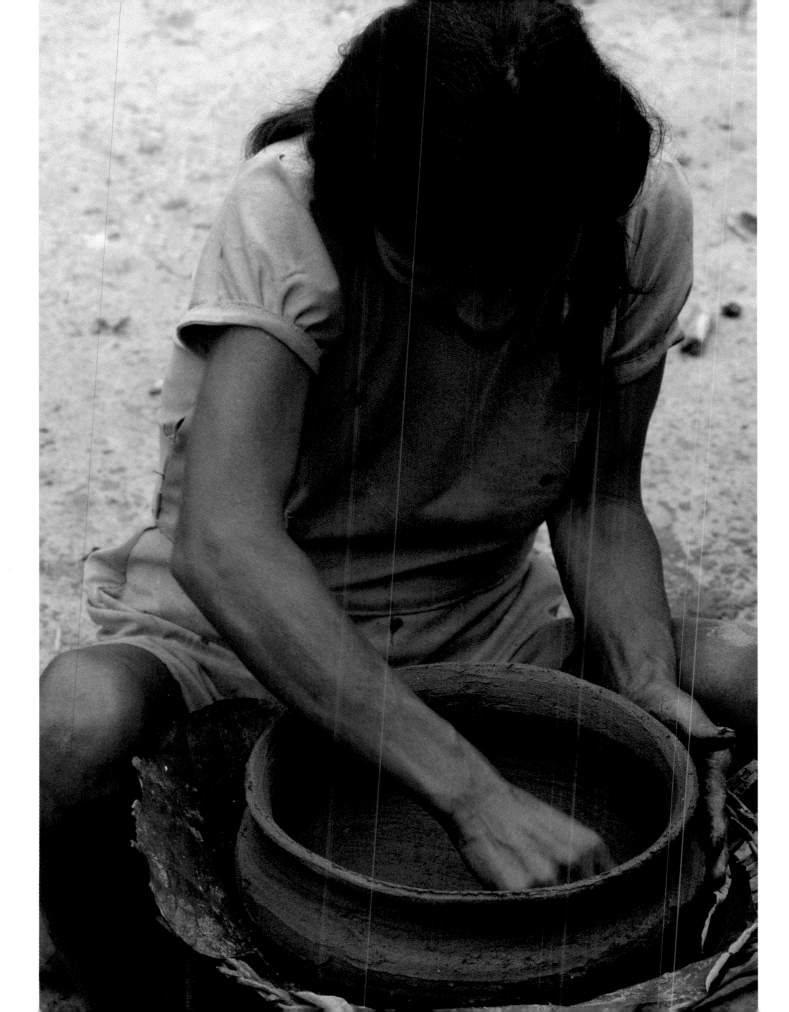

supreme female capacity of procreation, metaphorically associated with the transformative heat of the hearth.

The manufacture of the large manioc griddle, burned and blessed in the center of the maloca, is the supreme expression of female craftsmanship and the only work of pottery demanding a shaman's spiritual supervision.[4] In myth the earth is a huge griddle supported by clay pot stands. This griddle-earth is also the body of Romikumu, the Ancestral Mother herself, who by means of the transformative power of fire—the procreative fire contained in every woman's body—created, and continuously creates, the white, dry manioc cake: the Makuna bread of life.

Basketry, in contrast, is associated with the forest and the activities of men. The forest is a male domain; men hunt in the forest, clear land for gardens, cut trees for house construction and canoe building, and collect fruit for ritual consumption and canes for basketry. They are predators, tree fellers, house builders, and woodworkers. They cut, chop, carve, and weave the raw materials of the forest into tools, weapons, and ritual ornaments. By means of their creative craft, men turn plants of the forest into goods of the house. There is also an element of procreation and regeneration in men's relation to the forest and its produce; through controlled predation and the ritualized harvest of tree fruit, and through redistributive rituals and hunting shamanism, men ensure the renewal of nature and a continual supply of fruit, fish, and game. Weaving, cutting, and crafting in wood form part of this creative work of men and, as gendered tasks, draw their meaning from this wider cosmological context.

Makuna say that men make baskets in exchange for the manioc bread prepared by women. During the male initiation ritual, the boys are taught the craft of basketry by elder men. Toward the end of the initiate's seclusion period, they are expected to manufacture baskets, sieves, and trays, which are then given to the women as a kind of payment for painting the boys during the ritual. This exchange, which creates a ritual bond between young men and women, is sometimes a prelude to marriage. Baskets are also customarily given to prospective mothers-in-law. In general the art of basketry is seen as a prerequisite for male adult status. There is thus a chain of close symbolic associations between basketry, male sexuality, and marriage. Baskets were formerly exchanged between intermarrying groups, just as fish, meat, and forest fruit are still exchanged today in the *dabucurí* rituals.

Man weaving a fire fan from palm leaves. The fire fan is a multipurpose object serving as plate, pot lid, and baking spade for shaping and turning the cassava cake on the griddle. Weaving and basketry are male crafts among the Makuna.

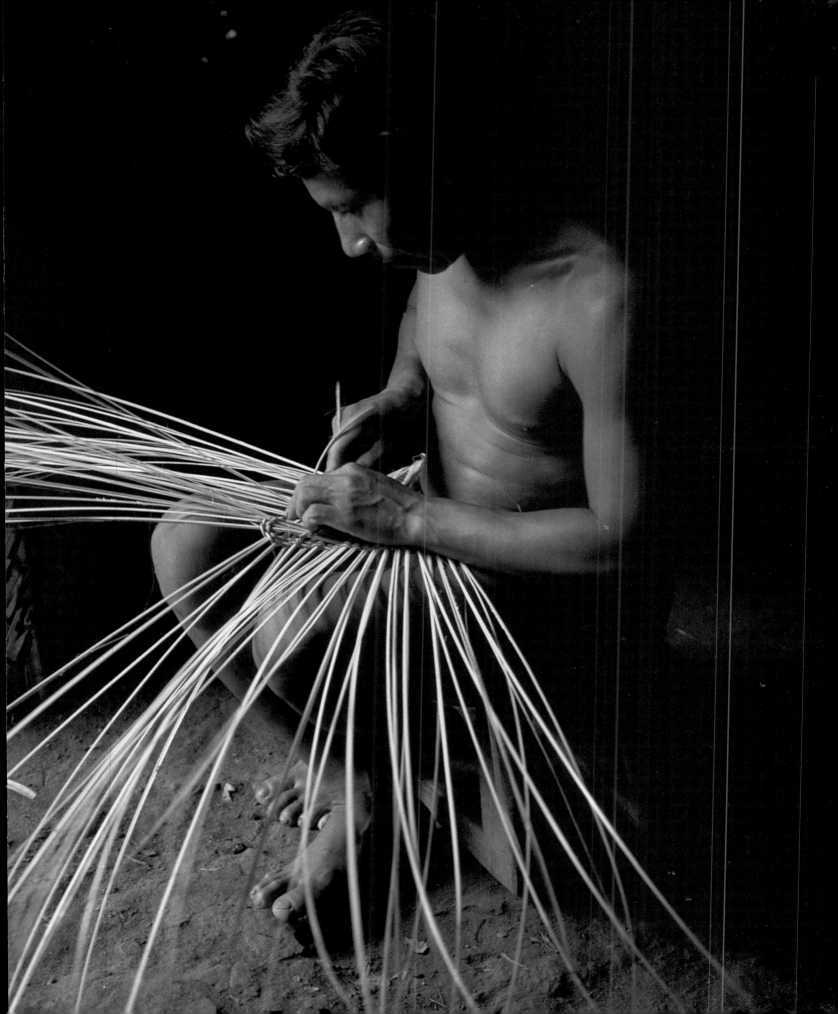

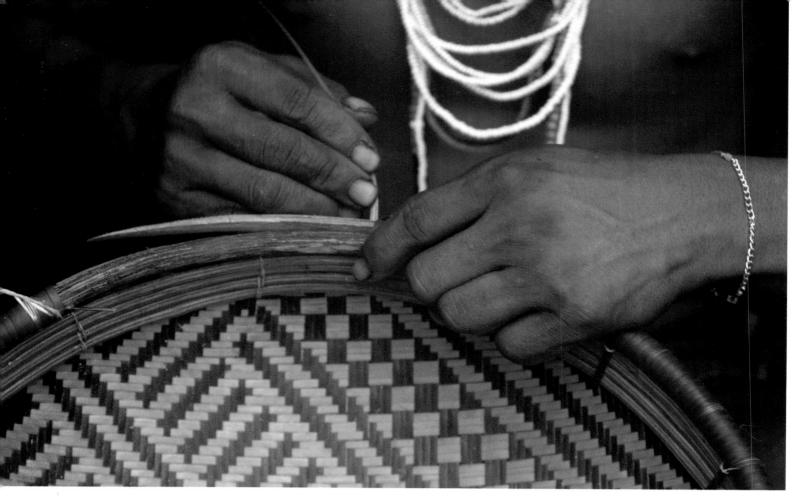

Though basketry is a male activity, the baskets themselves have strong female connotations—just as the round clay pots have. The word *hibü* (manioc basket) symbolically stands for the woman who uses the manioc basket in her agricultural work. Also the exchange of baskets between intermarrying groups of men appears as a metaphorical substitute for the exchange of women. The symbolic identity of baskets, pots, and women in Makuna thought can be traced to their common metaphysical function as vessels of life. In myth, baskets contain the children of the world, the ancestral anacondas, and the first fish and game born from the waste of the primordial artifacts; in the present, women's agricultural baskets contain their plant children—manioc tubers—and the cooking pots contain the fish and meat that become life-sustaining food. Thus, pots and baskets are symbols of female procreative power, they stand for the womb that transforms male semen and female blood into complete beings.

An equally rich meaning can be attached to the woven manioc press. Its Makuna name, *hinobü*—which literally means "basket anaconda"—not only alludes to its serpentlike form—an elongated tube open at one end and closed at the other—but also to its function of metaphorically swallowing the wet manioc mash and regurgitating the dry fiber pulp. The process of

Applying the finishing touch to a tray made from the slender reeds of the aruma plant (*Ischnosiphon aruma*). To obtain the ornamental pattern, the split canes are tainted black with *genipa* (a vegetable dye).

pressing the manioc mash is not only compared to the eating habits of the anaconda but also to the male initiation ceremony: the symbolic death and rebirth of the initiate.[5] In a Letuama myth the manioc press is explicitly identified with the ancestral anaconda vomiting up the first people on land.[6] The passage of the manioc mash through the press therefore symbolically evokes the mythical origin of people and the social rebirth of adolescent men into adulthood.

The stool, wicker stand, and gourds of coca and snuff grouped around one of the center house posts are part of the sacred riches of the house. The *kumuro* (stool), which literally means "the shaman thing," is the insignia of male spirituality. Elevating its occupant, the finely carved and painted stool also differentiates the sexes, since women sit directly on the ground, on woven mats, or on rough-cut, low seats. Every stool is blessed by a shaman, which enhances the spiritual powers of its owner when, during evenings, he sits invoking ancestral spirits, blessing food, and blowing curative spells.

The stool also figures prominently in Makuna myths. After giving birth to the anaconda children at the Water Door, Woman Shaman placed her children on rows of stools to dry. As they grew up, the ancestral anacondas traveled up the rivers of the earth and, in their turn, engendered the first people. In shamanic imagery the rows of stools, the ancestral anacondas, and the rivers of the earth are identical. The painted pattern on the men's stools is said to depict the journey of the ancestral anacondas. The design on the stool replicates the weave pattern of the manioc press (basket anaconda) and the painted designs on the legs of ritual dancers. Stools, baskets, and dancers all symbolically represent the creative powers of the ancestral anaconda. During rituals, when alternately dancing in the center of the maloca and chanting on their stools, the men become one with their ancestors. The stool transports them, like the anaconda it embodies, into the time and space of myth, the spiritual reality of the *he* world.

Made of palm splinters the hourglass-shaped wicker stand, called a *saniro*, supports the gourds of blessed coca, snuff, and beeswax. These gourds, called *tuga koa*, are sometimes decorated with carved designs similar to those painted on the yagé pot. The Makuna say that a wicker stand at the center of the world supports the various levels of the sky world. The mountains around the edge of the earth are described in shamanic language as stools or house posts holding up the roof of the cosmic maloca. The wicker

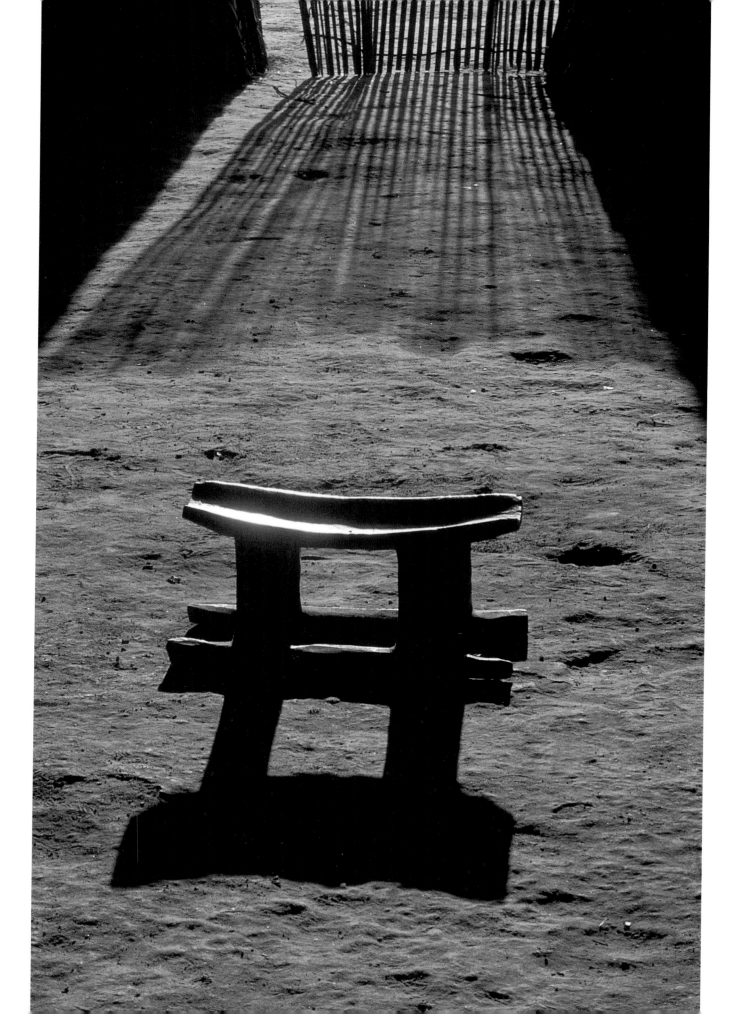

Charged with rich symbolic meaning, the stool—called the "shaman's thing"—is associated with maleness and spiritual powers.

stand, stools, and gourds at the center, and the clay griddle at the rear of the house, become synonymous with the multilayered world itself. The griddle is the earth, and the gourds of coca, snuff, and beeswax are the various sky levels sustained by the cosmic wicker stand and the mountain-stools around it.

The ritual goods are packed with symbolic significance. The cosmic wicker stand is also the gateway into the sky world through which shamans pass between the various levels of the universe during their silent chanting. The gourds symbolically represent the skulls of the ancestors, and the coca, snuff, and beeswax they contain are identified with different substances of the ancestors' bodies. These substances are collectively referred to as spirit food consumed by men and offered to the ancestors during rituals. As male ritual food, coca and snuff are symbolically opposed to the ordinary manioc bread, which has female connotations. Coca and manioc bread are to one another as soul to body, and just as men and women, they are equally important for the life of the longhouse community. Not only does the wicker stand support the gourds of coca and snuff at the center of the maloca, it also holds the tray of manioc bread outside each family compartment at the rear and sides. Symbolically uniting soul and body, male and female, the wicker stand is a profound life-sustaining symbol. Like so many other Makuna artifacts, it is gracefully simple in form but exceedingly rich in meaning.

SACRED SPACE

The Makuna term for maloca, *wi*, means more than simply house. It also has the connotations of *wiro*, the coat of an animal or the skin of a human being; *he wi*, a sacred ritual, as in the ritual of the ancient Yuruparí flutes; *büküa wi*, birthplace or a point of origin, procreation, and propagation, as in a place where animals are believed to breed and multiply; and *masa yuhiri wi*, the mythical birthplace and waking-up house of the clan. A maloca, then, is the protective skin of the clan, a sacred state of being, a space of procreation and rebirth, and a crossroad between this world and the *he* world.

In Makuna imagery the maloca is itself a model of the cosmos. Conversely the universe is conceived of as a cosmic house with doors, posts, beams, walls, and roof. The maloca's roof is the sky, the house posts are the mountains that support it, and the floor is the earth. The ridgepole under the roof is the path of the sun and the river of the sky. An imaginary river flows along the middle of the house, representing the Milk River of the earth, and below the earthen floor, where the dead are buried, is *bohori riaka,* the underground river of death and sorrow, where human corpses float through the Door of Suffering in the west. At the Water Door in the east, contextually identified with either the men's or the women's door in the maloca, the Milk River flows out of this world and into the upper and lower layers of the cosmos. The three imaginary rivers are all connected in the maloca cosmos forming a great circuit of celestial, terrestrial, and chthonic waters embracing the entire world.

Every Makuna maloca is constructed according to the plan of the primordial maloca. The house in this world thus has its counterpart in the spirit realm where the exogamous group with all its spiritual knowledge and tangible possessions originated. In Water Anaconda's underwater maloca, his descendants were taught the sacred dances and received the cultivated food plants and ritual goods—coca, tobacco, yagé, and the dance regalia. Every post and beam of the original maloca is named after an ancestral anaconda. The four central house posts in the Makuna maloca are thus identified with the four principal ancestors of the Land and Water People—*Yiba Hino* (Earth Anaconda), *Kome Hino* (Metal Anaconda), *Wai Hino* (Fish Anaconda), and *Ide Hino* (Water Anaconda)—all closely related by mythical ties of kinship and marriage.

The traditional roundhouse style of maloca perhaps most clearly expresses the symbolic identity between house and cosmos. Working among the Tukano-speaking Tanimuka, southern neighbors and close relatives of the Makuna, the Colombian anthropologists Elizabeth Reichel and Martin von Hildebrand have produced a rich account of the cosmic symbolism of the Tanimuka roundhouse, which also sheds light on the Makuna roundhouse.[7] As in the longhouse, the roundhouse's posts and beams reflect the multilayered architecture of the universe. The roundhouse has a great cone-shaped thatched roof erected over four pillars enclosing the central square and an outer circle of twelve posts. The maloca is oriented in an east-west direction so that the four pairs of posts in this outer circle form a cross pointing at the cardinal directions, each pair corresponding to the four gateways of the world. The horizontal and vertical spaces in the roundhouse are all named and attributed with cosmological significance. The

The four horizontal beams connecting the central pillars at the top are imagined as a curling ancestral anaconda, referred to as the Sky Anaconda. The horizontal space enclosed by the Sky Anaconda corresponds to the uppermost layer of cosmos, the abode of Thunder.

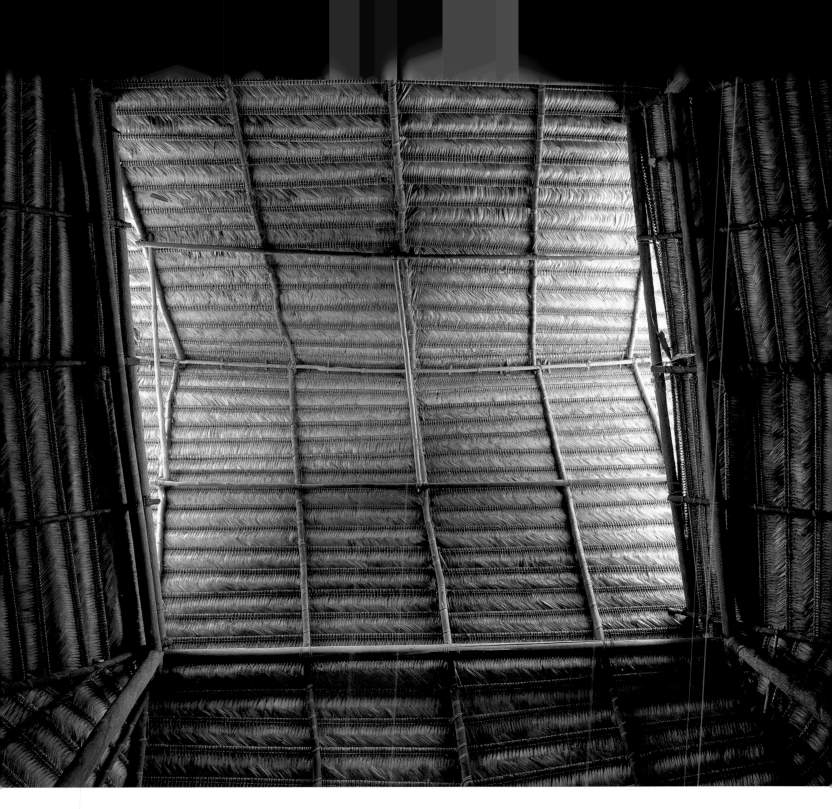

Tanimuka describe the ground in the center as the navel of the world and the four central posts as ancestral anacondas holding up the sky. The outer circle of twelve posts, called the Shaman's Path, represent the hills at the edge of the world. When a shaman blows protective spells, his soul travels along this path, encircling the world and protecting its inhabitants from outside evil forces.

The four central pillars are connected at the top by four horizontal beams, referred to as the Sky Anaconda. The twelve outer posts are also joined by various curved rafters lashed together to form a big circle on which the roof tilts rest. Between this circle and the four beams forming the Sky Anaconda is another supportive ring of lashed rafters called the Sun Rafter. Each of the horizontal spaces formed by these beams and rafters corresponds to a cosmic layer. The layer formed by the Sky Anaconda is the uppermost level of the cosmos, the abode of the Thunder. The space between the Sky Anaconda and the Sun Rafter is called the Path of the Sun. The lower layer corresponding to the Sun Rafter itself is called the House of Music, the origin of songs and dances and the abode of the spirits of deceased dancers and chanters who descend to possess the living during rituals. The layer formed by the wide, circular hoop of lashed rafters that connects the twelve outer posts is the home of the spirits of the dead, and the space between this layer and the Sun Rafter above is referred to as the Path of the Stars. Finally, the horizontal space below the intersection of roof and wall at the perimeter of the maloca is called the House of Vultures. Significantly, the Tanimuka bury their dead in the ground just inside the wall below the House of Vultures, where the thatched roof rots most quickly.[8]

During sacred rituals the maloca becomes one with the cosmos. Makuna rituals reenact the primordial events of myth, and the participants become the immortal actors of the cosmic drama. Identified with the powerful *he* spirits, they have the capacity to create and recreate the world. Social space becomes sacred space. By conflating house and cosmos and thus transposing cosmic structures and processes onto the house and its inhabitants, Makuna rituals engage with the ultimate forces of the universe.[9]

Collective dance rituals are held regularly throughout the year to celebrate the change of season, the initiation of young boys, the ripening of fruit, the migration of fish, the inauguration of a maloca, or for no other reason than that a shaman or headman considers the time appropriate for a particular ritual. Each ritual has its own particular set—usually a pair—of dances, songs, and accompanying musical instruments: decorated gourd rattles, hollow tubes of bamboo or painted balsa wood that are thumped rhythmically on the ground, and a whole series of different kinds of flutes.

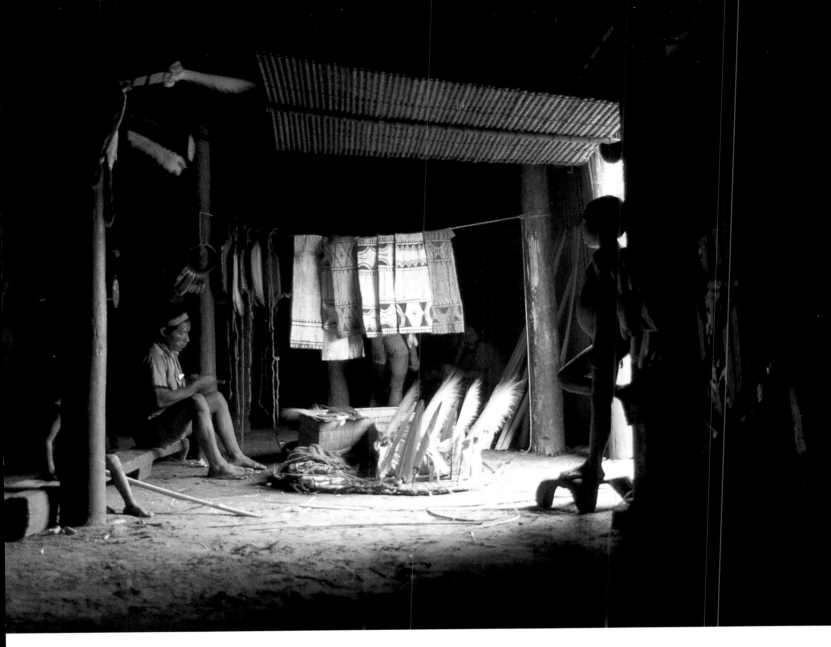

In preparation for a ritual, the sacred ornaments are carefully taken out of the woven storage box. In front, egret plumes and macaw tail feathers; hanging on a string above, decorated bark-cloth aprons.

In total the Makuna possess some fifteen distinct dance-songs sung in an archaic language only fully understood by the lead dancers, shamans, and knowledgeable old men.

The ritual is announced with blasts on clay trumpets that carry across the forest. It is said that, in the past, huge painted wooden slit-gongs beaten with rubber-headed sticks were used to call the guests. As they arrive at the dance house the guests are greeted and served large gourds of chicha. The men enter through the front door, chanting loud greetings, and then sit down to share coca and exchange news with their hosts. Women and children furtively walk in through the back door. The actual dancing usually begins in the late afternoon when the men, dressed in their ritual regalia and painted with black and red designs on their faces and bodies, line up

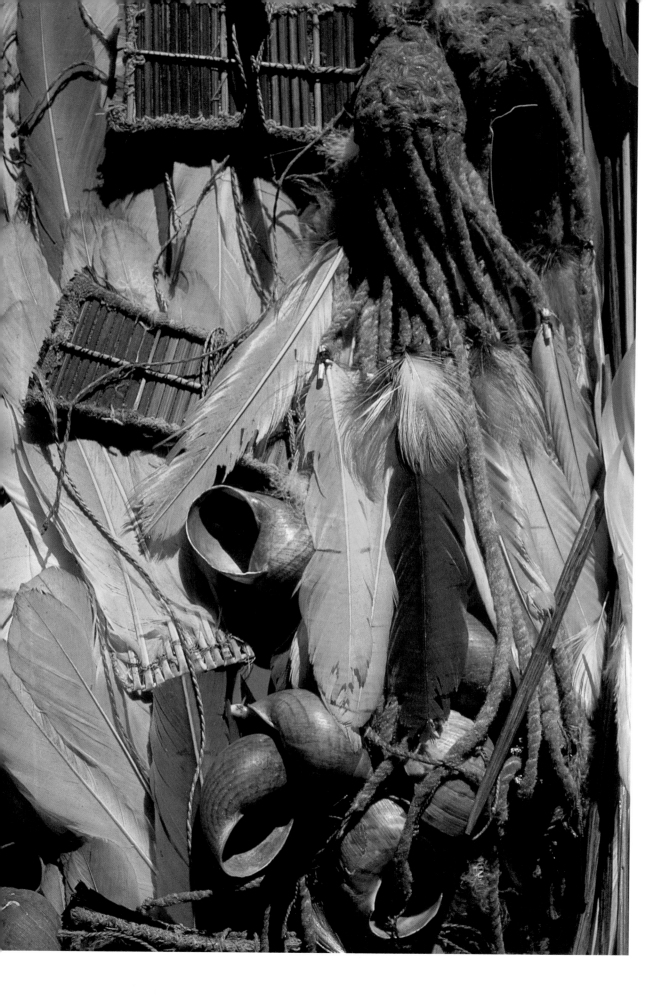

Ritual gear: elbow bracelets of monkey fur with snail-shell pendants and macaw feathers.

between the two central house posts and start moving, first slowly, then swiftly and forcefully, up and down the hall and around the dance path. The interior of the maloca is lit only by a burning torch in the center and the fires along the walls where more women and children gather as the night advances.

The fully adorned dancer—always a man—wears seed rattles tied to his right ankle and a belt of jaguar or peccary teeth around his waist with a painted, white bark-cloth apron hanging in front and sprigs of aromatic leaves tucked in over the buttocks. On the right elbow is a monkey-fur bracelet with feathers, snail shells, and metallic colored beetle-wing cases used as jingling pendants. Some men have a heavy cylinder of white quartz hanging from a necklace of black seeds around the neck, with another necklace of jaguar teeth and silver metal triangles on top.[10] The most important part of the dance regalia is the bright headdresses called *maha hoa* (macaw feathers), made from the deep yellow wing coverts of the scarlet macaw. A band around the head supports a banana leaf stalk at the back, a substitute for the old pigtail of hair bound with monkey-fur string, embellished by a plume of white egret feathers on a woven frame, a red macaw tail with white streamers, and a stick of down with a green feather topping. Onto the stalk is bound a hollow jaguar or eagle leg bone, and from this hang hanks of monkey-fur string, white egret wings, or fish-shaped objects with a mosaic of brilliant blue and purple cotinga feathers. Through his ornaments—derived from the most beautiful and conspicuous of nature's treasures—the dancer transcends ordinary human existence and becomes one with the forces of creation.

The dancing continues through the night. Each movement is initiated by the lead dancer, followed by a line of adorned men. Then women join in the dance, tucking their heads under the shoulders of the men. At interludes the men sit down on stools in a circle in the center, smoking, taking coca, and chanting. Yagé is prepared outside the front door; the vines are pounded in a mortar and the macerated bark is mixed with water, sieved, and the bitter brown liquid put in the decorated yagé pot. The yagé is then served in little gourd cups to the dancing men and ritual officiants. As the drug begins to take effect the men play cane flutes and whistles. It is said that their sound is that of yagé birds, spirits of the drug that bring brightly colored visions to the men.[11]

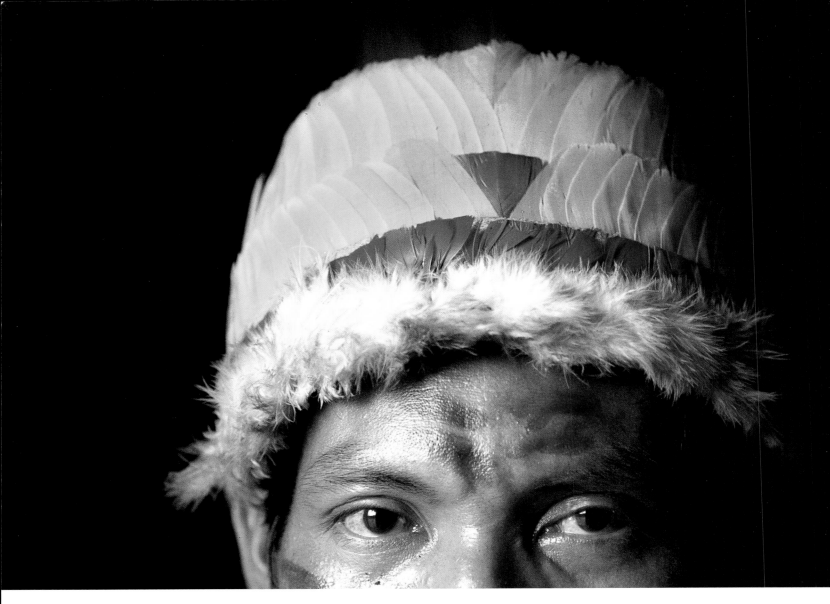

The crown of macaw feathers fringed with white down forms the most important part of the ritual attire, donned only by male dancers during the most sacred communal rituals.

As the main performers pause to chant, young men and women dance to the joyful tune of panpipes and weave in and out between the house posts. Children run around playfully imitating the adults, while women sit talking and laughing in the back of the house. When midnight approaches, the head chanter picks up the rattle-lance—a long staff decorated with a feather mosaic and small pebbles inserted in a swelling at the end—and strides to the rear of the maloca and back to the center. Holding the lance in the right hand, he hits it with the left to produce a sustained rattle that vibrates along its length. The dance proceeds until the morning, when it is called off and the weary dancers sit down on their stools to rest. The shaman collects the feather headdresses and other ritual regalia, and blows spells over the head and bodies of the dancers to ward off any dangers from having worn the sacred macaw feathers. The men then go down to the river to bathe and wash away their face paint. To purify their bodies, the dancers also drink water mixed with particular leaves until they vomit. Returning to the maloca, they sling their hammocks and go to sleep.

E very such ritual dramatizes and recreates events in the ancestral world. The participants are transported—through dance and songs, ritual food, and sacred ornaments—to the time and space of myth. The men dress in feathers, down, and plumes, jaguar bones and teeth, and the fur of sloth and monkey because in mythical times, humans, spirits, and animals were undifferentiated. In the ritual realm people become spirits, and animals become people. The archaic language of the songs is the voice of the ancestors, and the ritual food is the food of the spirits. The line of fully ornamented dancers represents the ancestral people, and the dance itself enacts their creative journey from the Water Door in the east to the center of the world where they gave birth to the present generation of people.

The sacred substances and ritual paraphernalia handled during the ritual are all body parts and substances of the *he* people. The beeswax is their liver and tongue, the snuff their brain, and the big, ceremonial cigar their penis. The metal ear ornaments that hang from the ears of the dancers are their eyes, and the crown of yellow macaw feathers worn by the dancers represents the Primal Sun, identified with the most senior of the Male Creators who, together with the Ancestral Mother, created the world and its original inhabitants. During dance rituals, when these sacred ornaments and substances are all assembled, the ancestral beings come alive and make their presence powerfully felt in the maloca.

Through the work of the shaman and the chanter, myth becomes real and ancestral order is recreated in the present. By blessing and blowing shamanic spells over the ritual substances, the shaman turns the dancers into spirits and protects the participants from the dangers of the potent *he* world. The ritual imparts new life to society and ensures that the human world—epitomized by the maloca and its inhabitants—is attuned to the wider order of the universe.

5
MAKING
A LIVING

When the Makuna wish to distinguish themselves from the whites, they call themselves *hoari ngana* (people of the forest). The term, which broadly corresponds to our notion of Indians, identifies a lifestyle and a mode of survival associated with the rain-forest environment. Indians belong to the forest, whites do not.

People of the forest are hunters, fishermen, cultivators, and gatherers. Men hunt and fish, women cultivate, and both men and women gather food in the forest. To the Makuna, hunting, fishing, and cultivation are a means of survival and part of a meaningful way of life. Grounded in an impressive practical knowledge of rain-forest ecology and charged with profound symbolic significance, their mode of living is a cultural whole, a worldview in practice.

Until recently the forest and the river provided the Makuna with all they needed for survival—animal and plant food; raw materials for their houses, weapons, tools, and household goods; large cedars for canoes; termite-resistant wood for house posts; palm fronds for thatching; bark for making walls and cloth; fibers for making ropes, fishing nets, and hammocks; poison for hunting and fishing; clay for pottery; and plentiful material for basketry. Though new needs are making their inroads in Makuna society and the demand for trade goods is growing, the forest and its yield are still the basis for their existence. In fact as the Makuna now become increasingly aware of the contrast in lifestyles between themselves and the whites, they tend to be even more committed to their identity as people of the forest.

The seasonal pulse of the rain-forest environment—the periodicity of flooding, the fruiting seasons of plants, and the reproductive cycles of animals—largely dictates Makuna subsistence activities. While the cultivated garden provides a fairly constant supply of manioc and other root crops throughout the year, the yields of wild plant food tend to be seasonal; cultivated tree fruit and berries are most abundant during the long dry season, while forest fruit generally ripens during the long wet season. The harvests of wild and cultivated plants thus form complementary seasonal cycles that together secure a

A Makuna hunter.

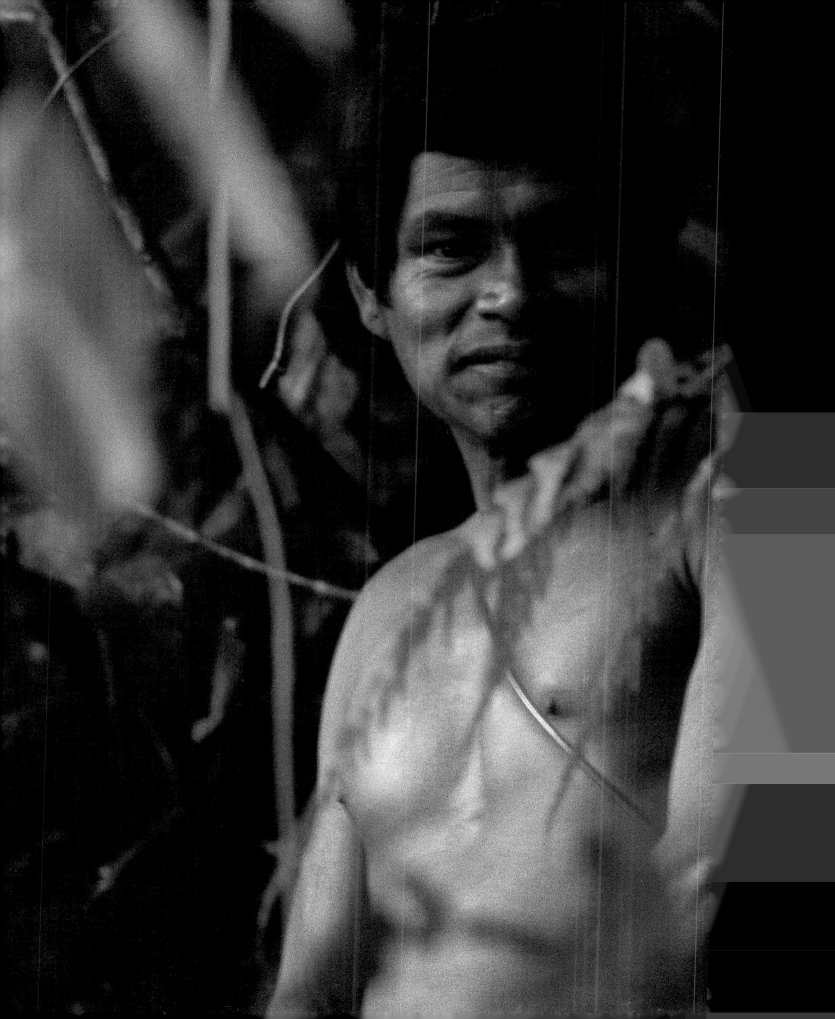

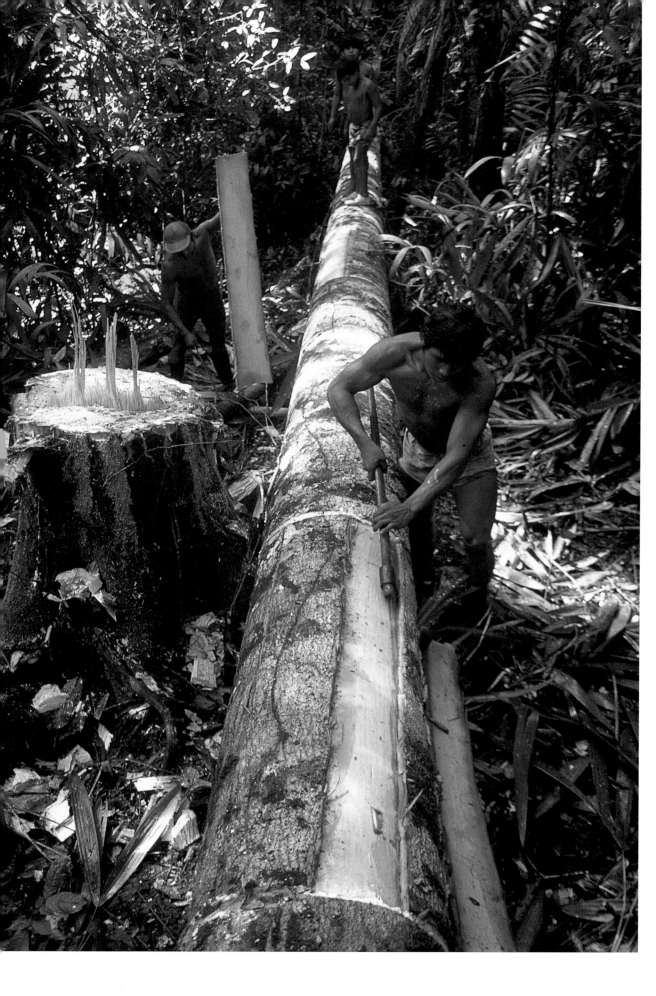

Left: Men extracting tree bark. The bark strips are flattened and used as wall planks in the maloca. The Makuna fetch practically everything they need for food and shelter from their immediate environment.

Below, right: Aerial view of recently burned forest clearing (swidden). The burning releases nutrients and helps fertilize the poor and sandy soils of the interfluvial forest.

regular supply of plant food all year round. The relative importance of hunting and fishing also vary seasonally. Game is generally more accessible in the dry season than during the long rains, when the forest is partially flooded and difficult to traverse. Conversely fishing appears to be more productive during the wet season, when forest fruit abounds and fish are easy to catch with baits and in weirs or traps in the flooded streams.

CHILDREN OF THE PLANT MOTHER

The dense vegetation of the interfluvial forest protects the fragile soils and reduces erosion and leaching. The roots of the trees act as sponges, absorbing the rain and releasing it slowly, counterbalancing the seasonal extremes of rain and heat. Consequently, if the protective forest is removed, the soil is washed away by the rainstorms and burned by the tropical sun. The Makuna are well aware of the limitations of their environment and put this knowledge into practice through an efficient system of shifting cultivation.

The bulk of the food in the Makuna diet comes from the cultivated garden—the swidden. Each year men cut clearings in the forest before the long dry season, so that the trunks have time to dry out before the land is burned toward the end of the summer. With the onset of the rains, the women plant the crops, manioc being the staple. Each household simultaneously cultivates several gardens in different stages of maturation. While a

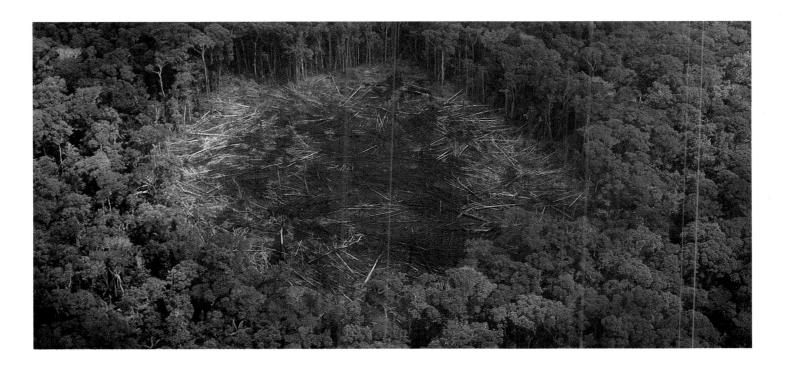

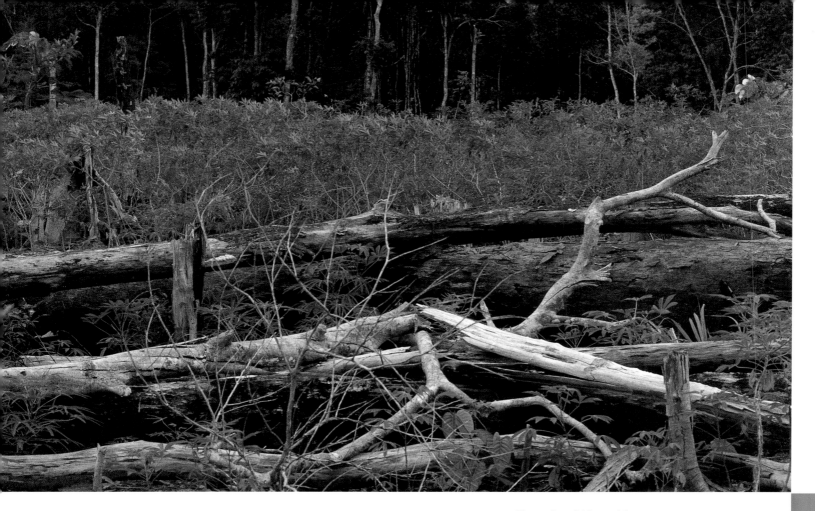

recently burned garden is being planted, older ones are harvested. Manioc provides good yields for only two to three years, but sweet potatoes, yams, pineapple, tree grapes, and several other crops are harvested for many more years. The transition from swidden to secondary forest is gradual, with the harvest tapering off over a long period.[1]

Conversely, a number of wild plants that are part of the forest regeneration process are tended and used by the Makuna. Plants may be transplanted from old to new garden sites and from primary forest to secondary forest close to human settlements. There is thus no clear-cut distinction between swidden and fallow, nor between fallow and natural forest. Rather there is a continuum from the swidden dominated by cultivated crops and old fallows composed entirely of natural vegetation.[2] Fallows also attract a number of coveted game animals—peccaries, agoutis, and deer, among others—making the overgrown garden an important hunting ground. Studies from a wide range of Amazonian groups show that Indians inventively manipulate and upgrade the secondary forest for their use, creating "artificial" resource concentrations—animal gardens and forest fields—that form part of an integrated system of forest management.[3]

Above: A swidden with standing manioc—the Makuna staple. The dry trunks and branches provide a store of firewood for the owner of the garden. As the wood quickly rots in the humid climate, it also adds precious compost to the soil.

Right: A single Makuna garden may contain thirty or more different crops, including plants used for ritual purposes. The diversity of plants reduces the risk for crop disease, and the interplanting of crops of different sizes and heights protects the fragile soils from the impact of the tropical rains.

In various significant ways the natural forest can be seen as a vast, overgrown garden. Walking along a forest trail or following a stream, the Makuna can name and point to different sites, which to the untrained eye are indistinguishable from the surrounding forest, but to them are old house sites, abandoned fields, or fallows. The forest is not as wild and virgin as it appears. It is quite literally a home and a garden full of memories and replete with human history; it contains traces of the lives and works of named and known relatives and bears the signs of remembered dead.

At first sight a Makuna garden does not seem an impressive feat. It is rarely bigger than one hectare (2.47 acres), with charred tree trunks and branches lying in heaps over the clearing, the crops struggling against the encroaching wilderness. It looks hopelessly entangled and presents an almost impassable obstacle to the untrained traveler. But to the Makuna the swidden is an open field. Balancing on stocks and branches, passing over and under felled trunks, they easily find their way. Among the trunks,

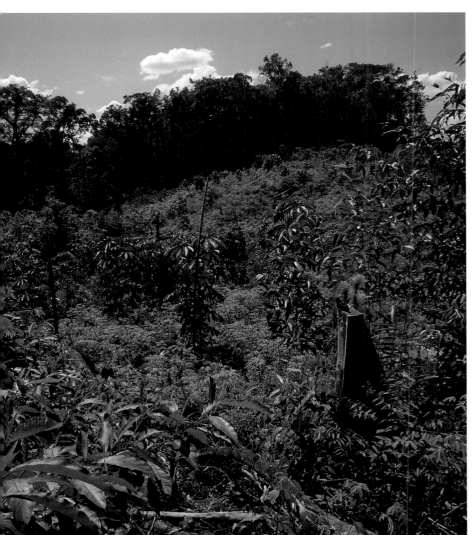

stumps, and heaps of branches grow a variety of roots and fruit trees of different sizes and heights. The Makuna cultivate more than thirty different food crops (most of them found in any single garden) including well-known aboriginal Amazonian crops such as manioc, sweet potato, yam, arrowroot, pineapple, chili pepper, plantain, banana, cashew, papaya, avocado, and squash. While the women plant food crops, the men grow coca and tobacco. The garden thus contains both male and female plants: the ordinary food crops, most of which are harvested by women, and the ritual food, reaped by men. As with every other aspect of Makuna culture, the garden expresses the fundamental complementarity of men and women.

Cleared garden land is said to belong to the male head of the household, but the cultivated plots—the "islands of manioc"—are owned by the women who planted them. Similarly, individ-

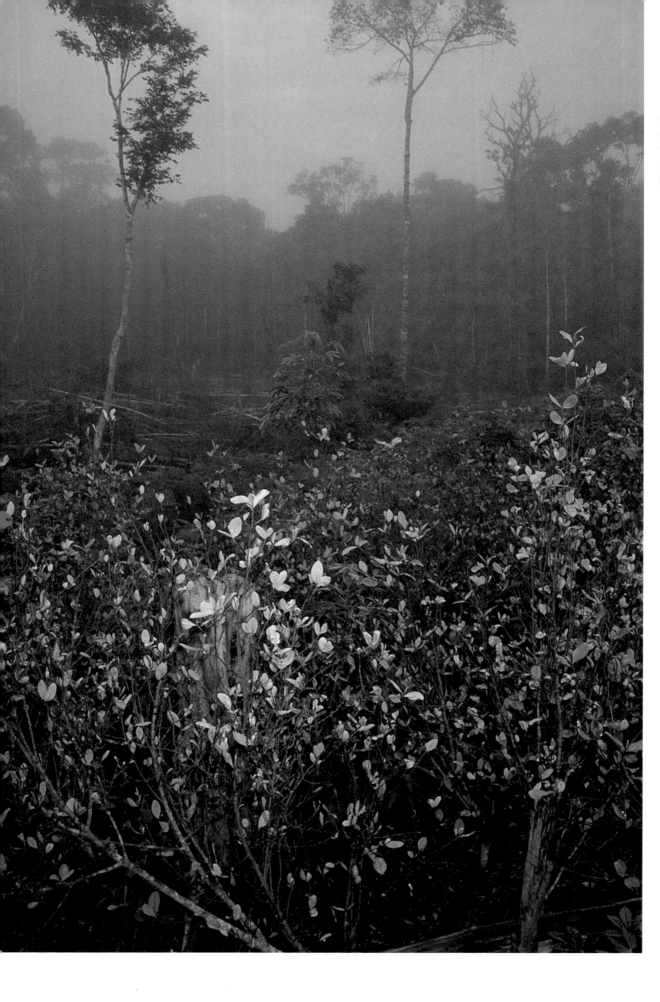

Coca bushes at the edge of the garden, planted in winding rows to imitate the wriggling body of the ancestral anaconda.

ual men own the coca and tobacco they have planted. Coca is usually planted in winding paths—"coca paths"—reminiscent of the body of the ancestral anaconda that originally supplied the clan with its stock of coca and tobacco. Fruit trees, peach palms, gourd plants, and bushes for preparing fish poison also belong to the individuals who planted them, whether men or women.

There are ecologically sound reasons for the chaotic appearance of the Makuna garden. The diversity of plants reduces the risk for crop disease and competition for nutrients. The interplanting of crops of different sizes and heights protects the fragile soils from the sun and rain. In important respects the swidden mimics the rain forest itself—its diversity, density, and multilayered structure. The small size of the garden allows secondary forest to conquer the clearing over a period of twenty to thirty years.[4] The burning of the felled trees and the slow decomposition of unburned debris release the vegetation's nutrients and fertilize the soil. Despite a widespread belief to the contrary, extensive swidden cultivation is probably the most rational form of agricultural land use in the tropical rain forest. The system produces a sustained yield of food crops in an environment where intensive field agriculture—even with the most modern techniques—would fail.[5]

Ecologically the swidden resembles the forest, but conceptually the Makuna sharply differentiate the garden from its surroundings. While the forest is the realm of men and spirits, the cultivated garden is the domain of women. As such it is intimately associated with female fertility and procreative power. There is a myth in which Yawira, the daughter of Water Anaconda and wife of Yiba, planted the first manioc by breaking her fingers and sticking them into the earth. The primal manioc crop grew, as it were, out of Yawira's own body. She is therefore also referred to as *ote hako* (mother of the cultivated crops or plant mother).

In their daily work in the garden, women identify themselves with their ancestress, the plant mother. They speak of the garden as a womb and compare harvesting to giving birth. The harvested crop of manioc is symbolically identified with their own children. Appropriately women actually give birth in the manioc garden—the fertile womb of the plant mother. After delivery the mother carries the new-born child to the maloca just as she carries her daily harvest from garden to house. This symbolic identity—

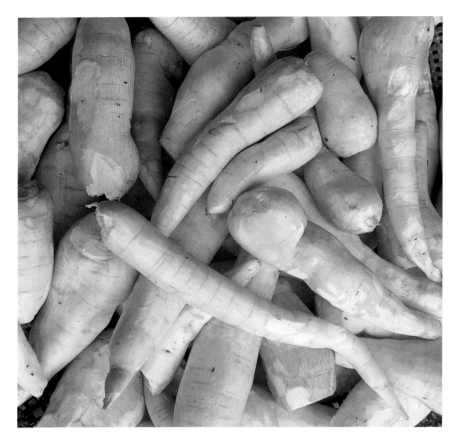

Left: Peeled manioc tubers. Manioc of the bitter variety is the staple among all horticultural groups of the Vaupés-Apaporis region.

Below: Peach palm fruit is extremely nutritious and provides one of the important cultivated food in the region.

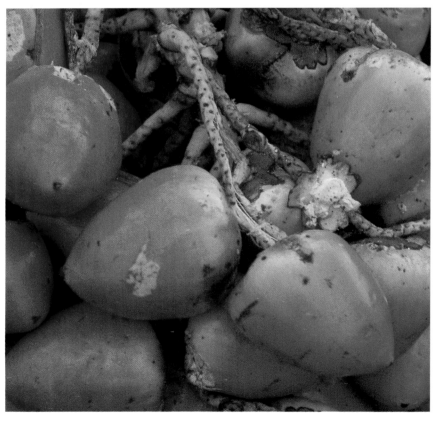

widespread in the Amazon area—between procreation and cultivation makes women the supreme agriculturalists: women are mothers and the crops their children.

The long process of preparing manioc bread is also deeply symbolic.[6] The process essentially involves the initial separation of starch and fiber (through grating, sieving, and squeezing) and their final recombination (through baking). The two significant components, starch and fiber, are metaphorically associated with different gendered substances of the human body: the liquid starch connotes female blood and the dry fiber the hard bone of male, seminal origin. Starch, then, is to fiber as blood to bone, female to male. Their final recombination in the process of baking symbolizes the formation of the human being. Baking, like harvesting, becomes an act of procreation. There is also in the manioc process a significant developmental sequence from origin to maturity reflecting the life cycle of human individuals: as the liquid, grated mass is progressively dried in the squeezer and baked on the griddle, the metaphorical child grows into a complete, mature being. The whole process, in fact, is a female counterpart to the male initiation ritual; turned into bread the plant children—like the initiates—are transferred from the domestic to the public domain and then delivered up to society.

The relationship Makuna women have with the land and its produce is one of intimacy and community. A woman relates to her crop as a mother to her children. The agricultural cycle and the domestic chores of women are symbolically associated with the women's reproductive cycle and thus constitutive of female identity—the cultivated crops are part of her body and being. Men, as we shall see, relate differently to their privileged subsistence domain—the forest and the river, and the animals they hunt and fish. If gardening is modeled on the relationship between mother and child, then predation is modeled on the ambiguous and agonistic relationship among affines.

NATURAL AFFINES

Just as cultivation is part of being a woman, predation—hunting, fishing, and in the past, warring—is constitutive of maleness. In practice, hunting and fishing are seen as a single productive activity; men usually carry both fishing and hunting gear with them on the same trip. A significant part of the hunting is done from the canoe, and some fishing is usually done in streams and rivulets along hunting tracks in the forest. Fish provide the bulk of the animal protein in the diet, but hunting is the quintessential male activity because of the dangerous and combative elements involved. While fishing may involve women and children, hunting is an all-male pursuit.

The Makuna view hunting and fishing as part of a continuous exchange between the human and nonhuman worlds of animals and spirits. The shaman has the power to release game animals and fish from their houses. In his mind and by means of his silent chant, the shaman travels to these invisible houses where he meets and talks with the spirit-owners and guardians of the animals. He asks them to deliver the game and fish, which later become the hunter's prey and the fisherman's catch. The deliberations between the shaman and the spirit-owners of animals are said to be like marriage negotiations, and the successful hunt is compared to a completed marriage—an exchange of women between exogamous groups.

By means of his chanting, the shaman negotiates the release of game animals from their houses in the forest, but it is the task of the hunter to actually find and kill the animals. The hunter uses his skills to attract and seduce the game; hunting, for the Makuna, is a form of courtship. Hunter and prey are related like man and woman, seducer and seduced. Conversely, the relationship between a man and his prospective bride—and any potential sexual partner—is compared to the hunter-prey relationship. Makuna men talk of capturing women like they talk of hunting. If the hunt symbolically is a form of courtship, capturing the bride is a kind of hunt— the man seduces, conquers, and symbolically kills his "prey."

Like marriage and sex, hunting for the Makuna has a double aspect of exchange and predation. The hunter will kill his prey only after the shaman— or the hunter himself if he is versed in hunting magic—has made a mystical pact with its spirit-owners. The slain animal, as with a woman obtained in marriage, has to be reciprocated. So the hunt is also an exchange of food between men and animals or, more appropriately, between humans and the guardians of the animals. What to outsiders looks like a hunter's bag full of game appears to the shaman to be a gift of food from the spirits. When the shaman chants in the center of the maloca, he in fact travels to the houses of the animal spirits and offers them coca and tobacco—the food of the spirits—in return for the hunter's bag.

The relationship between men and animals can be potentially antagonistic. Just as a marriage may easily break up and lead to strife between affines, the relationship between people and game animals may lead to metaphysical warfare. In Makuna anthropomorphic cosmology not only do people prey on animals but the spirit-owners of the animals also prey on people. Hunting has a price; men kill to survive at the risk of being killed and consumed themselves by the animal spirits. Only by maintaining a carefully negotiated relationship of reciprocal exchange between hunter and prey can humans avoid violent retaliation from their natural affines and their spirit guardians.

Most Makuna rituals aim at preserving or restoring this pact of reciprocity, ensuring peace and order in the cosmic society of men, spirits, animals, and plants. Ritual, marriage, and hunting are all variants of the same theme—the fundamental principle of exchange that pervades every aspect of Makuna life. At the seasonal *He* Fruit Ritual, for example, when ripe fruit are brought from the forest to the tune of the *he rika samara* (tree-fruit Yuruparís), the guardians of the fruit—embodied in the sacred Yurupari instruments—are invited to dance, drink, and feast with the men of the maloca. The guardians of the fruit are the fructivore animals of the forest, which compete with humans for the fruit. In return for the blessed coca and snuff he offers them, the shaman asks the guardians of the fruit to allot a fair share of the harvest to humans. At another great Makuna ritual, the Dance of the Spirits, men and young boys dress in bark-cloth costumes and painted masks to represent all kinds of animal spirits coming as honored guests to eat, drink, and dance with people, ensuring the regeneration of nature and the reproduction of society.[7] These, and other rituals, form part of a continuous exchange with nature that is fundamental to the Makuna way of relating to the world: animals are affines and nature forms part of society.

During a peccary hunt in the headwaters of Komenya in early 1973, I experienced the intense, mystical involvement with nature and the close community between hunter and prey that lie at the center of the Makuna way of life. After a long trek with Hacinto, a young Makuna hunter, we eventually smelled the peccaries near us. As we climbed a gentle hill, we came upon a herd of at least fifty animals. I was stunned by the sudden encounter, but Hacinto immediately fired his gun into the herd and wounded one as the rest scattered in all directions. He reloaded and fired again, this time missing entirely. Running after the fleeing animals, Hacinto shouted at me to stay and watch the injured one.

The peccary was now lying on the ground. With blood trickling from his side he looked at me intently. For a long while we just stared at each other. I felt strangely at a loss. Should I try to kill him or just wait for Hacinto to come back? My confusion was mixed with a feeling of compassion. His gaze made me feel pity, and something in his frightened eyes made him peculiarly human to me. Suddenly he rose to his feet and my pity gave way to fear—a fear of an utterly strange and unknown beast from another world. Was he going to attack me? I looked for a tree in case I had to climb to safety. But he stood quite still without taking his eyes from me. The thought crossed my mind that if I didn't kill him, he would escape. But kill him with what? Should I grab a stick and hit him? But what if he is stronger than me? As my tension and bewilderment grew, the animal started to move, first slowly, then faster. He ran away and disappeared into the forest. Only a faint trail of blood was left on the forest floor.

I stood rooted to the spot feeling foolish and yet relieved by his escape. After a while Hacinto returned empty-handed and irritated. He reprimanded me for having let the wounded animal escape: "He was almost dead! How could you let him go? You should have beaten him on the head with a stick and killed him. Now we have nothing to eat tonight." Hacinto soon calmed down. While following another peccary trail we came to a clearing in the forest after a while. "This is the house of the peccaries," Hacinto said. "It is their maloca. Over there is their eating place," he continued, pointing to a bare, trampled spot on the ground full of crushed seeds and nutshells. "And this is where they sleep. There is their path down to the stream where they bathe and drink water." A trail led down to a small stream. Indeed, the whole place resembled an abandoned Makuna hunting camp. We were tired and sat down to rest in the clearing. Leaning against a fallen tree trunk, I fell asleep. I woke up as Hacinto gently shook my shoulder saying that it was late and we had to go back to the maloca before nightfall.

Darkness had fallen when we arrived home. Hacinto told the others about our mishaps. I went to sleep hungry and gloomy. The next thing I remember was waking up in the middle of the night hot, sweating, and with a terrible headache. To my surprise I found the shaman of the house squat-

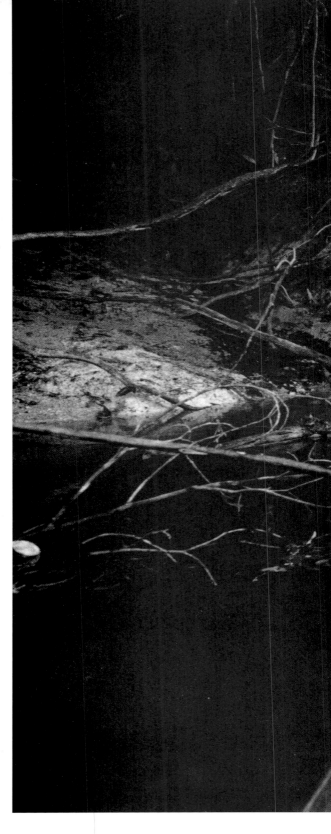

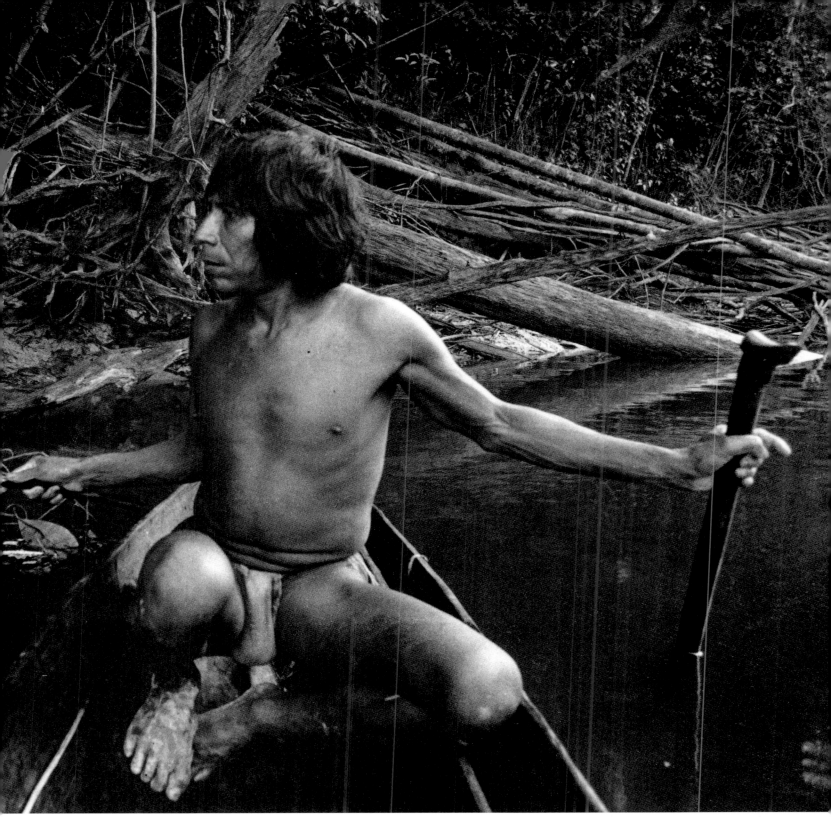

Dry season fishing along
the shore.

ting by my hammock. There was a fire burning and the old man was blowing and mumbling over a gourd of water. When he saw that I was awake, he looked up and said, almost in a whisper: "Don't worry, it will be all right. You have been grunting like a wild boar all night. The peccaries took your soul away. They took it to their house and turned you into a peccary. But I went there and brought you back. Your soul has returned, you are safe now. Drink this blessed water and you will be relieved." I drank the water. I must have been running a very high temperature. My shirt was drenched, and my head felt like it would explode. In disbelief and wondering whether in fact I had suffered from sunstroke, I fell asleep again. In the late morning I awoke feeling well, with no trace of the previous night's pain. The old shaman lay in his hammock smiling at me with an expression of pride on his wrinkled face.

My suffering that night made perfect sense to the Makuna. We had injured a game animal, and I had entered a particular relationship with one of them. As a result the peccaries had called me to their house, perhaps in revenge, perhaps merely out of curiosity. They had captured my soul, and I lacked the knowledge to protect myself. Fortunately a shaman was at hand to return my soul to my body.

In hunting and fishing the Makuna rely, to a great extent, on their knowledge of the local environment and the habits of the animals. They know the feeding habits, sounds, and tracks of every game animal. Hunting and fishing involve tracking and attracting animals—luring them near by imitating their sounds or by using seductive baits. The image of the hunt as courtship and deadly seduction makes very practical sense.

Of the available fish and game animals living in the Makuna territory, few are caught or hunted. In fact, only a small part of the great number of fish and bird species and, among the mammals, the large group of small rodents are actually utilized as food. Of some forty-five game animals considered edible, only about twenty are hunted on a regular basis; of some forty species of edible fish, only twenty-five to thirty are caught regularly.

The Makuna use the blowpipe and poisoned darts to hunt monkeys and large birds living in the canopy. They use the bow and arrow for other birds, peccaries, deer, rodents, and sometimes even tapir. Nowadays they use shotguns for all kinds of game. There is usually a gun or two in every

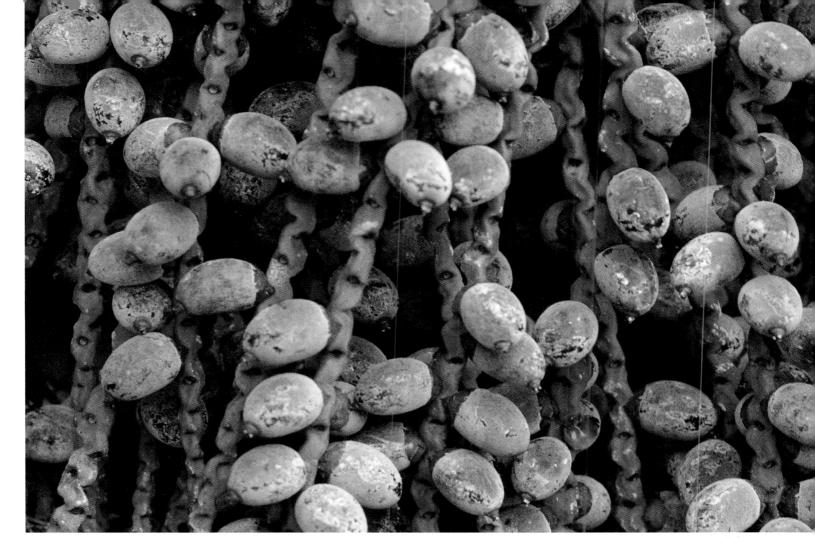

Edible fruit of the *milpe-sos* palm (*Jessenica poly-carpa*), which contain a tasty oil. Mixing the oil with water or manioc juice yields a nourishing drink.

settlement. If ammunition is available the gun is the preferred hunting weapon, carried along on all trips in the forest. Often, however, Makuna hunters are short of ammunition and must rely on their traditional hunting weapons or choose to redirect their subsistence efforts to the more regular and accessible supply of fish.

The most common game animals are the paca—a large rodent with tender meat—and its smaller relative, the agouti; the two species of peccary; monkeys, armadillos, and caymans; and a variety of game birds including toucans, curassows, guans, and tinamous. Hunted at night along the riverbeds, by canoe and with flashlight, the paca is by far the most important in their diet. Peccaries, which roam the forest in big herds, are most easily tracked down by hunting dogs and then killed by shotguns, spears, or even clubs. Big game birds such as curassows and guans are hunted at dawn; their presence is disclosed by their conspicuous calls and they are killed by blowpipe or shotgun. Tinamous are hunted at sunset or just after dark when they settle to sleep on the lower branches of the trees. Caymans are usually hunted at night, using torch or flashlight, and killed by shotgun or by a well-measured blow with the machete.

Because of its size and delicious meat, the tapir is perhaps the most coveted game animal but the least hunted. Tapirs are prototypical spirit animals, and as such, there are many rules and restrictions for hunting them. The Makuna believe that tapirs—like jaguars and anacondas—harbor the souls of dead people. The salt licks, where tapirs gather to browse and drink, are their birth and dance houses, and the waking-up houses of people. Only with the consent of the shaman and in preparation for ritual food feasts may they be hunted in the salt licks. Solitary animals may however be killed when occasionally met with in the forest.

While the hunting equipment is relatively simple, fishing tools and techniques are diverse and elaborate. Traditional Makuna fishing technology includes the use of rod and line, short hand lines, long lines, scoop nets, traps of all kinds, fishing spears, bows and arrows, and various types of fish poison.[8] There is an appropriate tool and technique for catching each particular species, at particular times and places. By far the most common and widespread method is fishing with rod and line. Steel hooks and nylon lines obtained from traders today form part of every fisherman's equipment.

The Makuna catch a variety of food fish.[9] The sábalo, sabaleta, palometa, and waracú are migratory characins with a tasty meat often caught in large quantities as they feed on fallen fruit in the flooded forest or travel in shoals between their up-river feeding grounds and down-river spawning sites. The taraira is a nocturnal, predatory fish, tasteless but easy to kill as it lies still in the shallow waters at the river's edge waiting for its prey. The pintadillo, a big, striped catfish often measuring one meter (3.2 feet) or more in length, is caught with baited line in the deepest parts of the rivers. A single specimen—smoked and cooked—can provide food for a family for several days. Apart from the big and medium-size fish, the Makuna regularly catch small and young fish, the fish children or *sardinas* (in Spanish), which is the basic source of protein for small children as well as adults during periods of ritual food restrictions—after important ceremonies, childbirth, and during illnesses.

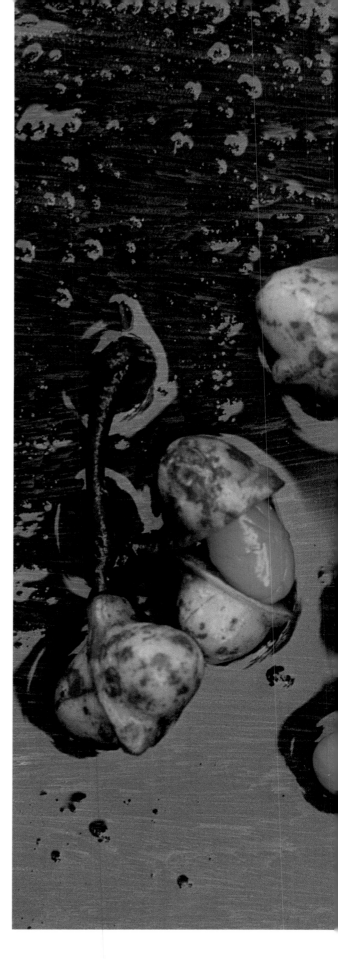

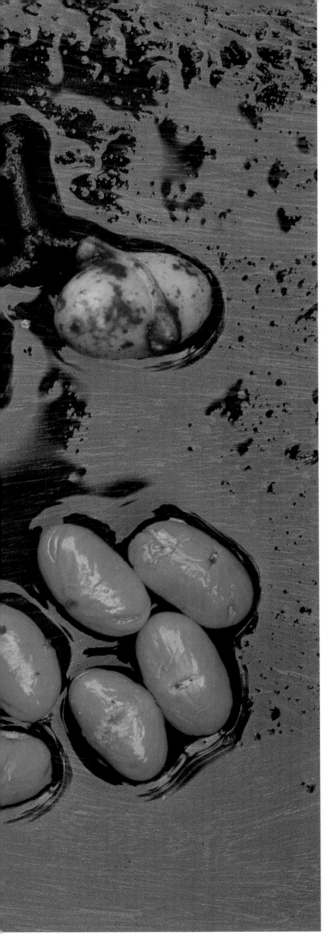

FOREST FRUIT

With its multitude of life forms the forest provides the Makuna with a variety of food gathered with comparatively little effort. The Makuna seasonally collect more than twenty varieties of wild fruit and nuts that complement their diet.[10] In a sense the forest is a natural garden. The fruit of the forest are explicitly described as the crop of fructivore animals—a vast number of birds, mammals, and fish. Forest fruit are also said to be the issue of the first ancestors, created in mythical times and continuously renewed through ritual and shamanism. The Makuna term *he rika* (tree fruit) alludes to this symbolic association between forest fruit and the *he* people.

The metaphysical connotations of forest fruit make them a focal object of various important collective rituals, and their seasonal harvest is a source of great concern. While walking through the forest the Indians constantly watch for fallen fruit and make long detours to collect a handful of fruit, which they examine and consume, commenting on their shape, color, and taste. When fruit abound in the forest, people from different localities come together in camps, at times cutting down whole trees, to collect the fruit on the ground. Men, women, and children also collect and consume fruit in smaller quantities as they hunt, fish, or wander in the forest.

During the long wet season, large-scale rituals are celebrated during which ripe forest fruit are shared and exchanged among groups. At the *He* Fruit Ritual great quantities of fruit are collected and redistributed among people from different settlements and local groups. The ritual is performed to ensure a plentiful harvest of fruit and to appease their spirit-owners—the fructivore animals of the forest. The shaman blesses and cools the fruit by blowing and chanting over them and, on behalf of his community, asks the guardians of the fruit for a fair share.

The forest not only yields plenty of plant food but also a seasonal abundance of edible ants, termites, larvae, and frogs. Certain edible caterpillars and wild fruit are symbolically equated; the *badi ia*, for example, feed exclusively on a single fruit-yielding host tree called *badigü*, and the two are seasonally synchronized in the sense that the former swarm when the latter

The edible *mamito* fruit of the nutmeg (*Myristicaceae*) family. From the bark of trees in the same family a strong hallucinogenic snuff is prepared.

come into season. Hence they are gathered together and their harvests jointly celebrated. When edible caterpillars abound in the forest, their harvest is embraced with the same or even greater enthusiasm than that of the forest fruit. A collective effervescence seizes the community as people collect as many as they can. Those who are too young or too old to collect the caterpillars go from house to house asking for a share of roasted, cooked, or raw larvae.

The nuptial flight of the ground termite and the seasonal reproduction of edible frogs similarly occasion protracted periods of domestic affluence; people collect and eat as much as they can, and often they get tired of the monotonous diet well before the supply is exhausted. Other forest food, including a variety of termites, ants, and grubs are available throughout the year and utilized as a source of food when needed or as another source for protein. A recent nutritional study of the Tatuyu on the upper Pirá-Paraná showed that insects are the second most important source of protein in the diet, after fish but well before game meat.[11]

Certain varieties of grubs, feeding on the decaying trunks of particular palm trees, are manipulated in a semidomesticated manner. Palm trees are selectively cut at comfortable walking distance from the settlement and left to rot to attract the parent beetles. The decaying trunks in which the eggs of the beetle develop into grubs thus serve as a store of protein-rich snacks, conveniently collected to supplement the diet.[12]

FOOD SHAMANISM

The blessing of food, *bare keare*, is a prominent feature of daily life among the Makuna. At all times, and in every place, men silently chant and blow spells over a piece of food or a gourd of liquid. Practically nothing is eaten unless first blessed, and virtually everything edible brought from the forest or the river passes through the hands of senior men, who by means of chanting or blowing convert the potentially harmful beings of nature into life-sustaining food for humans.

One particular incident comes to mind. A man, Amasio, sits on a stool in front of his thatched house of poles and woven palm fronds busily carving a wooden mask for a coming ritual. A woman comes up to him with a piece of meat on a small stick in her hand. She asks Amasio to bless the meat for her young son. Amasio receives the meat, places it on his lap, and continues carving. After a while he pauses, puts his tools aside, picks up the meat, and begins to blow as he holds the meat close to his mouth, breathing rhythmically over it and muttering a hardly audible chant. As he sits blowing and chanting another woman comes forward and asks him to bless some berries in a gourd. Amasio signals to her with his head to place the gourd on the ground in front of him. He stops blowing, calls on the first woman to come for the blessed meat. He hands it over to her while giving her some instructions and then returns to his woodwork. After a while he again pauses, takes the gourd of berries in one hand and begins to blow. When ready he calls on the second woman and hands the blessed berries over to her with instructions. He then continues carving. The scene is typical.

Blowing and carving, blowing and weaving, blowing and repairing fishing gear—so it goes with shamanic and manual labor continuously alternating, both forming equally important parts of a man's daily work. A considerable portion of men's time is spent in blowing over food. Some, like Amasio, are known for their skills in food shamanism. By specializing in different kinds of food, most men make themselves useful as expert blessers for the community as a whole.

To the Makuna, all food is both ambivalent and powerful; it sustains life and gives strength but may also kill and cause disease. Forest fruit, cultivated crops, fish, and game all share in the powers of creation. They contain the primordial substances from which the world was made—the powers of life and death. The Makuna say that plants and animals received powerful weapons or defenses from the substances out of which they emerged and, in the case of animals, through the food they eat. Forest fruit, for example, issued forth from the seminal fluids of the primordial ancestors and grew in the stained soil where Woman Shaman shed her blood, receiving the celestial fire of the Male Creators and the vaginal heat of the Ancestral Mother. Animals—insects, fish, and game—were born out of the materials the ancestors used to fabricate the first ritual goods: the ancient Yuruparí instruments and the sacred feather crowns. The animals that feed on the leaves, flowers, fruit, and insects of the forest thus contain in their bodies the blood and semen of the divinities and the potent remains of the primordial artifacts. Because they possess these powerful properties—their weapons—which derive from creation itself, plants and animals are considered inherently dangerous to eat.

The weapons of fish and game animals are visualized, like the *kūni oka* (defenses) of human beings, as their ritual goods and shamanic substances: Yuruparí instruments, feather crowns, dance regalia, and their own varieties of coca and snuff, chicha and yagé. Thus animals have their own spirit possessions, ritual dances, and knowledge—in short, their own soul. As such they are humanlike—a kind of people—and therefore particularly powerful and potentially harmful to humans.

These ideas about the weapons of all living beings form the basis of Makuna theories of illness and curing. Food shamanism amounts to a sort of preventive therapy, a mystical means of evading and removing the dangers of eating. All foods are blessed—by blowing and chanting—in a similar manner, each class of food requiring a distinct chant. The dangers of food are thereby controlled and the destructive weapons removed.

Only adult men have this knowledge. Some Makuna say that, in his mind and by means of silent chanting, the food blesser collects the weapons of the food, ties them together, breaks them, and throws them away through the gateways of the world. Others say that the blesser carefully collects the sacred goods of the killed animal and returns them to its birth and dance house. Or again, in Ignacio's words cited earlier: ". . . the powerful substances contained in the meat must be removed and restored to their proper places in the dance houses of the animals. The slain animal has to be converted into food by means of food shamanism. The person who knows how to bless food converts the tapir's meat into cassava bread or cultivated plants like plantain or pineapple. . . ." When blessing forest fruit a shaman may cool the fruit by evoking—in his chant—the juicy liquid from certain sweet berries, or he can mentally pass the fruit to fruit-eating animals like the *gake* (capuchin monkey). The monkey then eats the fruit instead of the human being, who thereby avoids its harmful consequences—a form of shamanic substitution.

Food blessing varies according to context, and from one blesser to another. Animals and plants from one part of the forest require their own particular chants different from those of another part. When blowing over peccary meat, for example, a shaman from the headwaters of Komenya said that he collects all the seeds, nuts, and fruit on which the peccary feed, and that makes up its armory; he ties them up, breaks them, throws them out of this world, and closes the doors so that the spirit of the peccary cannot return to haunt the people who eat its meat. If this is not done the heat of Woman Shaman's menstrual blood will cause fever, the grubs that the peccary has fed on will eat the victim's body from within and cause sores and boils. The spirit of the peccary may capture the soul of the victim and take him to the waking-up house of the peccaries; this means that the victim will fall sick and ultimately die.

In spite of individual and local variations a general pattern of food shamanism emerges. The weapons of slain animals are collected and removed. Not only must the food blesser collect the weapons that an animal acquired in the process of creation and continuously receives through the food it eats, he must also remove the danger derived from predators feeding on it and the animals living in association with it—its owners and helpers, to speak in the Makuna shamanic idiom. The same is true for the blessing of wild forest fruit, which also have their owners—the fruit-eating animals feeding on them. For each species the blesser must, in his silent chant, cover the entire food chain in which the species in question participates. The Makuna are acutely aware of the fact that a kill or a catch interferes with the complex web of life that constitutes the rain-forest ecosystem. They recognize in thought and action that human beings form an integral part of this grander community of living beings where the death of one means life for another.

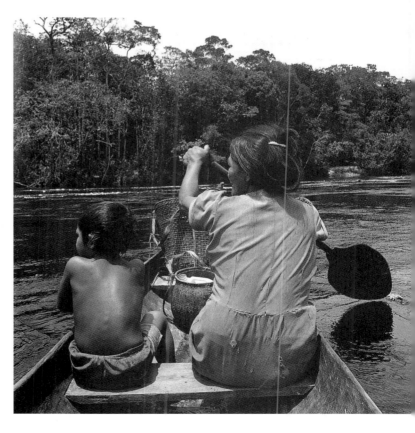

Paddling to the garden. The smaller basket contains provisions for a full morning in the fields.

Each category of food has to be blessed and subsequently introduced to every Makuna individual. In this way the young child gradually encounters all food, a process which takes some five to seven years. The sequence is then repeated in abbreviated versions during and after every collective ritual, particularly when the Yuruparí instruments are shown or yagé drunk.

Food restrictions are also imposed at the birth of a child, after a girl's first menstruation, and during serious illness. All these instances have in common the potentially dangerous contact with the *he* world. At birth the soul of the new-born child travels from the spirit world into this one. At every ritual, but particularly during male initiation, the participants establish a voluntary contact with the ancestral world in order to be reborn, to change souls, and to recreate in the present the cosmic order established in the

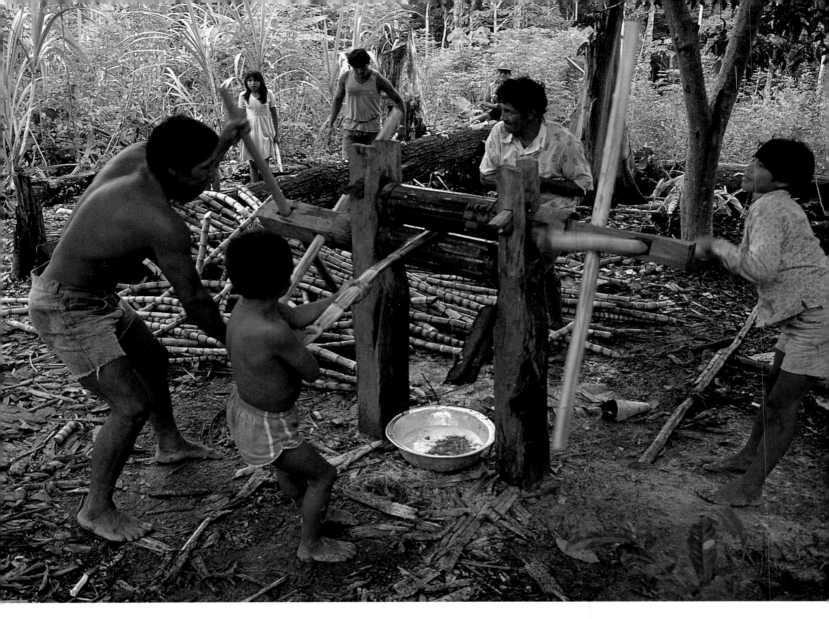

mythical past. While giving birth or menstruating, women are subject to in-voluntary contact with the *he* world.[13] During illness, the patient also faces the potentially harmful powers of the spirits. The Makuna attribute illness to many causes: eating of wrong, prohibited, or unblessed food; sorcery from evil shamans; or exposure to powerful and predatory spirits invoked during major rituals. If not properly treated the sick person, it is believed, is likely to die. The soul will be taken into the sky world, the underworld, or again, to the waking-up houses of the animals. To the Makuna all these other worlds are different dimensions of that single, fundamental, and alternative reality—the *he* world.

The food restrictions imposed at each of these occasions are gradually re-moved, and food is successively reintroduced by the blessing of each class in a fixed order. The sequence of food blessing following the male initiation

Men and boys pressing sugarcane. The robust wooden press is a requi-site of the longhouse set-tlement. The fermented sugarcane juice is a basic ingredient in the home-brewed *chicha* (beer) served at every ritual gathering.

ritual is perhaps the most complete one and provides a good example of the process. At first the diet consists exclusively of thin starch bread and raw or toasted ants and termites, always eaten cold and unspiced. After some time cold manioc juice, vegetable food—particularly palm heart and the boiled leaves of the manioc plant—and wild forest fruit are introduced. Then follows a ritual where pepper is shamanized. This ritual removes the danger of heat and fire, lifting the restriction on hot and peppered food. The pepper shamanism is followed by the blessing of fresh manioc bread and boiled sardinas. Subsequently other kinds of fish and small game are gradually introduced in the diet, roughly in order of size. The whole series culminates with the blessing of tapir meat at a communal ceremony, after which the initiates return to their ordinary diet.

The food-blessing sequence can be understood as a series of symbolic movements through various domains and dimensions of the Makuna cosmos.[14] The overall movement corresponds to a progression from bloodless food (plants and insects) to blood-rich animal food, and from food minimally processed (cold, raw, and unspiced) to highly processed food (hot, cooked, smoked, and spiced). This progression seems to allude to the process of initiation by which the initiate, symbolically killed and identified with the nonhuman spirit world, is reborn and gradually reintegrated into the social world of human beings. The food-blessing sequence can also be seen as a movement from underground root crops (manioc) and creatures living below the ground (ants and termites) to above-ground plants (vegetables and forest fruit). In the process the initiate symbolically emerges from the ground like a growing plant. The growth of a new-born child and a socially reborn initiate is thus metaphorically compared to that of a manioc plant.

After the pepper shamanism there is a clear progression from small fish to larger fish and game animals; the sequence of food blessing now describes a movement from water to land, which replicates the emergence of the ancestral people from river to land at the birthplaces of the different clans. In other words the rebirth of the young boys at the initiation ceremony evokes the mythic image of the collective emergence of the clan and also the chain of creative transformation of fish children into fish and ultimately into old fish—the land-living game animals. This food-blessing sequence also implies a movement from female to male; from food collected principally or exclusively by women to food exclusively procured by men—

the big fish and game. In the Makuna dietary idiom this process intimates that the initiate, like the small child, gradually grow away from the private world of the mother toward the male-dominated social world of adults. At the end of the sequence both male and female foods are eaten, emphasizing the interdependence between men and women in society. Just as men and women cooperate in life, no meal is complete without their complementary contribution. As a metaphor of society and the human condition in general even the ordinary meal is saturated with cultural meaning.

THE MAKUNA WAY

The Makuna mode of subsistence amounts to a specific, Tukanoan variety of an adaptive strategy common throughout the interfluvial forests of the Amazon basin. This general survival strategy, combining small and dispersed settlements with an integrated economy of shifting cultivation, fishing, hunting, and gathering has proven notoriously versatile in the tropical rain-forest environment.

In the wider context of Amazonian ethnography, the Tukanoan Indians of northwest Amazonia are unique in their strong emphasis on patrilineal descent, rank, linguistic exogamy, and territoriality. Emilio Moran has proposed that precisely these features—patrilineality, ranking, and territoriality—are adaptive adjustments to the limiting conditions of blackwater ecosystems, allowing control over critical fishing resources.[15] The complex system of food restrictions and a notorious ideological attention to place, along with ritually grounded notions of predation as exchange, regulating the use of river and forest resources, can be seen as cultural elaborations of this adaptive strategy.

The river territory of every community in the Pirá-Paraná area is divided into cosmologically defined sections where fishing is permitted or prohibited. Every bend, stretch, pool, and rapid is known by name and associated with a mythical story. Depending on the story it tells, each place is believed to be either harmless or harmful. Fish swimming in harmful waters are dangerous to eat; they cause illness and death, and fishing is consequently prohibited at these sites. A river section may be harmful because it contains the fire or blood of the ancestors or is polluted by ancestral yagé or dart poison. Particularly dangerous are the sites where the fish spawn and multiply— their birth and dance houses. Other sections of the river are said to be

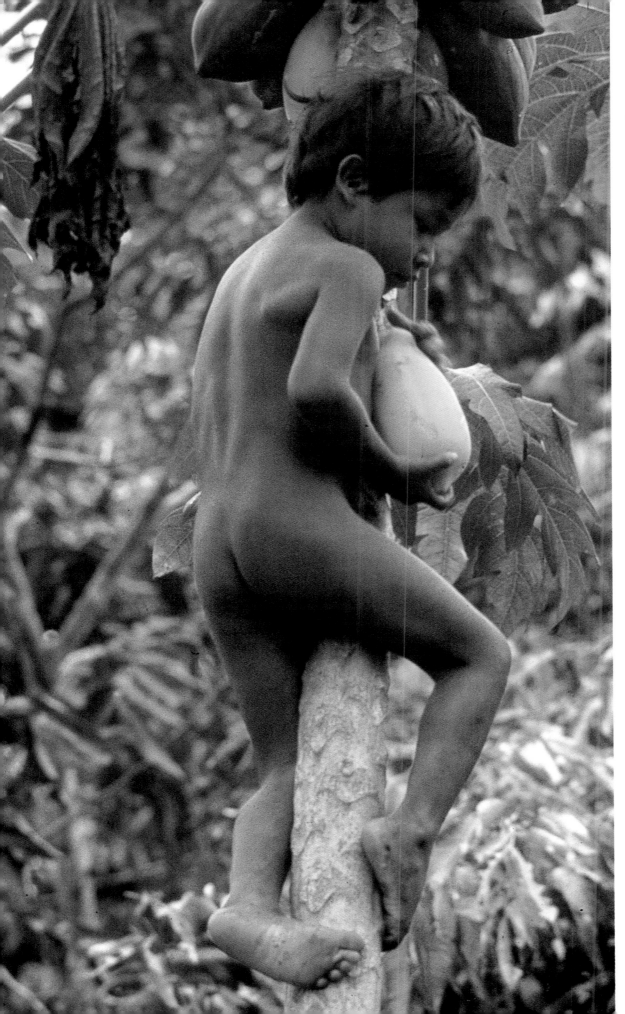

A boy fetching a papaya.

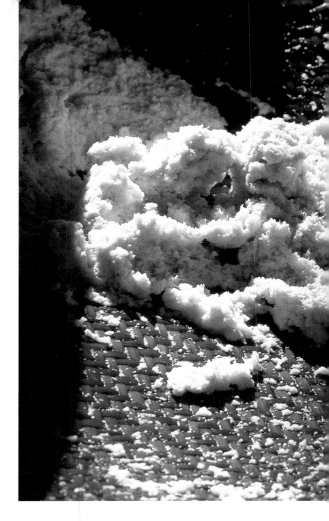

harmless because they are associated with the ancestor's benevolent deeds. In this way, by dividing the rivers into sections that are safe and others that are dangerous, the Makuna often exclude more than half the length of any river from fishing.[16] The harmful sections where fishing is prohibited are called *wai huna* (places where the fish cause pain) and as such constitute a kind of protected area or river reserve. Thus the mythical geography of each river territory has far-reaching implications for human land use. Myths, in effect, are land use plans—and extremely efficient ones at that since they are pragmatically informed, emotionally charged, and morally binding.

Subsistence efforts and food intake are not only tuned to the cosmological definition of place and the seasonal rhythm of the environment, but also to the life-cycle events of individuals and the collective rituals of the community. Some foods are periodically and selectively prohibited, depending on the age, sex, and ritual status of the individual. For example, at a particular point in time the male head of a family may eat meat and fish without restriction, while his nursing wife is allowed to eat only certain varieties of fish, their small children *wai ria* (small fish), and a recently initiated boy no meat or fish whatsoever. This metaphysically motivated practice implies that a hunter who comes home with a bag of meat after a long day in the forest may immediately have to set out on a fishing expedition, while his wife and children collect fruit in the forest and catch sardinas at the canoe landing. Though strenuous, this custom also has a very practical ecological consequence as it diversifies resource utilization, thus spreading out pressure on the environment.

In addition, a whole host of other rules and practices assure a balanced exchange between the human hunter and his prey. Male predation is regulated by an explicit norm of moderation—a code of adequacy—in hunting and fishing, prescribing that productive efforts should be attuned to the immediate subsistence needs of the household. Any sign of excess or overexploitation of the forest and river resources is strongly condemned by the community. Only in the context of collective rituals, such as the Peach Palm Ritual or the *dabucurí* (food-giving) ceremonies, when large amounts of fish, meat, and plant food are exchanged among different malocas, are kills and catches beyond the need of the individual households publicly sanctioned. At these occasions the services of powerful shamans are needed

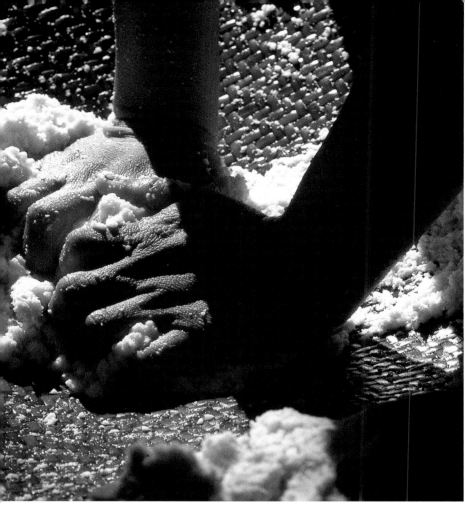

Left: The manioc mash being pounded through a sieve to remove the prussic acid. The mash is later squeezed dry in a woven manioc press and then baked into bread.

Below: Manioc or cassava bread. This coarse, rather tasteless cake is the Makuna bread of life, baked daily for every meal. It is usually served with thick, hot pepper sauce.

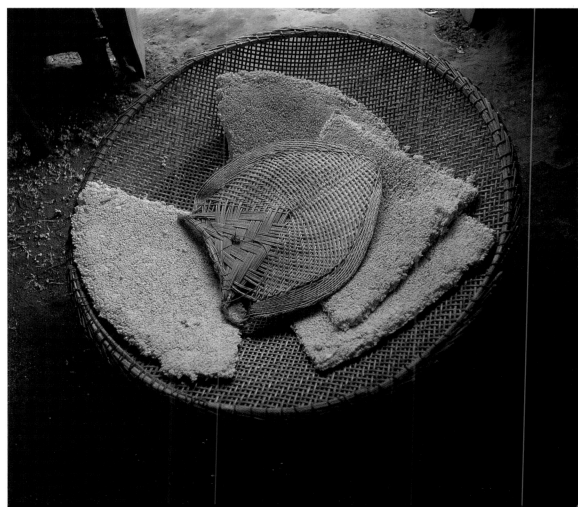

to secure abundant food supplies as well as to protect both those who procure the food and those who ritually consume it.

If this moral code is transgressed, the animals are believed to take revenge. Illness and misfortune befall the imprudent hunter or fisherman as his soul is captured by the animal spirits and taken to their houses in the forest or river. Unless retrieved by a shaman, the victim wastes away and dies. These shamanic beliefs imply a strong ideological sanction against the abuse of the living environment.

The integration of practical knowledge and cosmological beliefs turns the traditional Makuna mode of subsistence into an efficient system of resource management. Its compelling power derives from a particular mode of experiencing and relating to the world that posits a relationship of equality, continuity, and mutual implication between humans and their environment. In this view, plants, animals, and humans are conceived of as varieties of people in the community of all beings. Accordingly the rules and regulations that govern human interaction also govern the relationships with plants and animals. Subsistence activities are modeled on interactions in the social domain. Makuna men and women relate to their significant environment—cultivated crops, wild food plants, fish, and game—as they relate to one another.

While based on a detailed practical knowledge of the rain-forest environment gained over thousands of years of close interaction and careful use, the Makuna way of life also expresses a profoundly moral attitude toward nature. To cultivate, to fish, to hunt in the correct manner, and to eat the right food at the right time are all ways of maintaining good health and recreating social and cosmic order. To proceed in the wrong manner or to eat the wrong food at the wrong time destroys order and causes misfortune, disease, and death. By following their ancestral traditions the Makuna sustain and continuously reshape the meaningful world in which they live.

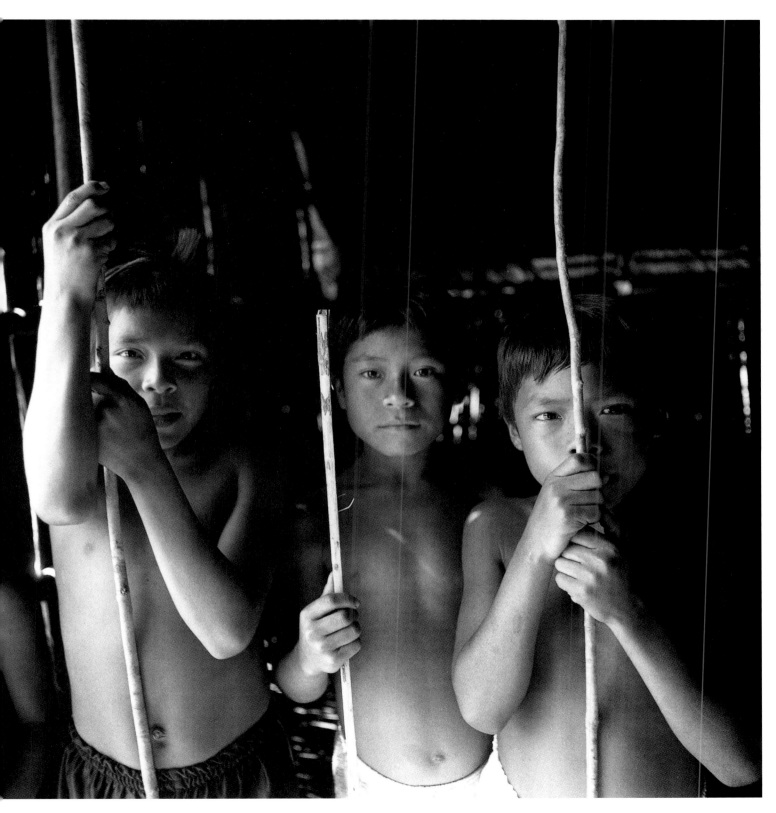

Boys with sticks used
for play.

6

THE DANCE
OF THE
SPIRITS

It is late afternoon in mid-March 1989. The peach palm fruit is ripe, the sabaleta is migrating toward its spawning grounds in the Apaporis River, and edible frogs abound in the forest heralding the beginning of the long winter rains. In the spare light of Ricardo's maloca on the upper Komenya people are hectically preparing for the great Peach Palm Ritual.[1] Ricardo, a young headman and chanter of the Ide Masa clan, is a paternal cousin (classificatory brother) of Ignacio. At the back of the maloca a group of women work at a tripod, preparing drink for the feast by squeezing the mash of grated peach palm fruit through a woven sieve into a huge clay pot. Nearby other women bake piles of manioc bread on the griddle. They laugh and chat as they work while small children dart around them, playing among the pots and piles of food and firewood.

At the front of the crowded maloca, newly repaired and decorated with fresh wall paintings for the feast, a group of men sit chanting and incessantly passing around cigars and bowls of coca. As a young boy runs between the back and front of the house serving peach palm drink to the men, the host ceremoniously greets the arriving guests. Along the sides other guests have already settled in with their pots and baskets full of food and drink. A multitude of hammocks fill the sleeping corridors of the maloca. A noisy group of youngsters—dressed in their finest clothes and faces elaborately painted—play panpipes, deer-bone flutes, and shell whistles near the men's door. After the greeting ceremony the officiating shaman—who happens to be Ignacio—withdraws behind a screen at the rear to blow silent spells over coca and snuff. As darkness approaches, the maloca takes on that paradoxical mixture of solemnity and triviality, order and disorder, tension and laxity, which characterizes all Makuna rituals.

Masked dancers moving rhythmically through the dark interior of the longhouse, red-hooded heads with their black, painted faces glowing in the moody torch light.

Suddenly there is a stir. Chatter and howling are heard in the distance, first faintly then louder. Children curiously peep through the door but are cautioned by the adults: "Come back, children, don't look out. The spirits are coming. If you see them, you may become blind." A line of masked dancers eventually appears, and one after another they enter through the front door beating the post

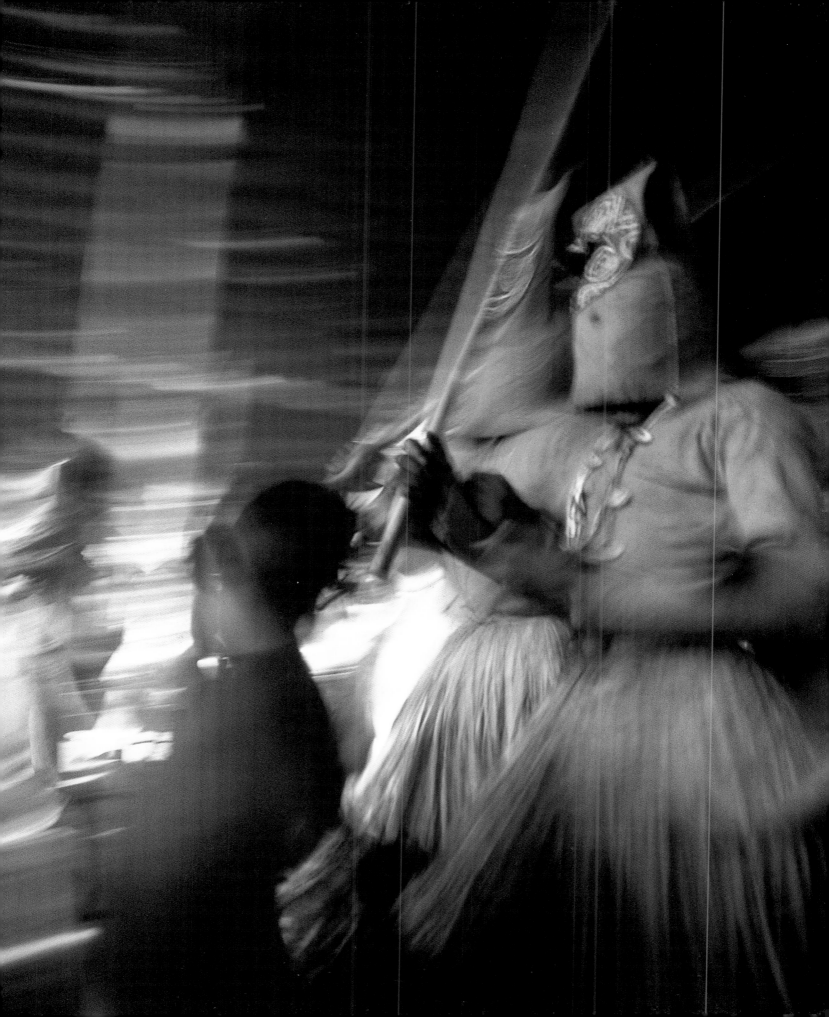

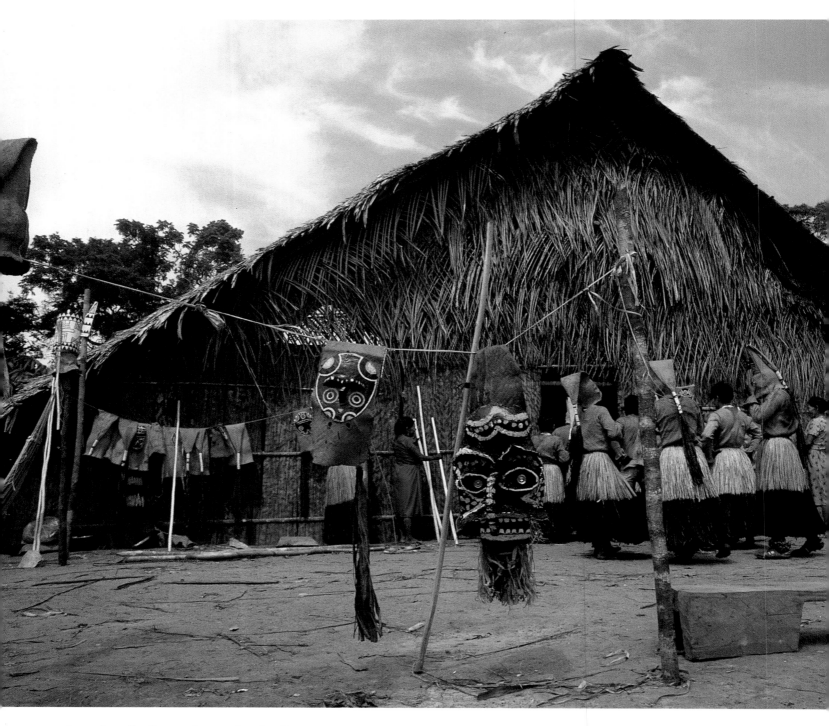

Scene from the Dance of the Spirits—one of the major ritual events among the Makuna—performed during the harvest season of the peach palm. Dancers resting in the plaza, their masks hanging on strings in the front of the dance house.

with branches. They howl and swagger toward the center of the maloca imitating a flock of capuchin monkeys. With the arrival of the monkey spirits, who come to eat, drink, and dance in the maloca, the ritual has begun.

Dressed in reddish bark-cloth hoods shaped like monkey heads, with protruding ears and charcoal designs on their faces, the masked dancers command the attention of the crowd. They wear a long-sleeve shirt of the same material and a whitish skirt with a pitch black fringe. Hands and feet are dyed black, and each dancer has a seed rattle attached to the right ankle, which produces a rhythmic sound as they move across the dance path.

As their performance continues the spirit dancers draw the onlooking crowd into the playful drama, turning the entire maloca into a stage. Bundles of food hanging from the roof beams and house posts are torn down by some of the masked dancers, while others rush and retreat from the attentive and laughing crowd. When the Monkeys finally move toward the rear where the hosts placate them with peach palm drink, another pair of masked dancers, very different in appearance and demeanor, steal into the maloca. Each wears a large, black resin mask painted with white and yellow stripes that form a monstrous head with a ferocious grin and lifeless, staring eyes made of metallic bits from torch batteries. These are the penis spirits, or *tori*. One of them is male, the other—oddly—female. Each holds a long stick with a rattle attached in one hand, while the other hand grasps another staff with its tip darkened red and held between the legs in the manner of a huge penis.

The penis spirits dance toward the amused onlookers with obscene movements. Children within reach are grabbed or pushed aside with mock bru-

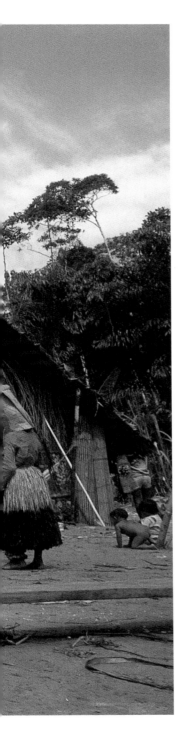

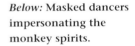

Below: **Masked dancers impersonating the monkey spirits.**

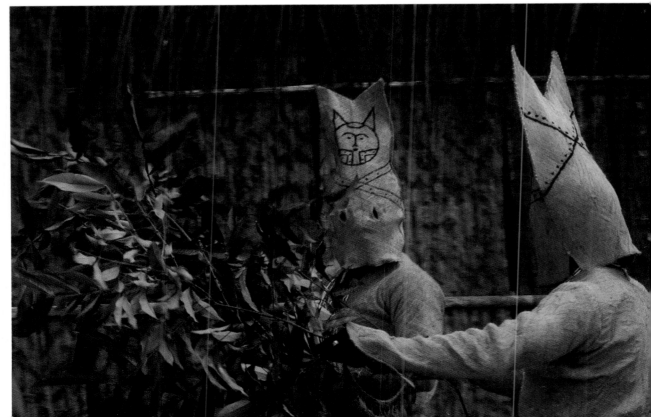

tality. The men fend off the dancer's attacks by striking the grotesque bodies and penises with sticks, while screaming women try to escape. After a while the penis spirits sit down in the center of the maloca. The men of the host group approach, greet, and jokingly touch and scrutinize them. The spirits remain silent, stirring only to accept snuff and drink. The Monkeys join them to receive the drink and trays of manioc bread offered. Then the penis spirits leave, soon followed by the monkey spirits, laden with food, drink, and blessed snuff.

Moments later several groups of bee spirits enter, dance, and leave, wearing black masks with protruding noses said to resemble the tube-shaped entrance to the bee's nest. Each strikes the ground with a branch as they dance across the middle of the house in a long, single line to the rear where they are also received by the hosts. Their performance is followed by a pause when the dancers remove their masks to rest, eat, and drink outside the maloca. Inside, young men and women begin another dance to the mournful tune of the *jota seru* (peach palm flutes) made particularly for this occasion from a pair of ordinary panpipes lashed together. In contrast to the swift movement of the usual pan-flute dance, the dancers now stride slowly and rhythmically, round and round in a wide circle.

At dusk there is a dramatic change in mood as twenty or more masked dancers reappear in a pair of long rows, again beating the door post upon entry. Their black masked faces are distinctively adorned with white and yellow designs, and sculptured noses and eyebrows protrude from the garish faces. These are the spirits of the *nokoro*—a small fish with a colored head living in streams and rivulets in the forest—dancing in line with long striding steps along the hall dimly illuminated by two flaming torches. As the dance continues they reassemble at the rear of the house with their backs toward the women's door and their heads facing the front entrance. The men of the host group greet the dancers, addressing them as "grandfathers" and asking who they are and from where they have come. The spirit dancers answer by moving their hands and hooded heads as if speechless. Anyone who would address them by name and thus reveal their human identities would waste away and die.

After the greeting ceremony, the hosts offer drinks and blow snuff up the noses of the visiting spirits. Reinvigorated they begin a solemn, circular dance very different from the playful appearance of those that preceded. Their

Nokoro (fish) spirits. The black faces and the *genipa* dye on hands and feet associate the dancers with the spirit world; as the dye gradually wears off, the dancers reemerge into the world of the living.

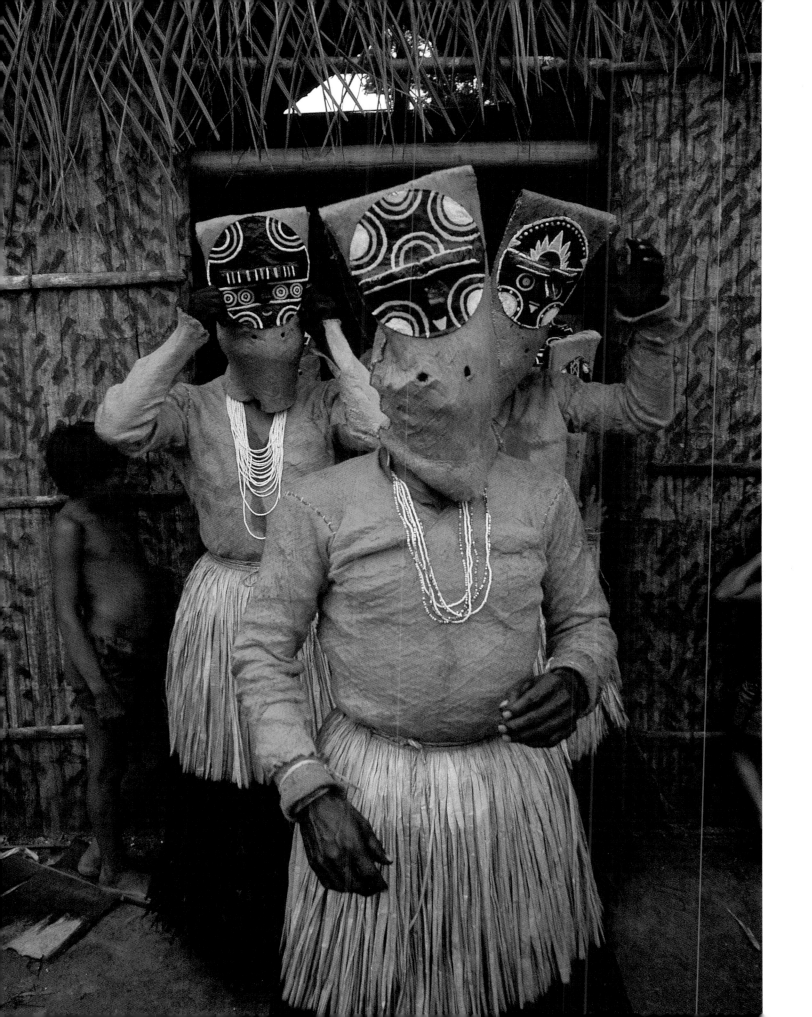

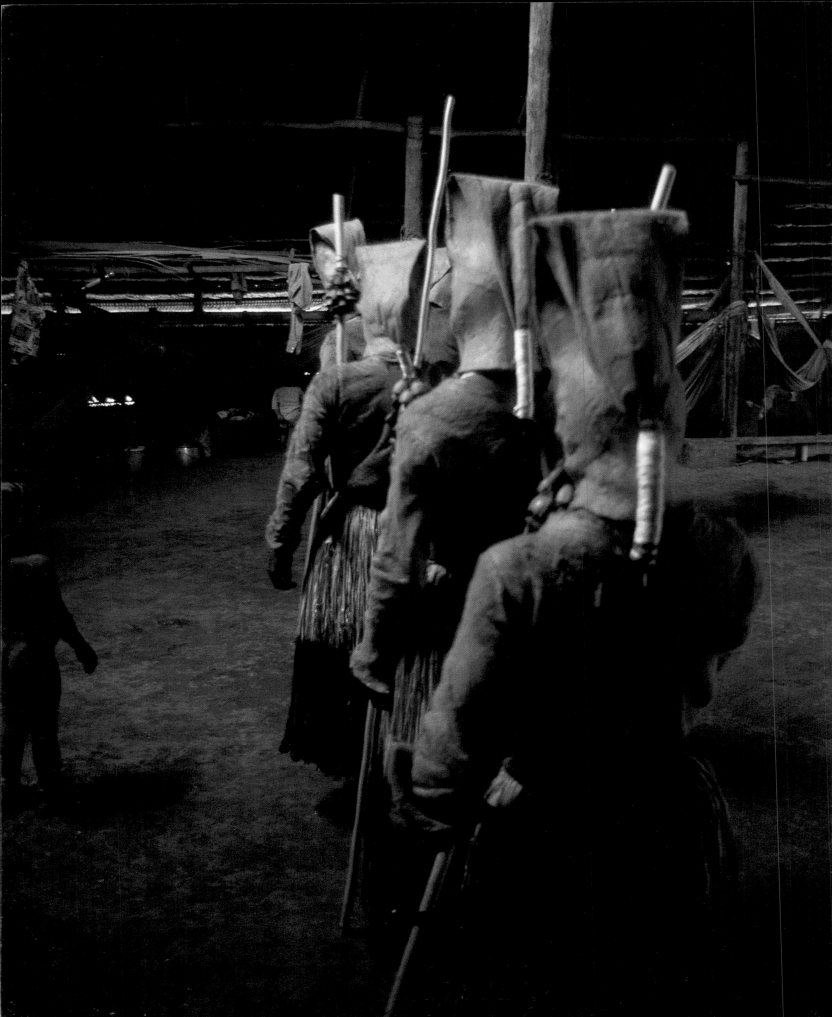

The fish spirits dance
solemnly in the center
of the longhouse.

forceful but monotonous performance is accompanied by a melancholic song as they dance, leave, and reenter several times. As the dancing becomes more intense women join the men; together they move in the interlaced manner typical of most Makuna dances. Yet the tune of the *Nokoro* Dance is singular, unlike any other Makuna song. In this deeply suggestive atmosphere the masked dancers move rhythmically through the dark of the longhouse; their red hooded heads with black, painted faces glow in the moody torchlight then fade into strangely figured silhouettes. The loud chorus of fifty or more men, the stamping of a hundred feet, and the sound of rattles and throbbing tube drums all combine to give the impression, as night wears on, that the spirit dancers indeed are visitors from another world.

In this way, alternating between jestful, dramatic play and solemn, sacred dance the spirits continue through the night and following day. In the interludes elders chew coca, smoke, and take snuff to keep sleep away, while the young pick up the paired panpipes and continue to dance. Neither the dancers nor the spectators are supposed to sleep during the ritual to avoid being carried away by the spirits. Though believed to be auspicious if properly performed and carefully supervised, the Dance of the Spirits is also potentially harmful. Like all Makuna rituals, the Peach Palm Ritual is a precarious encounter with the ultimate forces of reality. It is performed to bring life and fertility but may also cause death and misfortune.

Though the details vary according to its performative context, the general structure of the ritual is the same. It consists of two parts: the first, *rümüa sahare* (Dance of the Spirits), literally "the entry of the spirits," lasts for about twenty-four hours from late afternoon one day to nightfall on the following; the second, *hota basa* (Peach Palm Dance proper), which is also the name of the entire ritual, lasts for another night from dusk to dawn on the third day. For the Makuna the ritual as a whole is a celebration of the peach palm harvest. Yet, as will be seen, the ritual is more than a first-fruit ritual and food feast; fundamentally it is an engagement with the spirits of the dead. For the days and nights it lasts, time as we define it will be suspended, the past joined with the present and death symbolically transcended.

The ritual demands considerable preparation starting months before the actual feasting. As the peach palm fruit ripen, and then, as they are harvested and converted into a liquid mash, they are successively blessed by the officiating shaman. Closer to the agreed date of the ritual, masks and costumes are made, ample manioc bread baked, and large quantities of meat and fish procured for redistribution during the feast. As one of the great events in the Makuna ritual calendar, the Peach Palm Ritual requires an extensive investment of physical labor, material resources, and shamanic skills.

The host group sends word about its intention to sponsor the ritual well in advance. In response to the copious amount of food and drink anticipated, the guests, on their part, provide masks and costumes and lead the dancing during the ritual. This complementary division of tasks between hosts and guests is symbolically important and in itself part of the ritual. Ideally hosts and guests are supposed to correspond with intermarrying groups, and the ritual itself should strengthen the affinal relationship among them. In actual practice, however, hosts and guests are not rigidly separated and can jointly take part in most tasks before and during the event. The shaman, responsible for the mystical preparations and the supervision of the entire ritual, may belong to either group.

About two weeks before the ritual, the host group intensify hunting and fishing efforts to obtain an abundance of food, a labor that also demands shamanic expertise. The Peach Palm Ritual is a food feast that involves the redistribution of large amounts of fish and meat. The officiating shaman therefore seeks permission from the spirit guardians of the animals to hunt and fish beyond the everyday subsistence needs of the community. To avoid the animal spirits taking revenge and causing people to fall sick, the shaman offers them coca and tobacco. As the hunters return with their bags, the meat and the fish are smoked and stored on racks over large fires. Other men gather the peach palm fruit, while women harvest the manioc and boil and grate the fruit into a mash for storing in the ground inside the dance house.

At this time, the guests begin to prepare the various masks and costumes for the Dance of the Spirits. One important type of mask consists of a reddish bark-cloth hood with a tuft of black bark strips tied to the end. A

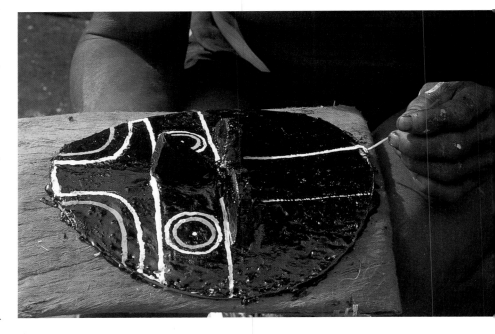

Above: The face of the spirit mask is made of an oval sheet of dried, black resin and painted with white and yellow patterns. Nose and eyebrows of balsa wood are glued onto the face, which itself is sewn to a reddish bark-cloth hood.

Above, right: Burero spirits taking a rest. The cylindrical balsa-tube mask and yellow face of the *bureru*—a wader bird—contrasts with the bark-cloth hoods and dark faces of the fish spirits.

Below, right: Mask of a *nokoro* spirit. The face of each individual mask is distinct but identifiable as belonging to a particular class of spirits.

round or oval face of black tree resin adorned with white and yellow circular or semicircular design is glued to the hood. Nose and eyebrows of carved bits of balsa wood provide a characteristic profile. This class of masks typically represents various kinds of fish, including the *nokoro,* and other animals closely associated with them in Makuna myth, such as the vulture. Together they enact the solemn parts of the ritual. Despite the common basic pattern, there are also individual artistic flourishes and local stylistic variations. It is difficult to identify a particular mask with a certain spirit character; only the artist can do so with certainty. The identification is doubly difficult since each mask may represent a whole series of different spirits in the course of a single ritual.

Another important type of mask consists of a hollow balsa-wood tube on which a yellow face is painted. The facial features are brought out by a stylized design in red and black. Oversized ears, also made of balsa wood and painted in abstract designs, are inserted in holes on the sides of the tube. The wooden mask is then fixed on a bark-cloth hood drawn over the head. This mask typifies the *bureru*—a wader bird living on the shores of the Apaporis River—who appears at dawn after the first night's dancing. By changing the forms of the ears the mask is made to represent the spirits of other animals who, like the *bureru,* all perform in pairs.

Several other kinds of masks are also made from the same basic materials to represent a single or a few conspicuous characters including termites, anteaters, and jaguars. The mask of the jaguar spirit, like those of termites and anteaters, consists of a carefully sculptured balsa head molded with black resin and decorated with yellow and white spots, which resemble the coloring of the animal.

The preparation of masks and costumes requires the close supervision of the shaman. Hoods and shirts are made from the bark of the *wasogü* tree;

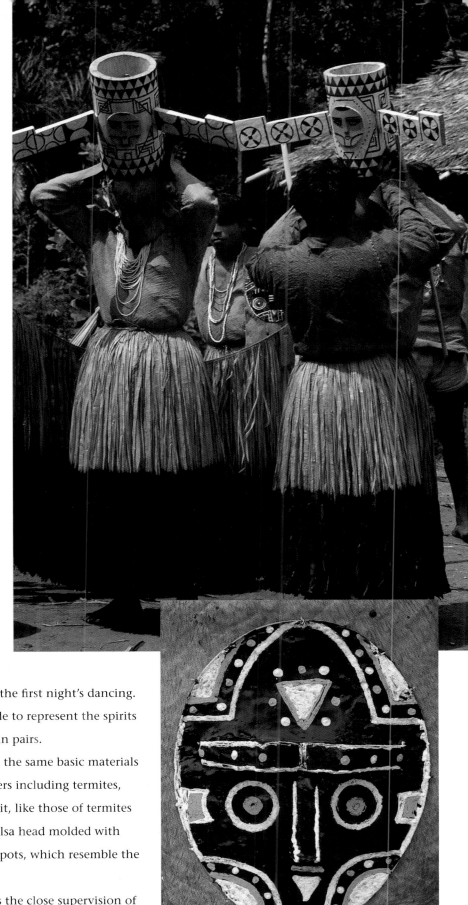

faces and heads are sculptured in balsa wood and resin. Before the materials can be collected the shaman blows over snuff to placate the spirit-owners of the *wasogü* tree—ancestral anacondas believed to inhabit certain named sites along the Apaporis River. The men inhale the blessed snuff before venturing into the forest. The same procedure is followed for collecting resin. When the material is blessed and amassed, the men collectively prepare the masks in a secluded place away from women and children. After the resin has been heated and molded into faces and heads, the masks are then addressed as *nyikü masa* (grandfathers). Henceforth the masks are carefully guarded until just before the ceremony when each dancer will add their final touches.

To prepare the cloth, a *wasogü* tree is felled and the lower, branchless part of the trunk cut into suitable pieces. Each section is then beaten with a heavy stick, until the crushed bark texture loosens, and is removed from the trunk. The thick, clothlike material is then washed in the river and dried in the sun before finally cut and sewn into hoods and shirts. Lastly, eye holes are burned out with a piece of glowing charcoal. The skirts are prepared from the inner bark of another tree that has been torn in long, narrow strips and dried. The strips are then tied to a fiber string, wound into bundles, and taken to the forest to be dipped in a certain clay that yields the black fringe of the final product. With the masks and costumes on hand the ritual may begin.

Some guests arrive a day early to settle in comfortably in the dance house. The dancers make a camp in a clearing away from the maloca where they may temporarily withdraw to rest and eat with their families during the ritual. In the maloca the hosts are busy making the final preparations. Women bake piles of manioc bread and complete the peach palm drink, while the men prepare sufficient amounts of coca and snuff to last them through the feast.

The host maloca and the dancers' camp in the forest form the spatial coordinates of the ritual. The division in space reinforces the symbolic separation between the hosts and the guests, between the people inside and the spirits outside. The spirit dancers move between the camp and the maloca, dancing in the house and on the plaza, and carry food, drink, and blessed snuff to the camp for their women and children.

Face of unidentified spirit. Masks are made with considerable artistic freedom. The same mask can be used to impersonate various spirits, including the penis and jaguar spirits.

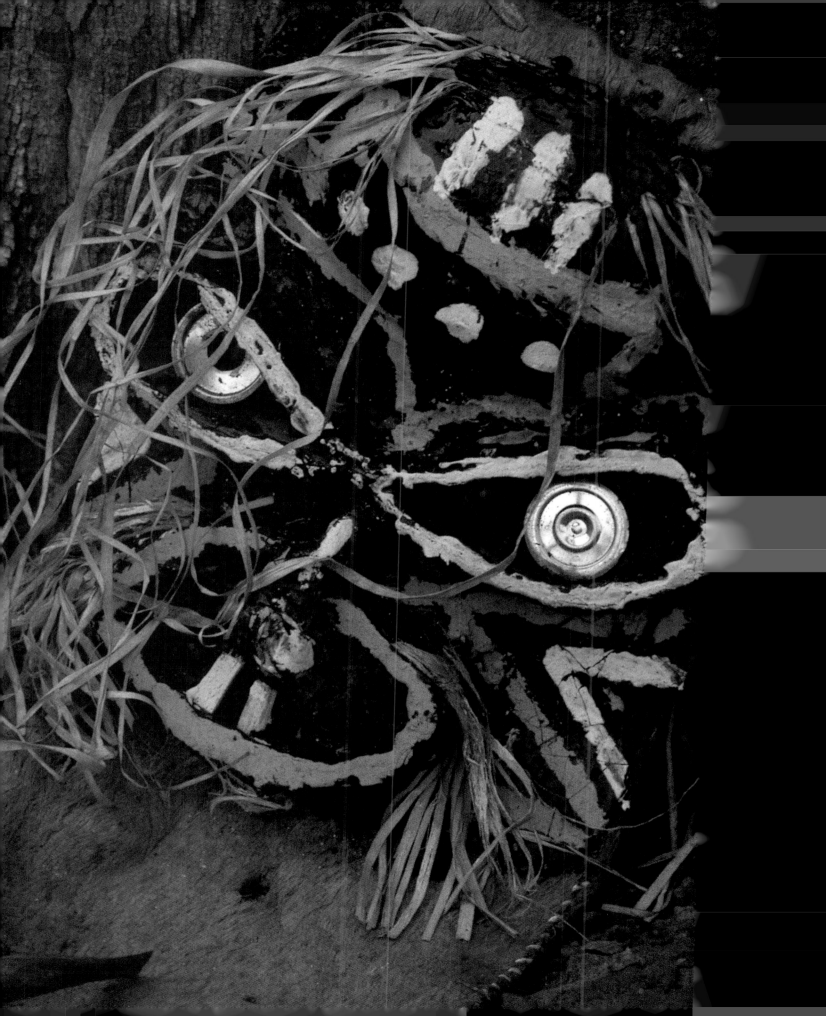

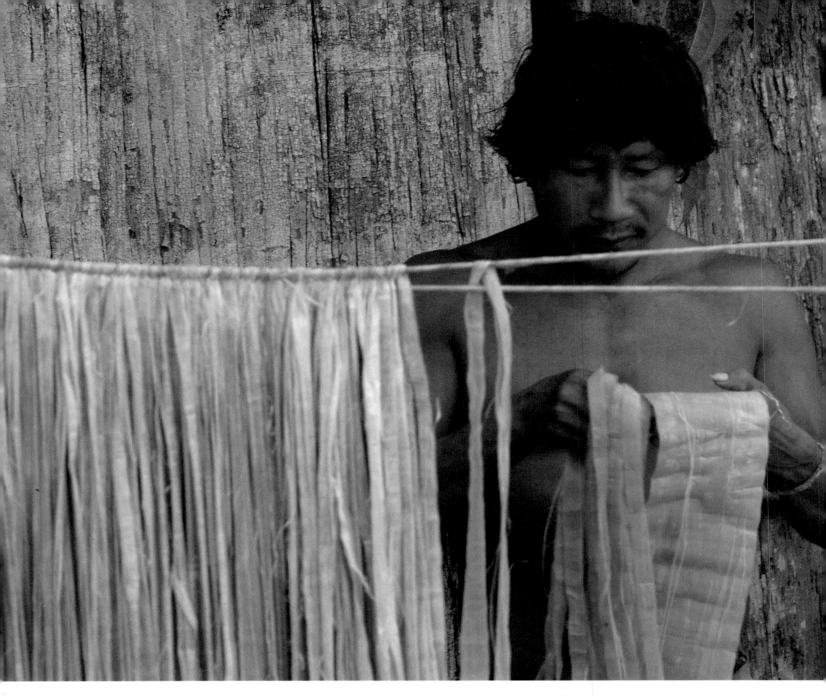

Above: Man preparing a skirt from bark strips tied to a fiber string. The strips are then died in clay to yield the characteristic black fringe.

Right: Portrait of a resting dancer.

Apart from all kinds of animal spirits the performers also impersonate a disparate collection of other odd characters including spirits of the male and female penises, tree fruit, fishnets, and bows-and-arrows. All in all more than one hundred distinct characters may figure in the ritual. Though the masks are changed to represent different spirits, the basic costume remains constant throughout as the performances alternate between *basa* (sacred dance) and *ahere* (playful acting). This dramatic tension between the solemn and the amusing, essential to the ritual as a whole, is underscored by the visual contrast between the stylized, black face of the fish spirits and the more realistic, yellow face of the playful *bureru* spirits.

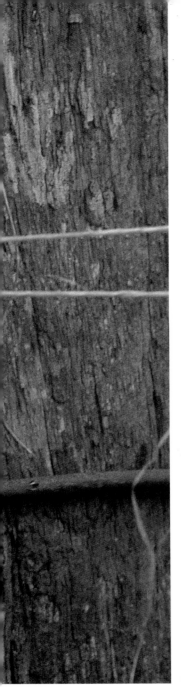

Depending on the masks prepared and the spirits impersonated, the ritual sequence varies from one occasion to another. Certain essential and fixed elements of the ritual sequence, however, structure the performance. The monkey spirits inaugurate the ritual, usually followed by the spirits of the penises, bees, and *nokoro*. The capuchin monkey is the *ühü* (head) of the forest animals, and as such also said to be a jaguar. He comes to collect food—meat, fish, and peach palm drink—from the host. The penis spirit, on the other hand, whose task is to receive shamanized snuff, is actually said to be a fish.

The following is an account of the ritual sequence on the upper Komenya in March 1989. After the long and mournful *Nokoro* Dance at dusk on the first day of the ritual, a more cheerful mood is ushered in by the appearance of a pair of Frog Catchers looking for frogs. These creatures stalk the ground and house posts of the maloca with burning torches in search of their prey. The Colored Toads follow in their footsteps, now and then jumping on an

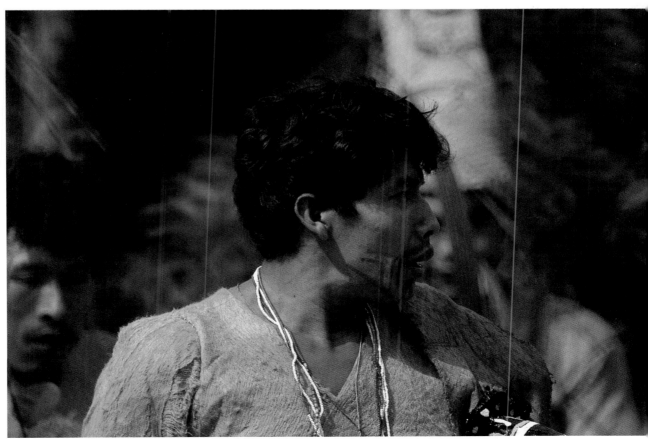

imaginary frog and threading it on an imaginary string as men do when they collect edible frogs.

A series of odd animal spirits, in pairs or small groups, follow in quick succession. Bats, Leeches, Piranha, Opossum, Peccary, Anteater, and Termites all enter in apparent disorder. They dance, sometimes several at a time, leave, and reenter. Each dance has its characteristic movement and song imitating the animal. The Bats move with waving arms, while the Leeches, as if they were trying to suck blood, fall upon the onlooking crowd. Some spectators shout mock insults at the spirits, while others shy away to avoid capture. Groups of Piranha move quickly like shoals of fish. The Termites, with huge masked heads, enter slowly and silently through the back door. They are *bare rinire masa* (food thieves) coming to eat the leftovers.

In the late evening the true *wai rümüa* (fish spirits) enter as the sacred dance starts anew. Then there is again a sequence of dramatic play featuring spirits of otters, jaguars, the small and large sloth, tree ants, anteater, and *wasogü* beetles, whose larvae feed on the tree from which bark cloth is made. The Otters persecute fish, swirling around and emitting a humming sound. Three growling Jaguars with big spotted heads run into the screaming crowd, aggressively attacking the central house posts. The Sloth, always solitary, walks exceedingly slow around the house with a penislike stick between his legs. Women strike at the stick, and the Sloth falls to the ground with a loud puff. A long line of Ants, followed by the Anteater, then enter. The Ants come to feast on the leftover food. The Anteater preys on the Ants; he is said to be the *ngamo* (godchild) of the Water Anaconda, and he has also come to offer ants to his godfather.

The mournful appearance of two *wasogü* beetle spirits at midnight provides a high point of the ritual. With huge sculptured heads dominated by curved wooden noses, the Beetles dance in the center of the house. Surrounded by the hosts, who illuminate the performance with torches in hand, the Beetles each attack the four central posts, beating them with sticks. The complex and graceful choreography of their dance and their melodious and sad song hold the crowd in suspense.

Between midnight and dawn the fish spirits reenter to perform the Fish's Night Dance. More drawn out and intense than their earlier appearance, the song and dance retrace the migration routes of the fish from the mouth of the Apaporis River to its headwaters, following all the major affluents up to their sources. Each important river segment has its own verse, tune, and

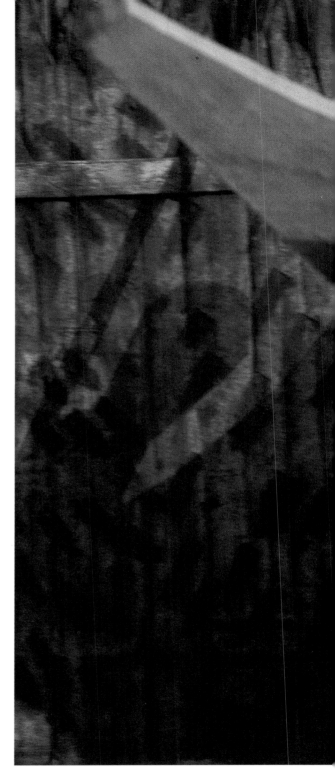

A pair of Frog Catchers looking for frogs.

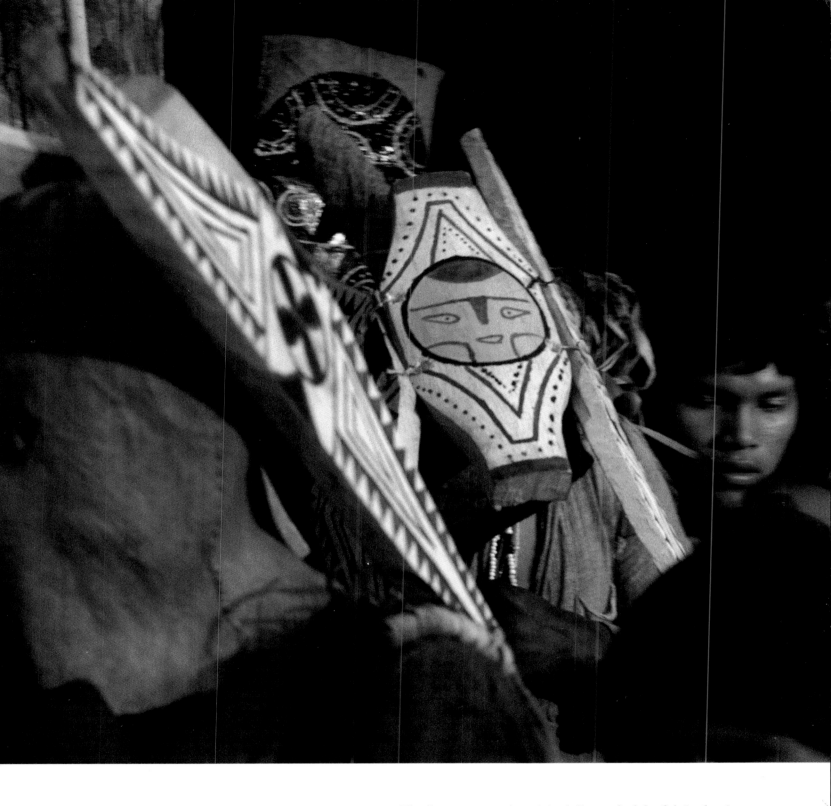

movement. The dance repeats the original dispersal of the fish in the rivers and recreates a moment in mythical time when they had no distinct, incarnate form, but were still spirit beings appearing both as fish and people. As dawn approaches the fish spirits leave and the Vultures—with the same masks—enter. Their song and dance similar to those of the fish spirits, the Vultures are said to follow the migration routes of the fish, feeding on their dead and rotting bodies.

The dawn of the second day is greeted by the *bureru* spirits, who, like the anteater, are godchildren of Water Anaconda and also owners of the fish. They dance in a pair, one leading the song, the other answering, and together they imitate birds playing on a beach. A whole series of bird spirits follow, wearing similar tubelike masks of balsa wood but with differently designed ears. As the morning wears on, other animal spirits, some in distinct masks, enter the house to dance and sing.

In the late morning the dancers take a break and a short rest. The shaman blesses an oversized cigar and offers it to the host who then leads the participants, dancers, and spectators in a long line, himself energetically puffing the cigar and blowing the smoke in all directions, down to the river. He exhales the smoke over the water, blessing the river and making it safe for bathing. The men then bathe and wash themselves before returning to the maloca to rest and eat.

At noon the dance starts anew with the reappearance of the fish spirits. A playful sequence follows as other spirits arrive to eat, drink, and dance: the Butterfly, Agouti, Otter, Cayman, Fish Children, Armadillo, Spider, Forest Fruit, Tapir, Wasps, Fishnet, and Bows-and-Arrows. The two Butterflies, wearing the cylindrical balsa masks and connected by a string, dance around and around like fluttering butterflies. The Spiders hold a strip of bark in their hands, which is used to tie up some of the spectators as if caught in their web. The spectators also stick leaves on the arrows of the Bows-and-Arrows, representing pierced fish, and the Tapirs dance in a wide circle with women, singing a deep humming tune.

In the late afternoon the fish spirits return for the last time. Their performance, the Fish's Day Dance, is a turning point in the ritual as the spirits now begin to return to their otherworldly abode. As the dancers, exhausted and intoxicated with snuff and coca, move in a circle and up and down the dance hall, the fish spirits descend the rivers and streams to their downstream homes and birth houses on the Apaporis River. They finally depart, dancing for a while in the plaza and bidding farewell to their hosts. When the sun sets the Vultures also come to take their leave.

A short pause follows, then chaos overtakes the maloca. The disparate spirits from earlier now reappear to say goodbye and get their last gulps of drink and portions of food. The *wai hosa* (fish servants)—the last born of the fish—appropriately come long after the other fish spirits have left. They

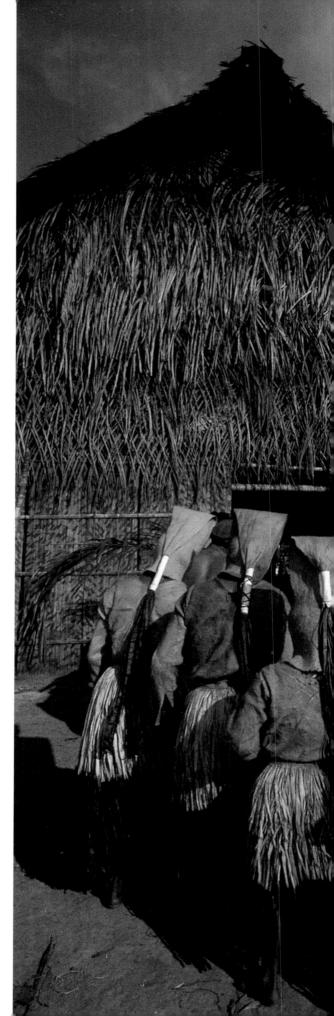

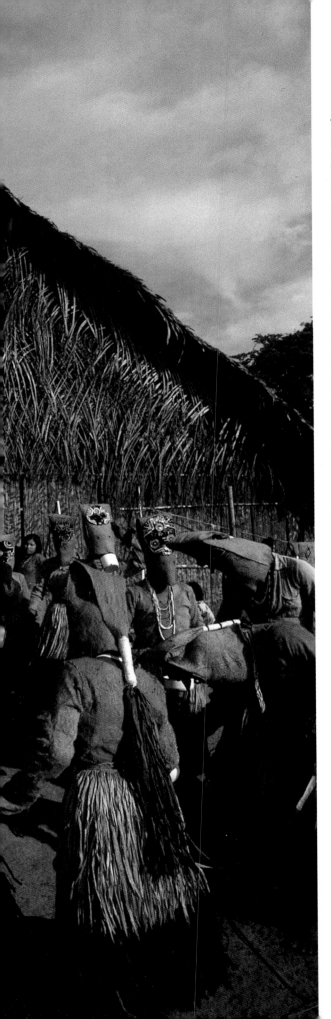

are closely followed by the Otters, who chase them around. The Jaguar and Deer—another predator-prey pair—turn up, then spirits of the ants and anteater, and the fish and the fishnet, group after group and occasionally all at the same time. The spectators now join in the play and the entire maloca boils. When the Hawk enters, wearing long sticks representing its tail, people know that the dance is about to end. The Hawk, chased around by men with blowguns, dances six times around the four central pillars. His appearance is followed by the Agouti joined by the rest of the spirit dancers in no apparent order. Except for the masks they wear, representing a mixture of all the spirits they have impersonated during the dance, they carry other masks in their hands or on sticks. Thus ends the Dance of the Spirits on the eve of the second day. All the participants—with and without masks, men, women, and children—simultaneously move around in the maloca and out through the front door, into the open plaza where the performance finally comes to a halt.

It is again dark when the host burns sweet-smelling beeswax inside and around the house to send away the dangers lingering after the spirits' visit. The dancers remove their masks and costumes and return to their camp to rest. Blessed food is communally served in the maloca; some eat and others pick up the paired panpipes and begin to play. Soon men, women, and children are again on their feet moving to the sorrowful melody.

After a few hours' break the Dance of the Spirits is followed by the Peach Palm Dance proper during which the men wear neither masks, costumes, nor headdresses. With a palm frond in one hand, rhythmically shaking a gourd rattle in the other, they dance until the morning of the third day. This concluding part of the ritual also recounts the deeds of the spirit people; the major characters are the same as in the preceding part, but the songs and the movements are now different. With the Peach Palm Dance the entire ritual is complete. The perishable bark-cloth masks and costumes are thrown away or burned, while the wooden masks are carefully stored away in the house until the next occasion.

During the Dance of the Spirits the masked dancers retrace the creative journey of the ancestors between the waking-up houses of the dead and the houses of the living.

The Peach Palm Ritual is part of an ideally fixed sequence of seasonal communal rites. The ceremony is succeeded by the *He* Fruit Ritual when forest fruit are brought to the house to the tune of the tree-fruit Yuruparí instruments at the beginning of the wet season, usually in April or May. This is followed by the ritual of the Ancient Yuruparís in June or July at the height of the wet season. According to knowledgeable shamans, this is the proper sequence of the three most important Makuna rituals. If the order is broken, or any of the rituals neglected, misfortune and disease will beset the community.

The Peach Palm Ritual is radically different from all other Makuna rituals. In no other ritual do men wear masks or bark-cloth costumes. Also in contrast to other important Makuna rituals, men do not drink yagé nor wear the sacred macaw feather headdresses. The Peach Palm Ritual, they say, is an occasion of feasting and amusement. Hence they cannot drink yagé or don the headdresses. Conversely, during rituals when men consume yagé and wear the complete ritual ornament, no ordinary food may be consumed, only chicha and spirit food—coca and snuff.

On the whole, masked dances are rare among the Tukanoan groups in the Vaupés region and today occur only on its northern and southern fringes where the Tukanoan live in close contact with neighboring Arawakan groups. The Cubeo to the north have masked dances in connection with their funerary rituals, and masked rituals similarly appear among the southern Tukanoan groups—the Makuna, Letuama, and Tanimuka on the Apaporis—and their Arawakan neighbors, the Yukuna and the Kabiyarí, in connection with the peach palm harvest. The names of certain key figures in the ritual—the *tori* (penis spirit) for example—are identical among these groups, suggesting a common archaic ritual language. In addition, masked dances occur among the Bora, Miranya, Witoto, Andoke, and Tikuna peoples farther to the south on the Caquetá, Putumayo, and Amazon Rivers. Significantly the Arawakan neighbors of the Makuna, the Yukuna and Kabiyarí, do not use yagé at all. Thus the characteristic ritual use of masks and the absence of yagé suggests an Arawakan cultural origin.

Yet the Makuna—specifically the Water People clans—consider the Peach Palm Ritual an important part of their own cultural heritage. The mythical context of the ritual is genuinely Tukanoan; it forms part of the cycle of

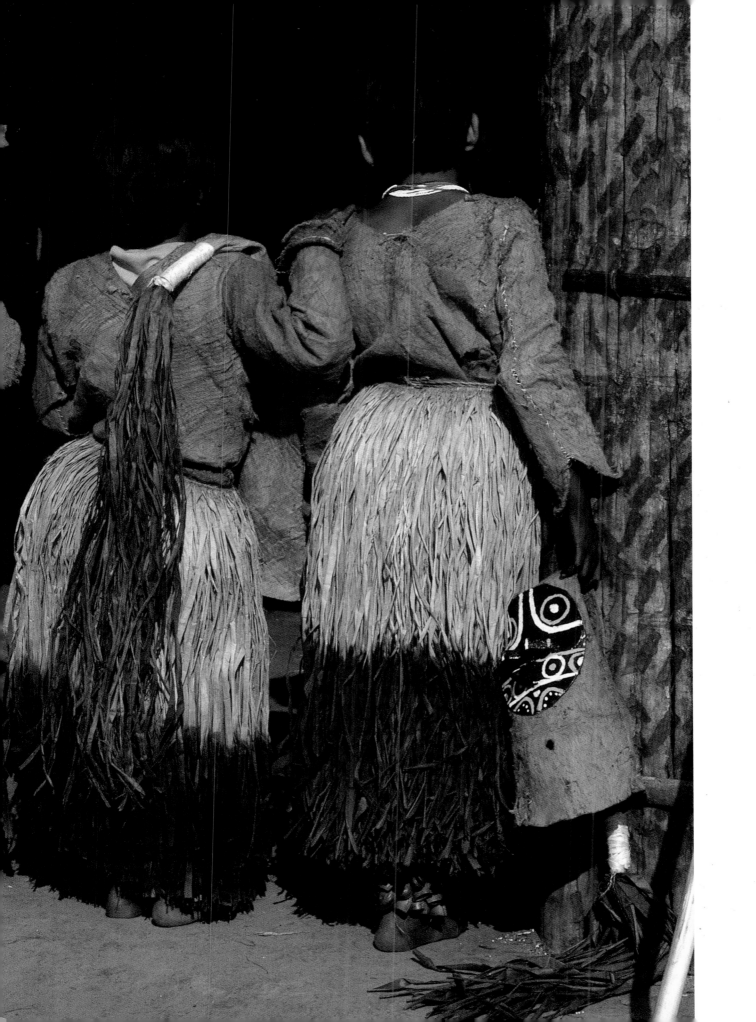

myths about the ancestral anacondas and—in the case of the Makuna—about the original alliance between Water Anaconda and Yiba. If the Dance of the Spirits has an Arawakan origin, it is certainly historically integrated into Makuna culture. All the above groups closely interact and share a fundamentally similar cosmology and mythic corpus, which facilitates mutual borrowing and the incorporation of new ritual elements and symbolic themes. In 1989, for example, a group of Makuna performed a Peach Palm Ritual for their Tuyuka allies, to whom it was previously unknown, with the express purpose of teaching them the ritual.

The mutually exclusive presence of masks and yagé in Makuna rituals is significant and may partly explain the easy accommodation of Arawakan elements into Makuna culture. The use of masks and the consumption of yagé are, in important respects, symbolically and functionally equivalent: both are ritual means of turning people into spirits, and, depending on the context, one takes the place of the other. When men take yagé and put on the sacred headdresses they turn into spirits, just as they become the spirits when they intone songs and dress in painted masks and bark-cloth costumes. Yagé allows men to see the spirits; the masks actually and tangibly depict them. The masks, as it were, externalize and objectify the inner visions produced by the yagé. Therefore it may not be incidental that the colors of the yagé pot, in which the sacred yagé drink is served, are identical to those of the black, ornate resin masks worn during the Dance of the Spirits. Indeed, the geometrical designs on the yagé pot and the spirit masks are conspicuously similar.

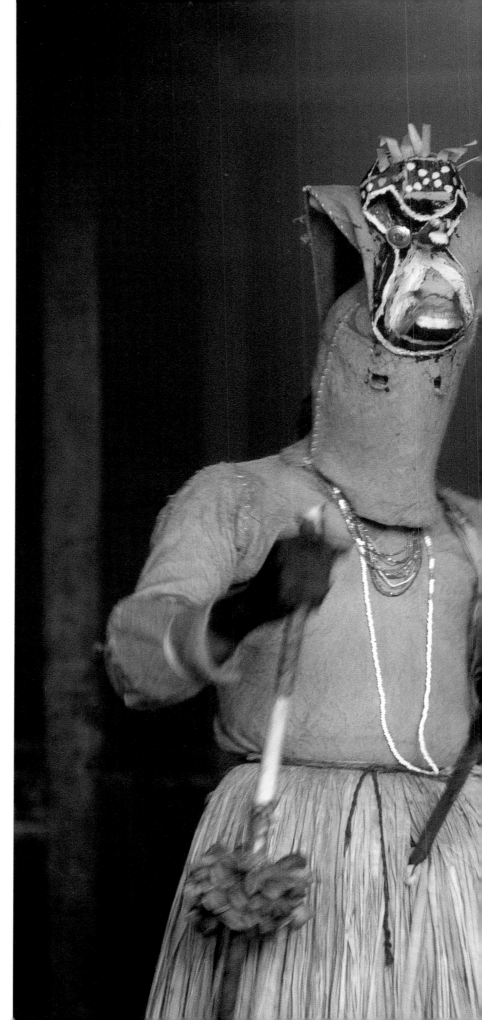

One of the *tori* (penis) spirits with an erect "penis" sticking out of his skirt.

SPIRITS OF THE DEAD, SOURCE OF LIFE

What, then, is this rich, colorful, and dramatic ritual all about, and who are the mysterious spirits impersonated by the masked dancers? The ethnographic literature gives little guidance, and the Makuna themselves give no simple answer.[2] However, from what various knowledgeable participants say about the ritual, and by placing it in a broader cultural context, it is nevertheless possible to offer a tentative interpretation.

After witnessing the entire ritual in March 1989, I asked Ignacio, who acted as the supervising shaman during the event, to explain the origin and purpose of the ritual. He responded, as usual, with a story:

The Dance of the Spirits is like a film showing something that happened a long time ago, at another place in another world.[3] It is performed to remember important events in the ancestral past. Before human beings existed the peach palm was owned by the Fish People.[4] It was first planted at the Water Door in the east. The Fish People went upriver, and, at various points along the journey, they stopped to dance and plant the primal peach palms. The first palms were planted at Boraitara, an island on the lower Apaporis and the birth house of the Fish People clans; then at Manaítara, the birthplace of the Water People clans below the mouth of the Pirá-Paraná River; then at Wasoturia above the mouth of the Pirá-Paraná; and lastly at Hasa hudiro (Jiri-jirímo Falls) on the upper Apaporis.

At each of these sites there is a great underwater maloca, around which groves of peach palm grow together with the other trees from which masks and costumes are made. The Fish People planted these trees. They also created the resin used for the masks and the clay used for painting them. The owner of the maloca at Boraitara is Fish Anaconda, and at Manaítara, Water Anaconda, the ancestor of the Water People clans. Fish Anaconda was the original owner of the *wasogü* tree. His descendants are today experts in preparing the white bark-cloth aprons used during certain other rituals but never learned to prepare the hoods and shirts from the red bark cloth. Instead the Water People received the knowledge to make masks and costumes for the Dance of the Spirits. They in turn taught the art to the Letuama, Tanimuka, and Yukuna. Together they are today the owners of the Peach Palm Ritual.

As the ancestral Fish People traveled up the Apaporis River they stopped to dance in the four malocas at Boraitara, Manaítara, Wasoturia, and Hasa hudiro. At each of these places they prepared the peach palm drink, made masks and costumes, and danced. All the animals of the forest and the rivers came to the dance. The first dance was held at Boraitara, the next at Manaítara, then at Wasoturia, and finally at Hasa hudiro. When the Fish People had danced at all four sites they returned downriver to the Water Door.

This somewhat cryptic explanation is apparently an outline of the mythical charter for the ritual. The Peach Palm Ritual of today repeats the dances of the ancestral Fish People at the four mentioned underwater malocas. For the Water People clans the mythical dance at Manaítara is of particular importance since it was given by their ancestor, Water Anaconda. Yawira—the

Plant Mother, daughter of Water Anaconda, and wife of Yiba—was the hostess and owner of the food and drink at this original feast. It is through her and her marriage with Yiba that the peach palm was later brought into this world and distributed among people. Owing to her, the Makuna say, the peach palm is today cultivated throughout the region.

The dance shows what happened in myth and, in this sense, is like a film. But there is obviously more implied. The ritual performance actually reenacts the ancestral dance and physically involves the participants in the mythical drama it recreates. During the ritual, the masked dancers become part of this drama and, indeed, identify with its actors. "When men wear masks, and sing and dance," Ignacio said, "it is the Fish People who sing and dance through them. The spirits of the Fish People enter their bodies. The dancers become the Fish People. The song of the fish spirits speaks about the ancestral journey of the Fish People, and each verse refers to a particular named site on this journey—a waking-up house of the Fish People. As a dancer begins a new verse, he calls the spirits from their underwater malocas. And as he calls them, they come to possess him. When the song is over the Fish People return to the sites from where they came." In the eyes of the shaman, then, the masked dancers are the Fish People, alive and present in the dance house.

The Fish People figure prominently in Makuna myths. They are spirits of the *he* world—the timeless world of myth where animals and men are undifferentiated, but also an invisible spiritual reality that exists parallel to the visible world of ordinary experience. In the ordinary world, Fish People appear as *wai* (fish), but to the shaman fish are really *masa* (people)—hence *wai masa* (Fish People). The peach palm harvest coincides with the migration of the sabaleta—a fruit-eating species and important food fish of the *Brycon* family. This coincidence is deeply significant to the Makuna; they say that when the sabaleta spawn at the beginning of the wet season in March and April the Fish People dance at their birth houses. During the harvest season of the peach palm, the fat sabaleta travel down in shoals from the tributaries of the Pirá-Paraná River to the Apaporis River to spawn along the shores of Manaítara. After the spawning period great numbers of exhausted fish die in the turbid waters around the island or perish on the journey back to their upriver habitat.

The migrating fish are the Fish People traveling to dance in Water Anaconda's underwater maloca at Manaítara. It is said that the sabaleta are men, the palometa—another important food fish—women. When traveling in the river, they appear as fish; when they go up on land, they turn into animals of the forest. As they enter the underwater maloca at Manaítara they become people, beautifully painted and dressed in ritual costume. There they drink the peach palm juice and receive blessed snuff from their host, Water Anaconda. Thus, when the fish spawn at Manaítara it is the spirit people who dance their own Peach Palm Ritual.

The mythical images of the dance in Water Anaconda's maloca account for the form and organization of the Peach Palm Ritual as enacted today. The first part of the ritual, *rümüa sahare*, represents the arrival of the Fish People in their various animal shapes at the underwater maloca. The animal spirits are greeted and received with food, drink, and shamanized snuff. The second part, *hota basa,* the Peach Palm Dance proper, enacts the actual dance of the visiting spirits as it was once performed in mythical times— and still is in the invisible *he* world when fish spawn and the peach palm bears fruit. The transition between the two phases of the ritual corresponds to a passage from one life world to another, an act of creation and transformation; when men remove their masks after the Dance of the Spirits and begin the Peach Palm Dance, the spirits shed their animal appearances and turn into people in the waking-up house of the ancestors.

A clue to the deeper levels of meaning of the ritual is suggested by the two Makuna words used to describe and address the masked dancers and the masks themselves: *rümüa* and *nyikü masa*. The word *rümüa* translated here as "spirits" properly means "ghosts," a term the Makuna use for the spirits of the dead. The phrase *nyikü masa* means "grandfather people," denoting living as well as dead ancestors two or more generations removed. There is a clear sense that the Fish People are identified with human ancestors. The spirits who come to visit the living during the dance are the souls of deceased relatives.

Manaítara is the waking-up house of the Water People clans. Here in the underwater maloca of their ancestor, the spirits of deceased Makuna men and women reside, leading a life parallel to that of the living. At the birth of a child, the soul of a dead grandparent travels from the waking-up house at Manaítara into this world and enters the body of the new-born child. The child receives the name of the soul-giving ancestor and becomes mystically identified with him or her. At death the soul returns to its point of origin and joins the spirit people at Manaítara. The journey of the soul at the beginning and end of life repeats the mythical journey of the ancestral anacondas when people were first created and the earth populated.

The waking-up house of the Water People is also, as we have seen, the major spawning ground of the sabaleta. The territory of the Water People clans corresponds to the migratory routes of the sabaleta. During their seasonal migrations, the fish of the lower Pirá-Paraná River and its tributaries repeat the journey of the human soul at birth, death, and rebirth, which was also the route the ancestors traveled between the margins and the center of the world. The myth of the creative journey of the ancestors and the journey of the soul in the life cycle of individuals are both patterned after the seasonal migration of fish.

In the shaman's vision, then, the fish descending from the headwaters of Komenya to the island of Manaítara on the Apaporis are the souls of the deceased returning to their point of origin, their waking-up house. The visiting spirits of the Peach Palm Ritual are the unborn children and the reborn spirits of the dead coming to fertilize the living. When men dance in this world, the spirits also dance in theirs. And as men and spirits dance, fish spawn, palms bear fruit, and people procreate. The Makuna say this ritual dancing actually causes animals and people to reproduce. In their view dancing creates and maintains life. Just as the ancestors sang and danced the world into existence, the Indians today—through their communal rituals—seasonally recreate the world. The Peach Palm Ritual is in its broadest sense a fertility ritual whose performance ensures the regeneration of nature and the fecundity of humankind. By inviting the spirits of the dead into the house of the living the Makuna unlock the generative power of death, which is also the ultimate source of life.

The Peach Palm Ritual speaks to us across cultural barriers; its most general message transcends frontiers of time and space. The Dance of the Spirits expresses the Makuna cultural wisdom that humans and nature are aspects of a single reality, that all living beings participate in a cosmic society structured by common relations of kinship and exchange, and that there is a fundamental unity of life behind the apparent disparity in form. During the ritual drama, this vision of humans and nature is transformed into a powerful personal experience for the participants, which shapes and

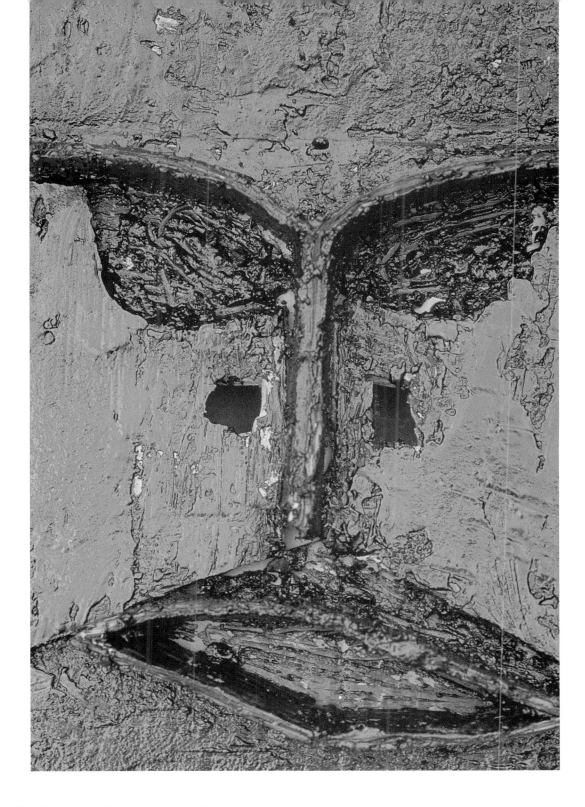

Close-up of the face of an unidentified spirit mask. Like all Makuna rituals, the Dance of the Spirits is a precarious encounter with the ultimate forces of reality; the spirits are believed to bring life and fertility, but may also cause death and misfortune.

reshapes their perception of reality. Processes of nature are brought under human control, and human actions are shown to have consequences for the working of nature. By turning ecology into ritual the Makuna people enable themselves to act upon nature within a meaningful context of moral values and sacred duties. The sacralization of nature provides a firm—perhaps the only—basis for a careful use of its resources.

7
THE THREAT

In 1986 gold was discovered in the hills along the Taraira River, only two days' walking distance from the Makuna territory. Over the years thousands of miners have entered the Taraira valley, and whole towns have appeared in what was once the heart of the forest. Encroaching on their ancestral land, destroying the forest, polluting the rivers, and increasingly eroding their culture, the gold mining at Taraira threatens the entire Makuna world.

CERRO ROJO: A GOLD MINING TOWN

In March 1990 I visited Cerro Rojo, one of the new mining towns in Taraira. Since 1989 a small airfield has served the goldfields, which earlier could only be reached by river and trail from La Pedrera and Mitú. With the airstrip and an army post that soon followed, the regional government has established a fragile foothold in the area. The Taraira River winds its way between hills and rocky outcrops in the dense forest marking the boundary between Colombia and Brazil. Scattered camps, clearings, and bare spots of red earth scar the forest revealing the presence of the miners. The airstrip, which looks like another patch of cleared and bare-scraped land, divides the town into two parts. On one side are the army post, a few administrative buildings, and shops; on the other side, the mining town proper is haphazardly spread out over the hill of Cerro Rojo. A footpath leading through a cleared and burned patch of forest connects the two parts. Along the path heaps of discarded beer and coke cans lay scattered among the charred tree stumps—sticking halfway up from the ashes looking like the strange crop of a recently planted Makuna swidden—a harvest of waste, the barren fruit of a different civilization.

The gold mining area along the Taraira River in 1990 was composed of three mining towns—Cerro

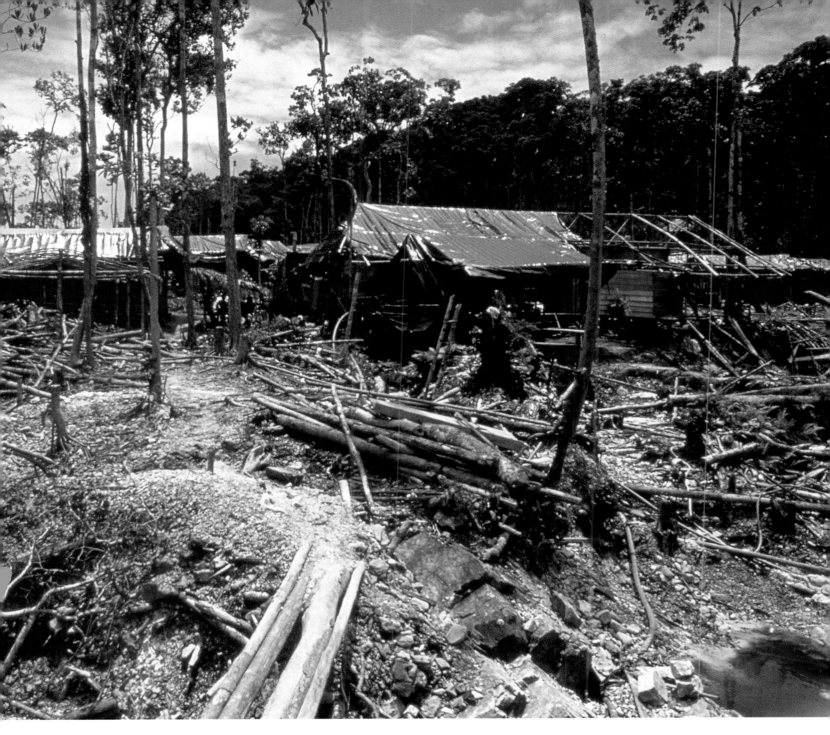

Mining camp in the hills
and streams of the
Taraira River basin, only
a few days' trekking dis-
tance from the Makuna
homeland, where in the
mid-1980s gold was
found. Thousands of
miners invaded the area,
and several mining
towns emerged in the
heart of the forest.

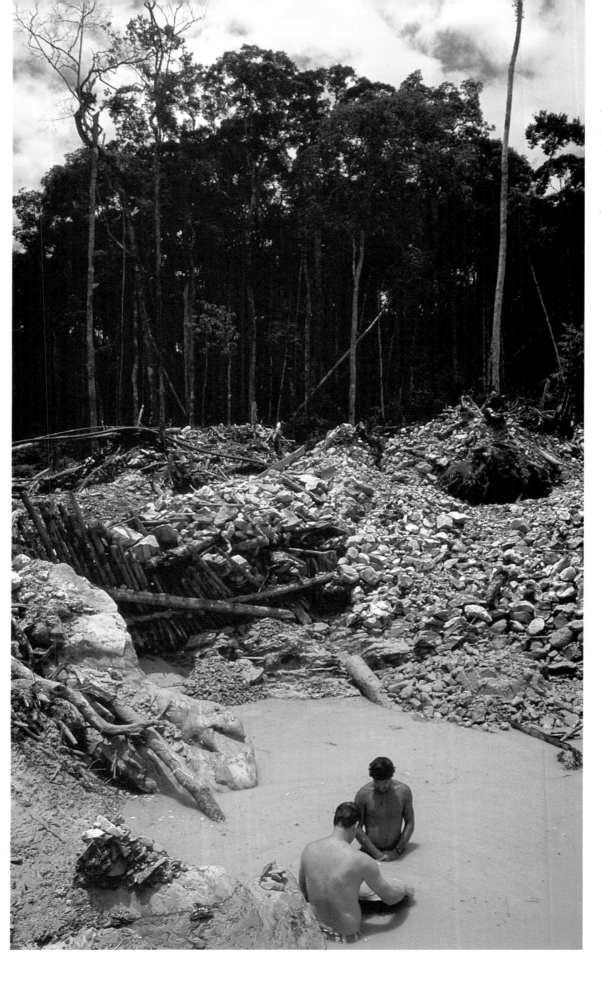

The mining activities are rapidly transforming the virgin forest into a wasteland of charred tree trunks, contaminated streams, heaps of gravel, and bare soil.

Rojo, Garrimpo, and Peladera—and scattered populations of miners moving between the towns and makeshift huts in the forest. Some 3,000 to 4,000 people (no exact figures are available) are believed to be making a living in the area, mainly by mining but also on all kinds of trade and commerce that flourish in the mining towns. During a few boom years in the late 1980s, when the gold was first discovered and easily available in the shallow streams, the population reached a peak of some 6,000 to 7,000. Today the easy finds are becoming scarce. Wealthy entrepreneurs with capital to invest in pumps, dredges, and other heavy machinery have taken over. Thousands of miners have left the area. Some of them were successful, but most left poorer than when they arrived. Of those who have remained, many work as day laborers for wealthy patrons.

The town of Cerro Rojo is a muddle of ramshackle buildings scattered over a hill. The houses—simple frames of poles with plastic or tin sheets for a roof—look as if they were erected overnight. Muddy footpaths connect the houses, shops, and bars. All sorts of trade goods can be found in the shops—from hoes and pans to cassette recorders and clothes of the latest Brazilian fashion. The bars serve beer cooled in petrol refrigerators and have shelves of liquor including *aguardiente* (the local Colombian liquor), Brazil-ian brandy, and imported Scotch whiskey—all brought in from Mitú and La Pedrera. Gold is the currency; every shop and bar has a scale for weighing gold dust and nuggets. Gold can buy anything, including *amor minera*—"gold miner's love." The girls of the local brothels evaluate prospective customers according to the quantity of gold they carry in small containers hanging from their necks.

The miners are a mixed lot of people—peasants, poor townspeople, and fortune seekers—from every corner of the country. Most are family heads who have left their wives and children at home far away from Taraira. "We

A gold-mining camp near the town of Cerro Rojo. The utter poverty of life in the camps contrasts heavily to the conspicuous wealth of a few successful miners.

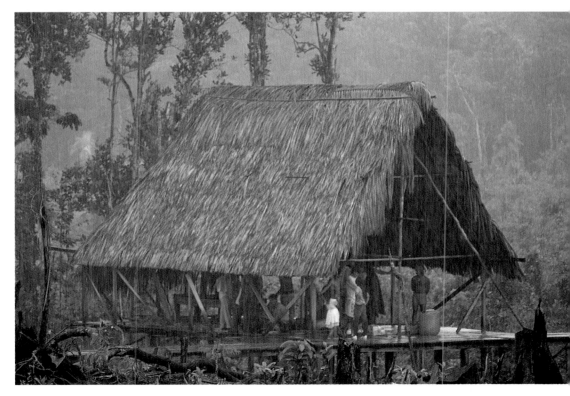

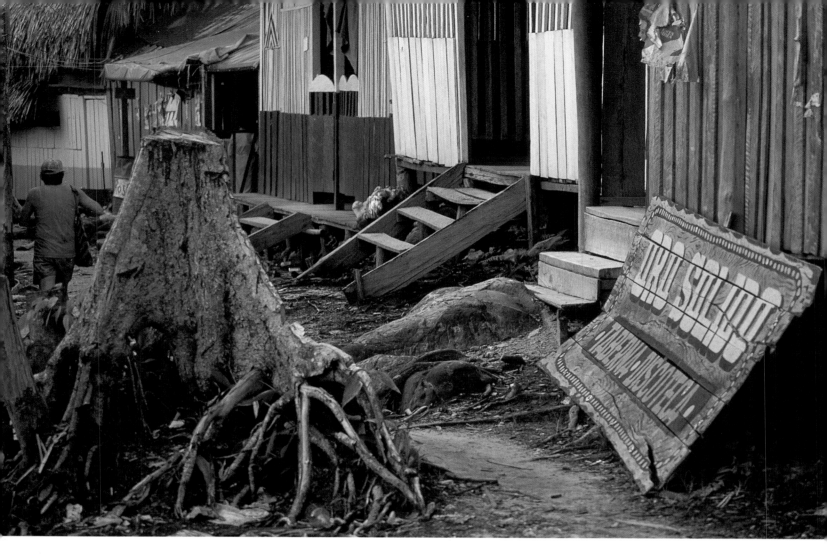

Above: Cerro Rojo is a typical frontier town with shops, bars, and brothels, but also with a chapel, school, and dispensary.

Right: Painted sign board advertising a local bar. After the hard days of work in the gold-fields, miners spend weekends in town, shopping, drinking, and dancing.

don't live here; we just work and suffer, and if we make some money we send it home to our families," one miner told me. "We stay until we have enough to return home with something in our pockets." Many of the miners have spent all their savings to come to Taraira, and many do not earn enough for the ticket back home. Others spend what they earn in the bars and brothels. Despite the rough surface and apparent companionship among the miners, there are deep social and economic cleavages in Cerro Rojo. Here, as elsewhere in the Amazonian mining towns, the big profits are not made by the miners but the patrons, traders, and entrepreneurs—the owners of capital and machinery.

The violence that accompanies poverty and quick fortune is ripe in Cerro Rojo. In the lawless mining towns tempers run high and brawls are commonplace. People fight over gold, merchandise, and women, and everyone carries a gun. Most miners spend the weeks working in remote camps and come to town only during weekends—to shop, drink, and drown the drudgery and hardships of their toil. The dream of making a fortune keeps the spirit high during long work days in the mines. At the outskirts of the town, rough wooden crosses stuck into the muddy soil testify to the vicissitudes of life in the mining towns. Several of the recently dead, I was told, were killed during bar brawls and shoot-outs among competing patrons.

At the far end of the town are the mines proper. In the scorching heat of the day, teams of miners scrape away the red topsoil that gives the hill its name; others work in the deep tunnels hacked into the rocky hillside. Wagons loaded with stone boulders emerge from the tunnels and trenches on wooden rails. Nearby are the work sheds and machines for crushing the boulders and sifting the gravel for gold. The forest is cut down, and the

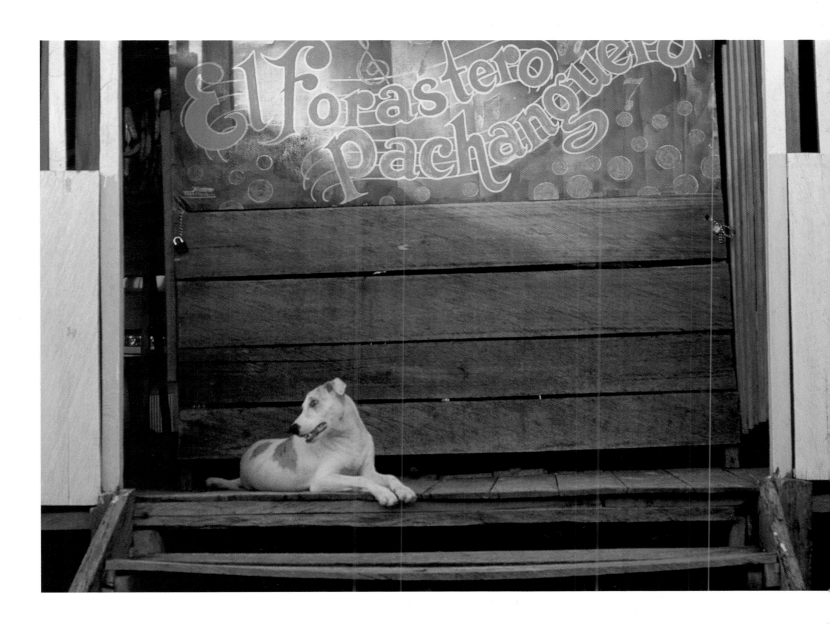

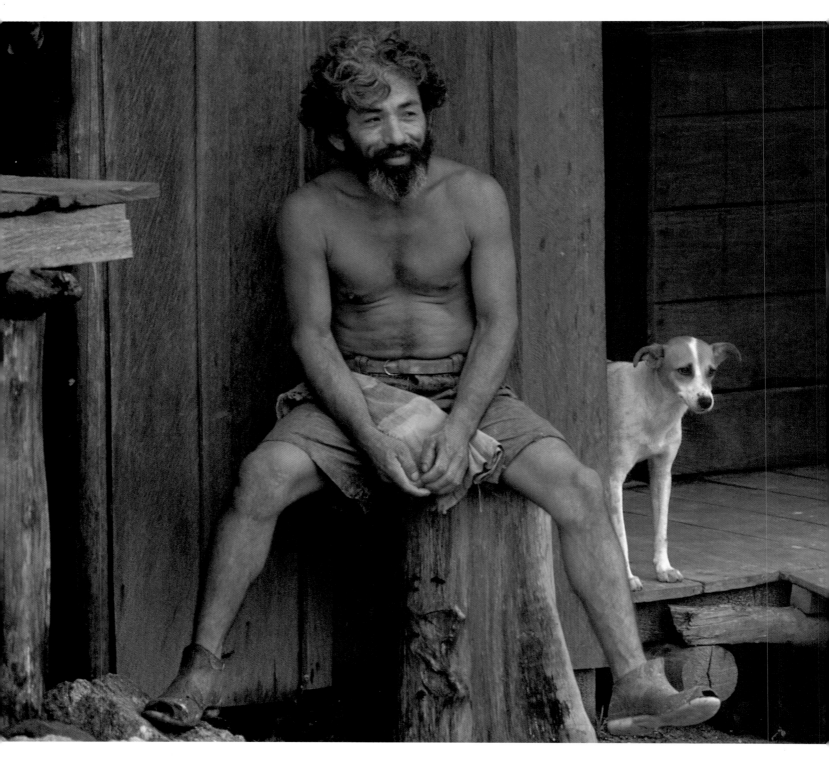

The miners are a mixed lot of people—peasants, poor townspeople, and fortune seekers from every corner of Colombia. Most of the Indians are family heads who have left their wives and children at home.

clear streams that once flowed from the hill into the Taraira River are now polluted with the mercury used by the miners to separate the gold from the sand and soil. The mines, in effect, are a huge factory for grinding the entire hill to gravel and dust. Heaps of crushed rock tower over the devastated land—a forest turned into wasteland.

The current developments in Taraira are but a part of a gigantic gold rush sweeping through the Amazon since the late 1970s with no signs of abating.[1] Several hundred thousand gold miners—inheritors of the early conquerors and colonists—have entered the region clearing the forest, building roads and airstrips, and establishing mining camps and towns in almost every corner of the Amazon. Invasions on native lands and violent confrontations with Indians occur frequently across the region. In the late 1980s the territory of the Yanomami Indians near the Brazilian-Venezuelan frontier was invaded by more than 30,000 miners.[2] Most of the invaders have remained on Yanomami land, presenting a continuing threat to the lives and lifeways of the native inhabitants.

The situation in Taraira is typical of the history of the Amazon as a whole. Native lands and resources suddenly become attractive to white entrepreneurs, colonizers, and miners, and the Indians—previously unimportant to the dominant society—become either a cheap labor force to exploit or an obstacle to be removed. As a result they are dispossessed, violently forced or unknowingly drawn into the commercial economy dominated and manipulated by the whites. The rubber boom at the turn of the century, the coca trade in the 1970s and 1980s, and now the gold rush all follow the same historical pattern.

A gold miner's ceremonial attire: a necklace with an ocelot fang and gold ornaments. This necklace displays prosperity and confers prestige.

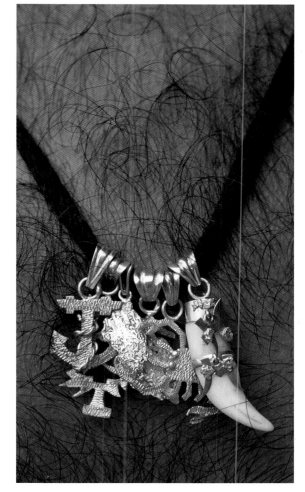

EYES OF THE SPIRITS

The Taraira valley is a wild and inhospitable tract of dense forest, steep hills, and violent streams. Twenty years ago, when I first came to the Makuna territory, the area was uninhabited and rarely visited by the Indians. According to the Makuna, it was sacred land never meant to be inhabited by human beings.

The hills where miners today dig for gold form part of the protective wall encircling the Makuna world and supporting the sky. In their cosmology, mountains and rocks are petrified ancestral beings, the transfixed mythical heroes that created the world and maintain all life on earth. The Hill of the Sun, overlooking the great Sun Fall in the middle course of the Taraira River, contains the light and heat of the Primal Sun. From the Sun Fall northward, a line of hills extends along the upper reaches of the river. The Jaguar Hill is said to be the ancestral Sky Jaguar with its rugged peak his petrified head. The Hill of the Stool is his stool in the cosmic maloca, and the Metal Hill his golden ornament. When shamans bless coca and snuff in the maloca they offer food to these hills. By caring for the spirits of the hills, they protect the people from illness and misfortune.

Gold itself is culturally significant to the Makuna as indicated by its many names and symbolic allusions. It is called *he kahea maküri* (eyes of the spirits) or "the shaman's vision" since it allows the shaman to see beyond the appearances of things into the world of the spirits. Gold, the Makuna say, contains the light of the sun and stars. Just as the sun and the stars are the visible manifestations of the ancestral beings in the sky, gold is the sign of ancestral life on earth. Therefore gold is also called "the stars of the earth." Another metaphor for gold is "the ornament of the ancestors" alluding to a myth about the beginning of time when the world was dark and chaotic. As the ancestral people dressed in ritual regalia, put on their sacred ornaments, and began to dance, the present world was created. *Ayawa*, the most senior of the mythical heroes, made a star descend to the earth to illuminate the cosmic maloca in which the ancestral people were dancing and singing. This star became the Hill of the Star on the lower Apaporis River, and its gold is the materialized reflection of its light.

In Makuna territory, myth and reality blend. The forest, hills, and rivers are visible features of the landscape, parts of the cosmic maloca, and manifestations of the living ancestors. What the whites call gold is a gateway

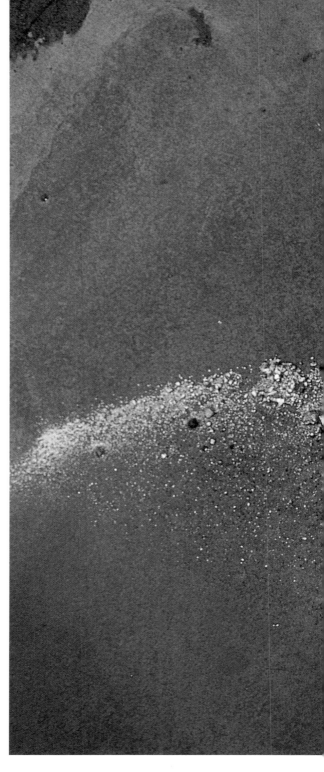

Gold dust on a stream bed. The Makuna speak of gold as the eyes or ornaments of the ancestors, or as stars of the earth. Gold, they say, contains the light of the sun and the stars and allows a shaman to see into the spirit world.

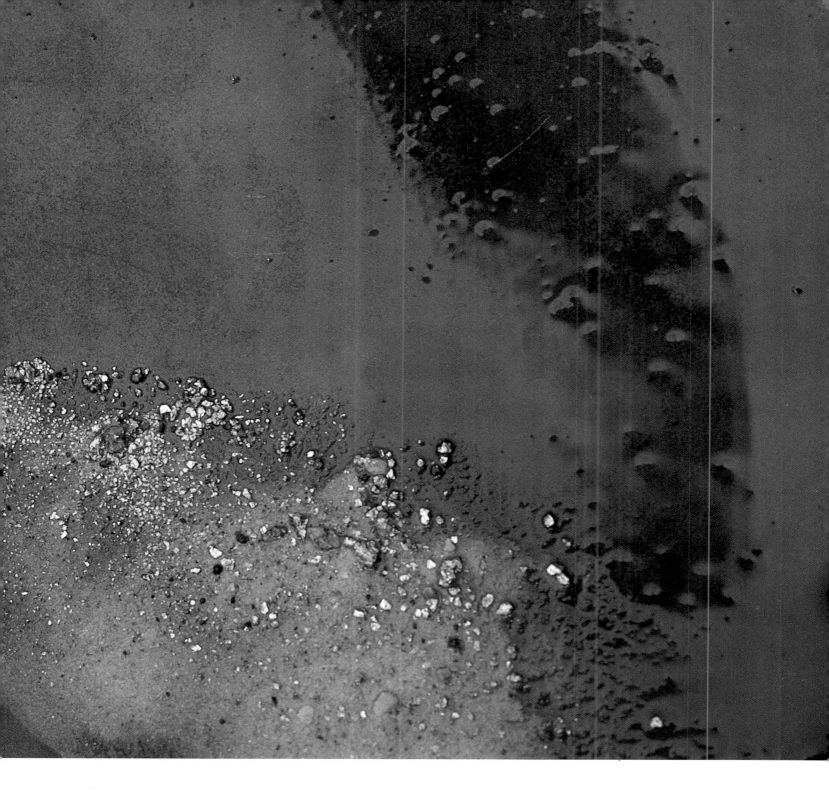

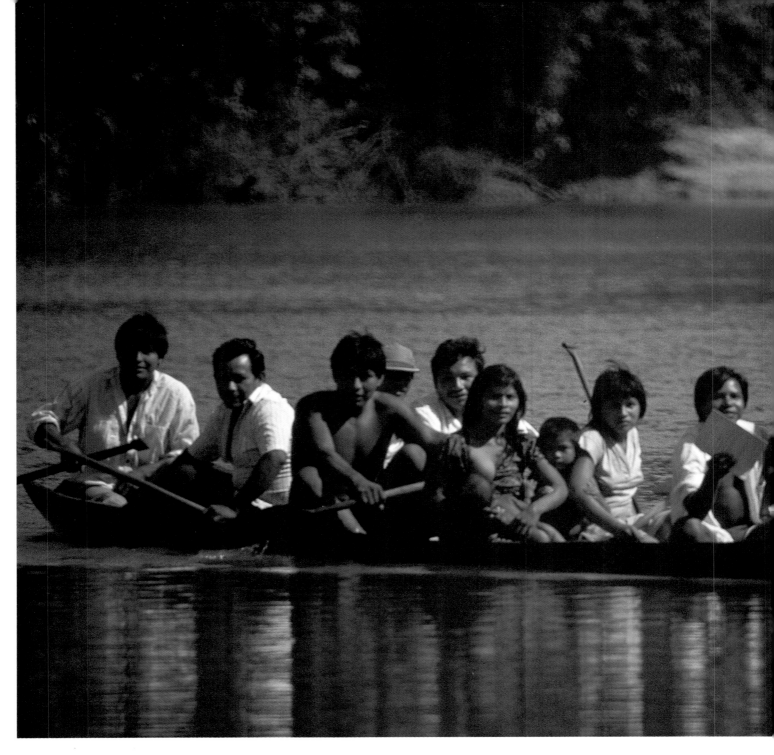

Group of Indians on the Apaporis River. The current gold rush has intensified the contact between Indians and whites.

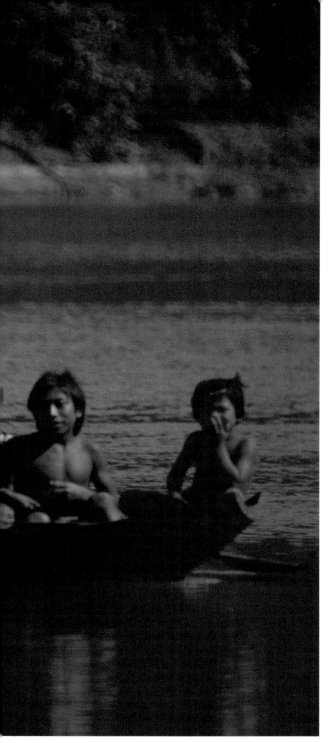

into the spirit world for the Makuna. The light it contains illuminates the world and bestows on the shaman his clairvoyant powers. According to the Makuna, gold belongs to the spirits of the hills, and therefore, should be left where it is. To the Indians the gold in the hills and streams of Taraira is a part of their spiritual legacy. In their minds and by means of their imaginative thought, Indians use the shining light of gold—the eyes of the spirits—to cure and prevent illness and to protect people from evil. As the miners now carve into the rocks of Taraira, they are literally cutting into the foundations of the Makuna universe.

AMAZONIAN APOCALYPSE

"The whites say we are poor," Ignacio once said to me, "but we used to be rich. We don't have money or trade goods, but our ancestors gave us another, *lighter* kind of wealth. They gave us our land, the forest, and the rivers, and they gave us the knowledge to use it, the myths and rituals to sustain ourselves and protect us from evil. But people no longer take care of the land, the young do not listen to what the elders tell them. Hunters kill game in excess. And when shamans visit the houses of the animals they see, hanging like old dresses along the inner walls of the maloca, only tattered skins perforated by bullets. The young are becoming like the whites, they have no respect for the old ways. . . ."

The gold mining in Taraira precipitates the processes of change among the Makuna and their neighboring groups. The mining towns now supply most of the trade goods flowing into the Makuna communities, and most young men today spend weeks or months away in the goldfields. For long periods the village of Santa Isabel on the Komenya is almost abandoned. When the men return, the village revives and there is plenty of food in the houses. Often groups of Indians from other communities pass through the village on their way to or from Taraira, staying for a few days to rest and socialize.

Gold brings trade goods into the communities, but mining takes time and effort from the daily subsistence activities. While the men are away in the goldfields, women and children are left to survive as best they can for months at a time. The periodic presence of outsiders—Indian miners from other villages and territories—represents a source of strain and additional pressure on scarce subsistence resources. The demand for trade goods has increased to a degree far beyond what is possible to satisfy. Young women today want men who can provide them with dresses, trinkets, and other trade goods. Economic differentiation is accelerated, and though some men are more successful than others in obtaining trade goods, all are poor according to national standards. The domestic economy is becoming more individualized, and the all-important principle of reciprocity is losing its force.

As miners begin to penetrate the Makuna world and extract its gold, many Indians feel increasingly threatened and unprotected. The vision of the shaman is blurred, they say, and his powers weakened. Ignacio and other elders see gold mining in Taraira as a sign of a pending apocalypse. They fear the imminent destruction of their world.

According to the Makuna creation myth, the present world emerged out of the ruins of a previous one. Woman Shaman destroyed the old world because its inhabitants did not respect her creation. People ate each other, brothers had sex with their sisters, plant seedlings bore fruit, and prepubescent girls gave birth to children. Woman Shaman therefore drowned the world, and as people desperately gathered on the hilltops at the margins of the world, jaguars, eagles, and huge anacondas killed and devoured them unsparingly. Then Woman Shaman set the world on fire and burned it to ashes. The earth was left like a swidden with only charred bones and skulls scattered on its devastated surface. The ruins of the old world sank into the underworld. The sky fell down and became the new earth from which a new generation of people emerged—the ancestors of the present-day Makuna clans.

The Makuna interpret their current reality in terms of this myth. During long nights, the elders sit smoking and chewing coca in the center of the maloca, commenting on the events of the day and the signs of the time. To them the encroachment of the whites on their ancestral land, the violence of the mining towns, the surging strife and division within their communities, and the children's increasing neglect of ancient traditions all forebode a catastrophic end to the world. Makuna elders fear that there will be no place for their people in the new world emerging out of the ruins of the present one.

Makuna elder in ritual attire. Many older Indians fear that the gold mining in Taraira will eventually destroy their world; in the eyes of local shamans, it threatens to tear down the entire cosmos.

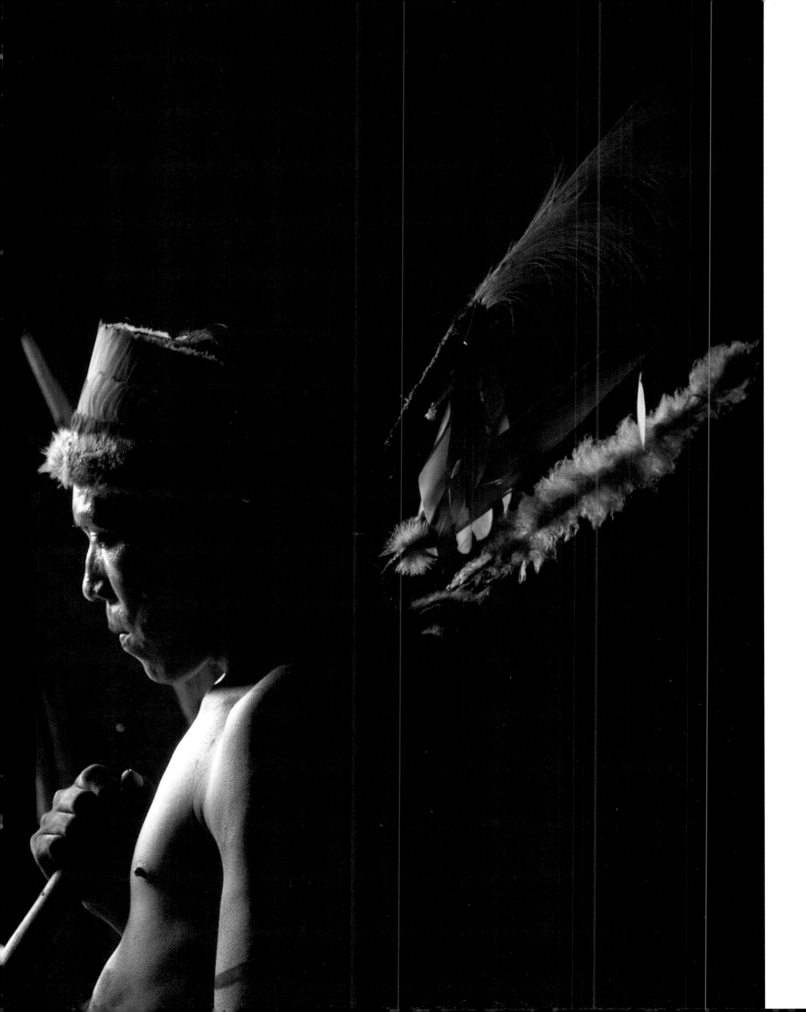

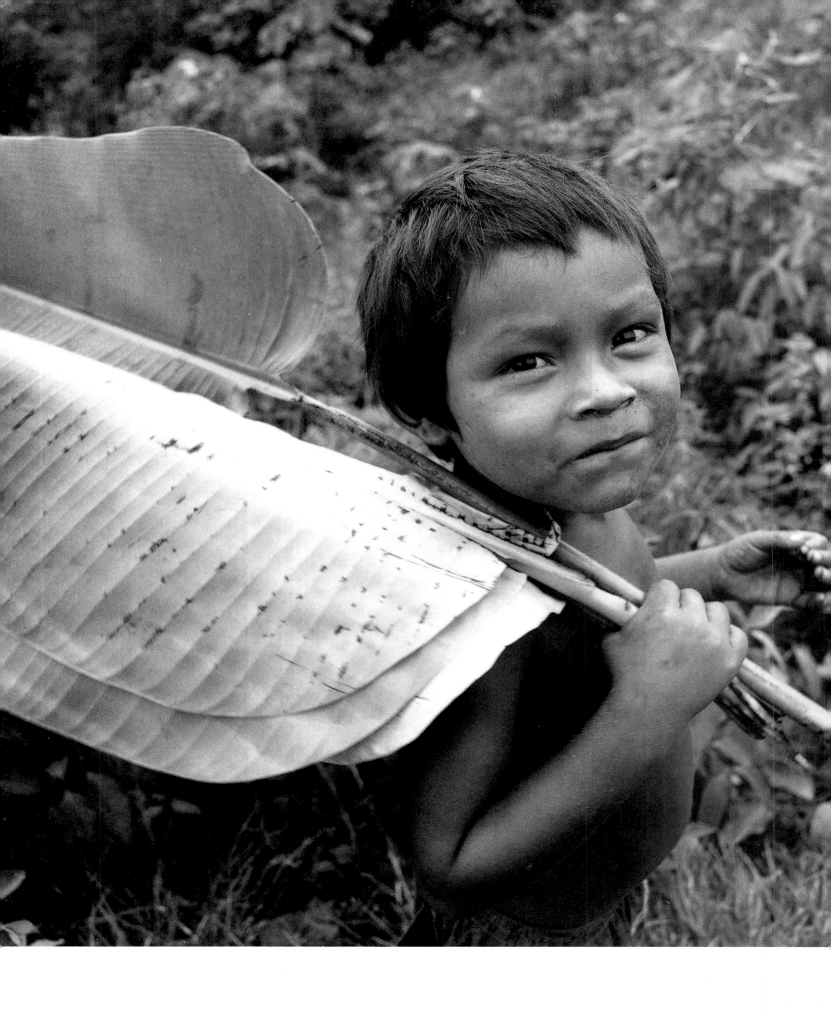

NOTES

CHAPTER 2. THE MAKUNA WORLD

1. For ethnographies of Tukanoan groups of the Vaupés, see Århem 1981; Bidou 1976; Chernela 1993; Correa 1996; Goldman 1963; C. Hugh-Jones 1979; S. Hugh-Jones 1979; Jackson 1983; and Reichel-Dolmatoff 1971, 1996a.

2. The social and political importance of the maloca is declining with the current breakup of longhouse communities and the formation of nucleated villages. Yet in Pirá-Paraná society the maloca is still very much a ritual center. In other parts of the Vaupés, however, there are today few traces of the Tukanoan maloca tradition.

3. Men are expected to consume only ritual food during feasts, while women and children also eat ordinary food. Though particularly associated with the men, elderly women may also take snuff and coca in modest quantities. Men, women, and children all drink chicha.

4. The drink is prepared from a mixture of leaves and bark of the yagé vine (*Banisteriopsis caapi*).

5. For a full description of the Yuruparí cult, see S. Hugh-Jones 1979.

6. The name Yiba refers to an ancestral being associated with the forest and terrestrial, fructivore animals, particularly the tapir. In Barasana the term *yeba* means "earth" or "soil."

7. The number varies depending on where the line is drawn between mature clans and segments of clans growing into autonomous units.

8. The evangelical mission, represented in Vaupés by the North American–based Summer Institute of Linguistics, may also have played a role in this development.

9. As traditionally used by the Indians in the region, coca (not to be confused with the chemically refined cocaine) consists of a green, powderlike substance prepared from the leaves of the coca plant (*Erythroxilon coca*). The preparation of coca is described in chapter 4.

10. Basuco, cheap and in abundant supply during the boom days, is a vicious, hallucinogenic by-product of the process of cocaine production.

11. For detailed references regarding the history of Vaupés, see S. Hugh-Jones 1981.

12. For a comprehensive account of the atrocities of the rubber barons in the northwest Amazon, see Pineda Camacho 1987.

13. These intertribal hostilities may partly have been a consequence of the slave-raiding that ravaged the northwest Amazon between 1750–1850, but it was probably also inherent in the indigenous cultures of the time. Warfare apparently had a ritual character and was part of the relationship among socially distant groups. Just like hunting is today, warfare in the past may have been seen as a male regenerative activity, a sort of cosmic fertility ritual, creating new life through the killing of socially distant people.

14. The hierarchical ideology of the Tukano-speaking groups of Vaupés is thoroughly described and analyzed by Stephen and Christine Hugh-Jones in their works on the Barasana, neighbors of the Makuna. See particularly C. Hugh-Jones 1979 and S. Hugh-Jones 1979, 1995.

15. For more information on the idea of imaginary chiefdom, see Århem, 1990b. Cf. S. Hugh-Jones 1995.

16. For a summary of the history of missionary activities in the Amazon, see S. Hugh-Jones 1981.

CHAPTER 3. THE LAND

1. Schultes 1988, 20. Cf. Moran 1991, 1993.

2. Schultes 1988, 11. It is estimated that the average four-square-mile patch of rain forest may contain up to 1,500 species of flowering plants, and as many as 750 tree, 125 mammal, 400 bird, 100 reptile, 60 amphibian, and 150 butterfly species. Insects are so abundant and so little is known about them that it is difficult to

Boy carrying *Heliconia* leaves. The leaves have multiple uses among the Indians, particularly as temporary rain cover and protective covering in general.

provide even an estimate, especially when a single tree can support some 400 insect species unique to that tree alone (Caufield 1984, 60).

3. Caufield 1984, 244; Chernela 1982, 1985, 1987.

4. Mejía Gutierrez 1987, 87.

5. By way of comparison, all rivers of Europe combined support fewer than 150 species of freshwater fish. See Caufield 1984, 244. Cf. Smith 1981, 18, cited in Clay 1988, 15.

6. For the ecology and migratory behavior of characins in central Brazil, see Goulding 1980. His findings confirm my own observations of the Pirá-Paraná drainage system and accounts given by expert Makuna fishermen.

7. Moran 1993, 22.

8. Ibid., 27–30.

9. Moran 1991.

10. Cf. Århem 1977.

11. For current views on the prehistory and paleoecology of the Amazon, see Meggers 1988 and Reichel 1987.

CHAPTER 4. THE LONGHOUSE

1. The two types—as well as various intermediary forms also found in the region—are really transformations of one another, as will be seen in the description of the spatial structure of the maloca. Cf. S. Hugh-Jones 1985, 1995.

2. This account of the maloca inauguration draws freely on S. Hugh-Jones 1985.

3. Wallace 1892, 190.

4. For a description of the manufacture of the clay griddle among the Tanimuka, see Reichel 1976.

5. C. Hugh-Jones 1979, 180.

6. Palma 1984, 229.

7. Reichel and von Hildebrand 1984.

8. A peculiar feature of the roundhouse is its two openings, or windows, in the roof through which sunlight enters. According to Reichel and von Hildebrand (1984), this architectural feature turns the Tanimuka roundhouse into a solar calendar and clock, indicating both the season of the year and the time of the day. The two windows just under the roof crest face east and west. As the sun moves over the sky during the day, its rays—entering through the two windows—describe a regular trajectory across the wall and the floor inside the maloca, which allow the inhabitants to judge the time of the day. In the morning the light is projected onto the western part of the interior, at noon the house lies in shadow, and in the afternoon the sunrays light up the eastern wall. The seasonal changes in the position of the sun in the sky have a similar effect. The sunrays entering the house through the windows in the roof describe a pendular movement on the floor, lighting different parts of the house according to the season. Only the sacred center of the house lies constantly in shadow.

9. For a fine analysis of spatial symbolism, see C. Hugh-Jones 1979.

10. This section draws on the description of Barasana rituals and ritual ornaments in S. Hugh-Jones 1985.

11. S. Hugh-Jones 1985, 92.

CHAPTER 5. MAKING A LIVING

1. Among some groups of Amazonian shifting cultivators, fallows may be productive for fifteen years and selectively harvested for even longer periods (Denevan et al. 1984, cited in Clay 1988, 28).

2. Clay 1988; Denevan and Padoch 1987; Denevan et al. 1984; and Posey and Balée 1989.

3. Clay 1988, 51 and Posey 1982, 1985.

4. Any estimate of the period of forest recolonization is at best approximate. In poor soils of blackwater ecosystems, for example, the full recovery of natural vegetation may take over one hundred years (Moran 1991).

5. Abundant evidence for this increasingly accepted contention is supplied by Clay 1988. Cf. Caufield 1984, chapter 7.

6. For a detailed description of the symbolism of manioc preparation among the Barasana, see C. Hugh-Jones 1979.

7. The ritual is described in full in chapter 6.

8. Århem 1977.

9. Sábalo (*Brycon*), sabaleta (*Colossoma*), palometa (*Myleus*), waracú (*Leporinus*), taraira (*Erythrinus*), and pintadillo (*Pseudoplatystoma*) are some of the most important food fish.

10. The Hupdu Makú identify at least forty species of edible forest fruit and nuts (though only about one quarter is harvested in any significant quantity), and the Bará Makú recognize fifty-four different kinds of edible fruit (Reid 1979 and Silverwood-Cope 1972, both cited in Moran 1991).

11. Dufour 1987, cited in Moran 1991.

12. Grubs (predominantly of the species *Calandra palmarum*) are known in Makuna as *wadoa* and in Vaupés as *mojojoy*. The custom of breeding grubs is widespread in the Amazon. Cf. Clay 1988, 6.

13. When a woman gives birth, the Makuna say that she sees the *he* spirits (*he tigo yamo*).

14. For a fuller account of food blessing among the Barasana, see C. Hugh-Jones 1979 and S. Hugh-Jones 1979.

15. Moran 1991, 1993.

16. This estimate tallies well with findings from related Tukanoan groups. Thus, Chernela (1987, 50) has calculated that among the Uanano of the upper Río Negro, fishing may be restricted to less than 40 percent of the river margin available in their territory. See also Clay 1988.

CHAPTER 6. THE DANCE OF THE SPIRITS

1. The peach palm (*Guilielma gasipaes* or *Bactris gasipaes*) is known in Vaupés as *chontaduro* or *pupunha*.

2. To my knowledge the Dance of the Spirits has never been systematically described nor analyzed in the literature.

3. Ignacio, in his youth, participated in a documentary film about the Pirá-Paraná peoples. Today young Makuna are familiar with television, cinema, and video through visits to frontier towns and trading centers (see Århem 1993).

4. The Fish People refers contextually to spirit beings (*wai masa*) and to a named exogamous group (*Wai Masa* or *Bará*) reckoning descent from the mythical Fish Anaconda (*Wai Hino*).

CHAPTER 7. THE THREAT

1. For a comprehensive study of the Amazonian gold rush, see Cleary 1990. Hecht and Cockburn (1989) provide a very readable account of the economic history of the Amazon to the present and its social and environmental consequences.

2. The situation of the Yanomami Indians is continually reported in newsletters and documents by IWGIA (International Work Group for Indigenous Affairs) in Denmark and other international organizations concerned with the plight of the world's indigenous peoples such as Cultural Survival in the United States and Survival International in Britain.

BIBLIOGRAPHY

In addition to the works referred to in the text, a selection of recent publications relevant to the themes of the book have been included in this list as a guide to the interested reader.

Århem, K. 1977. "Fishing and Hunting among the Makuna." In *Annals, the Ethnographical Museum of Gothenburg.* 1976 Annual Report. Göteborg: Ethnographical Museum of Gothenburg, 27–44.

———. 1981. *Makuna Social Organization: A Study in Descent, Alliance, and the Formation of Corporate Groups in the North-Western Amazon.* Stockholm: Almqvist and Wiksell International.

———. 1984. "Vida y muerte en la Amazonía colombiana: un relato etnográfico Makuna." *Anthropos* 79 (1–3): 171–89.

———. 1987. "Wives for Sisters: The Management of Marriage Exchange in Northwest Amazonia." In H. O. Skar and F. Salomon (eds.), *Natives and Neighbors in South America: Anthropological Essays.* Etnologiska Studier 38. Göteborg: Ethnographical Museum of Gothenburg.

———. 1989. "The Makú, the Makuna, and the Guiana System: Transformations of Social Structure in Northern Lowland South America." *Ethnos* 54 (I–II): 5–22.

———. 1990a. "Ecosofía Makuna." In F. Correa (ed.), *La Selva Humanizada: Ecología Alternativa en el Trópico Húmedo Colombiano.* Bogotá: Instituto Colombiano de Antropologia.

———. 1990b. "Los Macuna en la historia cultural del Amazonas." *Informes Antropologicos* 4: 53–59.

———. 1992. "Dance of the Water People." *Natural History,* January, 46–53.

———. 1993. "Millennium among the Makuna: An Anthropological Film Adventure in the Northwest Amazon." *Anthropology Today* 9 (3): 3–8.

———. 1994. "Amazonområdet." In S. Howell and M. Melhuus (eds.), *Fjern og Naer: Sosialantropologiske Perspektiver på Verdens Samfunn og Kulturer.* Oslo: Ad Notam Gyldendal.

———. 1996a. "The Cosmic Food Web: Human-Nature Relatedness in the Northwest Amazon." In P. Descola and G. Pálsson (eds.), *Nature and Society: Anthropological Perspectives.* London: Routledge.

———. 1996b. "Powers of Place: Territory and Identity in Northwest Amazonia." Paper presented in the workshop on "Locality and Belonging" at the 4th EASA [European Assocaition of Social Anthropologists] Conference, Barcelona, July.

Balée, W. 1992. "People of the Fallows: A Historical Ecology of Foraging in Lowland South America." In K. Redford and C. Padoch (eds.), *Conservation of Neotropical Forests.* New York: Columbia University Press.

———. 1994. *Footprints of the Forest: Kaápor Ethnobotany.* New York: Columbia University Press.

Beckerman, S., and R. A. Kiltie. 1980. "More on Amazon Cultural Ecology." *Current Anthropology* 21 (4): 540–46.

Bidou, P. 1976. "Les fils de l'anaconda céleste (les Tatuyo): étude de la structure socio-politique." Thèse de troisième cycle, University of Paris.

Caufield, C. 1984. *In the Rainforest.* Chicago: University of Chicago Press.

Chernela, J. 1982. "Indigenous Forest and Fish Management in the Uaupés Basin of Brazil." *Cultural Survival Quarterly* 6 (2): 17–18.

———. 1985. "Indigenous Fishing in the Neotropics: The Tukano Uanano of the Blackwater Uaupés River in Brazil and Colombia." *Interciencia* 10 (2): 78–86.

———. 1987. "Endangered Ideologies: Tukano Fishing Taboos." *Cultural Survival Quarterly* 11 (2): 50–52.

———. 1993. *The Wanano Indians of the Brazilian Amazon: A Sense of Space.* Austin: University of Texas Press.

Clay, J. W. 1988. *Indigenous Peoples and Tropical Forests: Models of Land Use and Management from Latin America.* Cultural Survival Report 27. Cambridge, Mass.: Cultural Survival, Inc.

Cleary, D. 1990. *Anatomy of the Amazon Gold Rush.* London: Macmillan.

Colombia Amazonia. 1987. Bogotá: Universidad Nacional de Colombia.

Correa, F. (ed.). 1990. *La Selva Humanizada: Ecología Alternativa en el Trópico Húmedo Colombiano.* Bogotá: Instituto Colombiano de Antropología.

———. 1996. *Por el Camino de la Anaconda Remedio: Dinámica de la Organización Social entre los Taiwano del Vaupés.* Bogotá: Universidad Nacional/Colciencias.

Crocker, J. C. 1985. *Vital Souls: Bororo Cosmology, Natural Symbolism, and Shamanism.* Tucson: University of Arizona Press.

Denevan, W. M., and C. Padoch. 1987. *Swidden Agroforestry.* New York: New York Botanical Garden.

Denevan, W. M., J. M. Treacy, J. B. Alcorn, C. Padoch, J. Denslow, and P. Flores. 1984. "Indigenous Agroforestry in the Peruvian Amazon: Bora Indian Management of Swidden Fallows." *Interciencia* 9 (6): 346–57.

Denslow, J. S., and C. Padoch (eds.). 1988. *People of the Tropical Rain Forest.* Berkeley: University of California Press.

Descola, P. 1994. *In the Society of Nature: A Native Ecology in Amazonia.* Cambridge: Cambridge University Press.

Descola, P., and A. C. Taylor (eds.). 1993. "La Remontée de l'Amazone: Antropologie et Histoire des Sociétés Amazoniennes." *L'Homme* Special edition. 33: 126–28.

Dufour, D. 1987. "Insect as Food: A Case Study from the Northwest Amazon." *American Anthropologist* 89: 383–97.

Goldman, I. 1963. *The Cubeo: Indians of the Northwest Amazon.* Urbana: University of Illinois Press.

Goulding, M. 1980. *The Fishes and the Forest: Explorations in Amazonian Natural History.* Berkeley: University of California Press.

Guss, D. M. 1989. *To Weave and Sing: Art, Symbol, and Narrative in the South American Rain Forest.* Berkeley: University of California Press.

Hames, R. B., and W. T. Vickers (eds.). 1984. *Adaptive Responses of Native Amazonians.* New York: Academic Press.

Hammen, M. C. van der. 1991. *El Manejo del Mundo: Naturaleza y Sociedad entre los Yukuna de la Amazonía Colombiana.* Utrecht: ISOR.

Hecht, S., and A. Cockburn. 1989. *The Fate of the Forest: Developers, Destroyers, and Defenders of the Amazon.* London: Verso.

Hildebrand, M. von. 1983. "Vivienda Indígena, Amazonas." *Revista PROA* 323: 12–21.

Hill, J. 1984. "Social Equality and Ritual Hierarchy. The Arawakan Wakuenai of Venezuela." *American Ethnologist* 11: 528–44.

———. 1993. *Keepers of the Sacred Chants: The Poetics of Ritual Power in an Amazonian Society.* Tucson: University of Arizona Press.

Hugh-Jones, C. 1979. *From the Milk River: Spatial and Temporal Processes in Northwest Amazonia.* Cambridge: Cambridge University Press.

Hugh-Jones, S. 1978. *A Closer Look at Amazonian Indians.* London: Hamish Hamilton.

———. 1979. *The Palm and the Pleiades: Initiation and Cosmology in Northwest Amazonia.* Cambridge: Cambridge University Press.

———. 1981. "Historia del Vaupés." *Maguare* 1: 29–52.

———. 1985. "The Maloca: A World in a House." In E. Carmichael, S. Hugh-Jones, B. Moser, and D. Taylor, *The Hidden Peoples of the Amazon.* London: British Museum Publications Ltd.

———. 1995. "Inside-out and Back-to-front: The Androgynous House in Northwest Amazonia." In J. Carsten and S. Hugh-Jones (eds.), *About the House: Lévi-Strauss and Beyond.* Cambridge: Cambridge University Press.

Jackson, J. 1983. *The Fish People: Linguistic Exogamy and Tukanoan Identity in Northwest Amazonia.* Cambridge: Cambridge University Press.

Koch-Grünberg, T. 1909–10. *Zwei Jahre unter den Indianern: Reisen in Nordwest-Brasilien 1903–5.* Berlin: E. Wasmuth.

Lathrap, D. 1970. *The Upper Amazon.* New York: Praeger.

Meggers, B. 1988. "The Prehistory of Amazonia." In J. S. Denslow and C. Padoch (eds.), *People of the Tropical Rain Forest.* Berkeley: University of California Press.

Mejia Gutierrez, M. 1987. "La Amazonía colombiana, introducción a su historia natural." In *Colombia Amazonica.* Bogotá: Universidad Nacional de Colombia, 53–126.

Moran, E. (ed.). 1983. *The Dilemma of Amazonian Development.* Boulder: Westview Press.

———. 1991. "Human Adaptive Strategies in Amazonian Blackwater Ecosystems." *American Anthropologist* 93: 361–82.

———. 1993. *Through Amazonian Eyes: The Human Ecology of Amazonian Populations.* Iowa City: University of Iowa Press.

Palma, M. 1984. *Los Viajeros de la Gran Anaconda.* Managua: Editorial America Nuestra.

Pineda Camacho, R. 1987. "El ciclo del caucho, 1850–1932." In *Colombia Amazonica.* Bogotá: Universidad Nacional de Colombia, 181–210.

Posey, D. 1982. "Nomadic Agriculture of the Amazon." *Garden* 6 (1): 18–24.

———. 1983. "Indigenous Ecological Knowledge and Development of the Amazon." In E. Moran (ed.), *The Dilemma of Amazonian Development.* Boulder: Westview Press.

———. 1985. "Indigenous Management of Tropical Forest Ecosystems: The Case of the Kayapó Indians of the Brazilian Amazon." *Agroforestry Systems* 3 (2): 139–58.

Posey, D., and W. Balée (eds.). 1989. *Natural Resource Management by Indigenous and Folk Societies of Amazonia.* Advances in Economic Botany Monograph Series. New York: New York Botanical Garden.

Ramos, A. 1995. *Sanumá Memories: Yanomami Ethnography in Times of Crisis.* Madison: University of Wisconsin Press.

Reichel, E. 1976. "La manufactura del budare entre la tribu Tanimuka." *Revista Colombiana de Antropología* 20: 177–200.

———. 1987. "Asentamientos prehispanicos en la Amazonia colombiana." In *Colombia Amazonica.* Bogotá: Universidad Nacional de Colombia, 127–54.

Reichel, E., and M. von Hildebrand. 1984. "Vivienda indígena, grupo Ufaina, Amazonas: función socio-politica de la maloca." *Revista PROA* 332: 16–23.

Reichel-Dolmatoff, G. 1971. *Amazonian Cosmos: The Sexual and Religious Symbolism of the Tukano Indians.* Chicago: University of Chicago Press.

———. 1975. *The Shaman and the Jaguar: A Study of Narcotic Drugs among the Indians of Colombia.* Philadelphia: Temple University Press.

———. 1976. "Cosmology as Ecological Analysis: A View from the Rainforest." *Man* 11: 307–18.

———. 1985. *Basketry as Metaphor: Arts and Crafts of the Desana Indians of the Northwest Amazon.* Occasional Papers of the Museum of Cultural History 5. Los Angeles: University of California, Los Angeles.

———. 1996a. *The Forest Within: The World-View of the Tukano Amazonian Indians.* Foxhole, Dartington: Themis Books.

———. 1996b. *Yuruparí: Studies of an Amazonian Foundation Myth.* Cambridge, Mass.: Harvard University Press.

Reid, H. 1979. "Some Aspects of Movement, Growth, and Change among the Hupdu Makú Indians of Brazil." Ph.D. diss., Cambridge University.

Roosevelt, A. 1994. *Amazonian Indians from Prehistory to the Present: Anthropological Perspectives.* Tucson: University of Arizona Press.

Schultes, R. E. 1988. *Where the Gods Reign: Plants and Peoples of the Colombian Amazon.* Oracle, Arizona: Synergetic Press.

Schultes, R. E., and R. F. Raffauf. 1992. *Vine of the Soul: Medicine Men, Their Plants and Rituals in the Colombian Amazonia.* Oracle, Arizona: Synergetic Press.

Seeger, A. 1981. *Nature and Society in Central Brazil: The Suya Indians of Mato Grosso.* Cambridge, Mass.: Harvard University Press.

Silverwood-Cope, P. 1972. "A Contribution to the Ethnography of the Colombian Makú." Ph.D. diss., Cambridge University.

Smith, N. J. H. 1981. *Man, Fishes, and the Amazon.* New York: Columbia University Press.

Sponsel, L. 1986. "Amazon Ecology and Adaptation." *Annual Review of Anthropology* 15: 67–97.

———. (ed.). 1995. *Indigenous Peoples and the Future of Amazonia: An Ecological Anthropology of an Endangered World.* Tucson: University of Arizona Press.

Trupp, F. 1975. "Makuna Masks." *Review of Ethnology* 4 (15–16): 113–24.

———. 1977. *Mythen der Makuna.* Acta Ethnologica et Linguistica 40. Series Americana 8. Wien: Institut für Völkerkunde.

Umúsin, P. K., and K. Tolaman. 1980. *Antes o Mundo nao Existia.* São Paulo: Livraria Cultura.

Viveiros de Castro, E. 1992. *From the Enemy's Point of View: Humanity and Divinity in an Amazonian Society.* Chicago: University of Chicago Press.

Viveiros de Castro, E., and M. Carneiro da Cunha (eds.). *Amazonia: Etnologia e História Indígena.* São Paulo: Universidade de São Paulo.

———. 1984. "Notas etnograficas sobre el cosmos Ufaina y su relación con la maloca." *Maguare* 2: 177–210.

Wallace, A. R. 1892. *A Narrative of Travels on the Amazon and Rio Negro.* London: Ward, Lock, Bowden, and Co.

INDEX

Page numbers in bold indicate photographs

chili pepper, 99
clan territories, 43
clearwater rivers, 50
climate: in Amazonian rain forest, 45, 47, **51**; identification with hunting and fishing, 97
clothing styles, **37**
coca, 54, 66, 70, 85, 86, 89, 131; chewing and smoking of, **9**; cultivation and trade of, **20**, 27, 31–32, **100**, 101; preparation of, 74, 75, **76–77**
coca paths, 101
collective dance rituals, 88–89, **89**, **90**, 91–93, **92**
Colombian Amazon, 2
Colored Toads in Dance of the Spirits, 137
continuity, 62
coqueros, 31–32
crafts, sexual division of, 78, **79**, 80, **81**, 82, **82**
creation myth, 23–25, 27, 52–55, 162
Creators of the World, 53
cross-cousin marriage, 17–18, 32
Cubeo people, 17, 43, 142

D

dabucurí (food-giving) ceremonies, 19, 120, 122
dance of inauguration, 66–67
Dance of the Spirits, **25**, 105, 124, **125**, **126**, 126–28, **127**, **129**, **130**, 131–34, **132**, **133**, **135**, **136**, 136–42, **137**, **138–39**, **140–41**, **143**, **144**, 144–49, **149**; bee spirits in, 128; Colored Toads in, 137; costumes in, 136, **136**; dawning of second day in, 140; end of, 141; fish spirits in, 138–39, 140; Frog Catchers in, 137; general structure of, 131; masks for, **132**, 132–34, **133**, **135**, 136–37; meaning of, 148–49; monkey spirits in, 124, **125**, 126–27, **127**, 137; *nokoro* spirits in, 128, **129**, **130**, 131, 137; origin and purpose of, 145–49; other animal spirits in, 138, 140–41; Peach Palm Dance proper in, 141–42; penis spirits in, 127–28, 137; preparation for, 132, 134; role of shaman in preparation of masks and costumes for, 132–34; symbolic separation between hosts and guests in, 134; visual contrasts in, 136. *See also* Peach Palm Ritual
darts, **29**
death, 24, 61, 147–48
diet: animal protein in, 49, 104, 108–9; caymans in, 109–10; daily, 29; edible insects in, 111, 112; fish in, 15, 29, 110; game birds in, 109; *mamito* fruit in, **110–11**; manioc in, 15, 25, 27, 29, 74, 97–98, **98**, 99, 101, **102**; from *milpesos* palm, **109**; paca in, 109; peccaries in, 105–9; tapirs in, 110; timing of daily meals, 74–75; tinamous in, 109; wild fruit and nuts in, 111–12. *See also* agriculture; Makuna garden
Door of Suffering, 42, **42**, 86
drug trade, 31

E

educational customs, 30, 35–36
egalitarian political practice, 34
Emilia, **8**
estuary, 50

F

face painting, 71, 73
fallows, 98, 99
fish, life cycle of, 57–58
Fish Anaconda. *See Wai Hino* (Fish Anaconda)

fishing: association with wet season, 97; dry season, **107**; equipment for, 109
Fish People. *See wai masa* (Fish People)
fish poison, 110
fish-poison plants, 64
Fish River. *See* Pirá-Paraná River
Fish's Day Dance, 140
Fish's Night Dance, 138–39
fish spirits in Dance of the Spirits, 138–39, 140
food chain, 29, 56–58
food-giving rituals, 19, 120, 122
foods: blessing of, by shamans, 56; human, 56; ritual, 19; spirit, 19, 85. *See also* diet
food shamanism, 112–18
forest fruit, metaphysical connotations of, 111
forest management, integrated system of, 98
Franciscan missionaries, 36
Frog Catchers in Dance of the Spirits, 137
fur trading, 30

G

gaheoni (goods of the house), 78
gake (capuchin monkey), 114
Garrimpo, 153
gender division of labor, 27, 29
gold: discovery of, 150; mining camps for, 150, **151**, 153; mining of, **160**, 161
gourds, 64
güdareko ngana (people of the center), 43
Guiana highlands, 50
Guiana shield, 43–44

H

Hacinto, 105–6
hakoria (mother's children), 17
Hasa hudiro (Jirijirímo Falls), 42, **42**, 55, 58, 145
hawa (stingrays), 59
he, 12
he büküra (sacred Yuruparí instruments), 19, 21
He Fruit Ritual, 105, 111, 142
he kahea maküri (eyes of the spirit), 158, 161
he people, 12, 53, 55, 58, 61
he rika (tree fruit), 111
he rika samara (tree-fruit Yuruparí instruments), 21, 105
he wi, 85
he world, 19, 146; spirits of, 53, 88, 146
Hildebrand, Martin von, 86
Hill of the Star, 158
Hill of the Stool, 158
Hill of the Sun, 158
Hino (anaconda), 17, 59
hinobü (manioc press), 67, 82–83
historical traditions, 33–35
hode ngana (headwaters people), 43
hosa masa (servants), 15
hota basa (Peach Palm Dance), 131–32, 147
hot pepper sauce, 7
House of Music, 88
House of Vultures, 88
humans, relationship between animals and, 104–5
hummingbirds, 47
Huna sohe (Door of Suffering), 40
hunter, reciprocal relationship with prey, 105
hunting: association with dry season, 97; equipment for, 108; mystical nature of, 104

I

Icana River, 50
Ide Hino (Water Anaconda), 24, 25, 27, 66, 86, 101, 138, 145, 147
ide ma (water path), 24
Ide Masa (Water People), 23–25, 24, 27, 35, 66, 86, 148
Ide sohe (Water Door), 23, 40, 42, 49, 53, 54–55, 86, 93, 124, 145
Ignacio, 7, **8**, **10**, **11**, 27, 35, 124, 145, 146
illness, food restrictions at serious, 115–16
inauguration, dance of, 66–67
integrated system of forest management, 98
Itara, 24

J

Jaguar Hill, 158
jaguar people, 33–35
jaguars, 25, 48, 56
Javerianos, 36
Jirijirímo Falls. *See Hasa hudiro* (Jirijirímo Falls)
Joaquín, 36
jota seru (peach palm flutes), 128

K

Kabiyarí people, 17, 42, 142
Katarina, **8**
keti bare (spirit food), 19
Koch-Grünberg, Theodor, 33
Kome Hino (Metal Anaconda), 86
Komenya Makuna, 17, 27
Komenya River (Axe River), 2, 17, 23, 24–25, 27, 35, 37, 43, 161; fish in, 58
kumua (protective shamans), 18–19, 60
kumuro (stools), 83; symbolism associated with, 83, **84**, 85
küni oka (defenses), 24, 114

L

land, 40–62
Land People. *See Yiba Masa* (Land People)
La Pedrera, 16, 29, 35–36, 40, 150, 153
Letuama people, 17, 142, 145
linguistic exogamy, 17
longhouse. *See* maloca (longhouse)
lower floodplain, 50
Luis, 7

M

macaws, 47, **58**
maha hoa (macaw feathers), 91, 92, **92**, 93
Makú, 15
Makuna: ancestral territory of, 43; anthropomorphic cosmology of, 105; attribution of illness, 116; concept of nature, 62; cosmos of, 40, 61, 85–86; daily life and chores of, 27, 29; diet of, 97–98, 101, **102**, 103; as distinguished from whites, 94; early encounters with whites, 33; educational customs of, 30, 35–36; fishing tools and techniques of, 110; food restrictions placed on, 115–17; hierarchy ideology of, 34–35; hunting tools and techniques of, 108; land inhabited by, 16, 40–62; in making a living, 94–122; predation practices of, 103–11; shifting cultivation practices of, 97–99, **98**, **99**, 101, 103; subsistence activities